This book is a cond  ook, *The Coming Great (* *1.* It contains some of the (.ional new content.

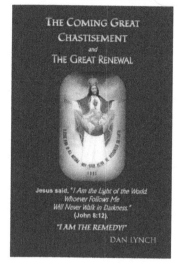

You have two options as to how you may read this book. You will notice that many of the words are in bold. The first option is a quick and easy read by going through and reading only the words that are in black bold. Then do a subsequent read of the entire book to get more information and a better understanding.

The second option would be to just read the entire book.

This condensed version is intended to be reader-friendly for all those who want to practice the Jesus King of All Nations Devotion and learn the prayers, promises, and prophecies of the Coming Great Chastisement and the Great Renewal that Jesus has revealed for the protection of His people, now living in the wicked darkness of this end-times Culture of Death.

Jesus is coming soon to manifest His justice and His mercy, as symbolized by His golden scepter. However, it will not be His Second Coming when He will come in glory at the end of the world to judge the living and the dead.

We are living in the end-times, but not at the end of the world. It is a time when God will once again enter into history through signs, miracles, warnings, and chastisements. These will make the reality of God and His truth self-evident to all souls and give humanity an opportunity to choose between the Kingdom of God and the Kingdom of Satan.

These events will happen through the intercession of the Blessed Virgin Mary and the Triumph of her Immaculate Heart — the sinful world will be purified. The Church itself will be purified and renewed. Those who repent, convert, and survive the chastisements (the remnant) will live in the Era of Peace, with the Great Renewal of the Holy Church, of Mankind, and of All Creation. They will be filled with God's grace and love for Him and one another. "When the storm has swept by, the wicked are gone, but the righteous stand firm forever." (Proverbs 10:25).

Jesus King of All Nations said,

How greatly I love my people! It is for your good, O mankind, that I allow my justice to be poured out in order to awaken your conscience and correct your sinful behavior. Yet you see how dearly I love you in that I continually warn you and even seek to comfort you in the pain of the cleansing which is almost upon you. (*Journal* 414). (See pg. iii for an explanation of the *Journal*.)

Awake! Lift up your heads, my people! Do you not see the signs all around you?! A great catastrophe is about to befall you! (*Journal* 664). Great is the chastisement that is ready to descend upon this sinful world to correct the consciences of individuals and the conscience of mankind as a whole! (*Journal* 366).

Hear me at last or the state of the world will continue to decline yet further until one day the Great Chastisement will fall upon you and you shall cry, 'Blessed is He who comes in the name of the Lord!' (*Journal* 734).

Wake up, my people! Come to the foot of my throne to receive mercy, peace, and forgiveness. Come to receive protection from what is soon to come upon the world.

"Because you have kept my message of endurance, I will keep you safe in the time of trial that is going to come to the whole world to test the inhabitants of the earth. I am coming quickly. Hold fast to what you have, so that no one may take your crown." (Revelation 3:10–11). (*Journal* 852).

My children, dear children, do not despair. There is always hope. (*Journal* 319). I have told you of the remedy. That of the public practice of my Devotion and veneration of my Image. (*Journal* 671).

SO, AS JESUS REQUESTS OF US, LET US NOT DESPAIR, BUT RATHER LET US ACCEPT HIS REMEDY OF THE PUBLIC

PRACTICE OF HIS DEVOTION AND THE VENERATION OF HIS IMAGE.

AS GOD SAID, "STAND UP! WHAT ARE YOU DOING DOWN ON YOUR FACE?...SANCTIFY THE PEOPLE SO THAT THEY WILL BE FORTIFIED FOR THE BATTLE!" (Joshua 7:10, 13).

Front Cover

On the front cover, we see the Image of **Jesus King of All Nations**. He revealed in His *Litany in Honor of Jesus King of All Nations* that He **is "the Light beyond all light, enlightening us in the darkness that surrounds us."**

This is represented on the front cover by the light emanating from His Image enlightening the darkness that surrounds it.

On December 17, 1988, Jesus appeared to His "Secretary," the mystic of the Jesus King of All Nations Devotion. She described Him as follows,

> **He had come in majesty. He was clothed in a long white tunic with a mantle of red draped over His shoulders which reached gracefully toward the floor.** His tunic was gathered at the waist which had a gold band around it. Both His tunic and mantle were trimmed in gold. The wounds in His hands were clearly visible. His right hand grasped a beautiful golden scepter. His left hand was open in a gesture of mercy. (*Journal* 3).

> **Jesus' Sacred Heart was also visible.** There was a wound on the right side, out of which flowed drops of blood. Flames issued from the top of His Sacred Heart and licked up upon a small image of the earth. (*Journal* 4).

> His wounded feet were also visible beneath His tunic. **He wore a solid crown of gold set with rows of pearls,** surmounted by a Cross in the middle of which was a red gem. (*Journal* 5).

The drops of blood flow from His Sacred Heart upon the large earth globe below. These and **the rays of light that emanate from His wounds symbolize Our Lord's mercy and love poured out upon all nations.** The flames that issue out of His Sacred Heart lick up upon the small earth globe above which is a small Cross. This symbolizes His perfected Kingdom won by the triumph of His Cross and enveloped by His love.

Kings have all authority. Jesus is the King of All Nations because, as He said, "All authority in heaven and on earth has been given to me." (Matthew 28:18). The crown and scepter are traditional symbols of royalty.

The crown represents the authority of Jesus King of All Nations and the scepter, when held aloft, symbolizes the exercise of His mercy, as in the Book of Esther. "Then the King extended the gold scepter to Esther and she arose and stood before him." (Esther 8:4).

We see on the front cover that Jesus pierces the darkness and appears as the risen and glorified Christ. He is the light of the world. He said, "I am the light of the world. Whoever follows me will never walk in darkness, but will have the light of life." (John 8:12).

Around the Image appears the prayer, "O JESUS, KING OF ALL NATIONS, MAY YOUR REIGN BE RECOGNIZED ON EARTH."

The Reign of Jesus King of All Nations has not been fully recognized on earth since the French Revolution. Before that, His Reign was recognized for almost 1300 years.

To "recognize" means to "know again" as, for example, you knew and acknowledged a friend before, but, in the interim, forgot about him. Then later you saw him again and recognized him.

So, it has been with Jesus King of All Nations. He was known and acknowledged as a legitimate king in the line of King David from the Reign of French King Clovis for almost 1300 years until 1789 when the French revolutionaries no longer knew and acknowledged King Louis XVI as the legitimate King of France. They beheaded him and made themselves their own kings through their own power.

As a result, they no longer knew and acknowledged Jesus as King of All Nations.

Now, in these end-times, Jesus King of All Nations wants to be known and acknowledged as such so that His Reign will once again be *recognized* on earth.

We recognize His Reign by submitting to His sovereign authority, obeying His commandments, receiving His sacraments, and leading a virtuous life.

Testimony of Fr. Peter M. Damian Fehlner, OFM Conv., S.T.D., Author and Theologian

The late Fr. Peter M. Damian Fehlner, OFM Conv., S.T.D., was the author's spiritual director and the spiritual director of the Jesus King of All Nations Devotion and of Jesus' "Secretary," the mystic who received the revelations.

Fr. Peter believed without any doubt all of the revelations of the Jesus King of All Nations Devotion.

He **studied all of the revelations of the Devotion and wrote that he believed in "the authenticity of these revelations as revelations directly dictated by Jesus to His Secretary and the truth of their content."**

He wrote that the revelations were "a remedy for the imminent chastisement under way."

He predicted that promoters of the Devotion will "realize the love of Jesus for all those assisting Him in its revelation and promotion among the faithful."

On August 12, 1951, Fr. Peter entered the Franciscan Friars Conventual Novitiate in Middleburg, New York. He was ordained to the priesthood, on July 14, 1957, at the Basilica of St. Alessio in Rome, Italy. He was an avid scholar and received a Doctoral Degree in Sacred Theology (S.T.D.) from the Seraphicum in Rome in 1959. He was one of the world's leading experts on the writings and theology of St. Bonaventure.

Fr. Peter taught dogmatic theology at St. Anthony-on-Hudson Theological Seminary in Rensselaer, New York, for over 25 years. During his tenure, the theological library became a world-class collection. Through the years, he also held a position on the Pontifical Faculty of St. Bonaventure in the Seraphicum in Rome. In 1984, he moved to Casa Kolbe, in Rome, where he became the Assistant International Director of the Militia Immaculata and editor of its publication, *Miles Immaculatae*. In this position, he became renowned worldwide as a speaker at conferences, retreats, symposia, and media events.

From 2008 to 2014, Fr. Peter served as Rector of the Shrine of Our Lady of Guadalupe in La Crosse, Wisconsin. In 2015, Fr. Peter's scholarly genius was recognized by academics at Notre Dame University at a symposium dedicated to his theological writings, including the 6-volume, critical edition of the *Collected Writings of Father Peter M. Damian Fehlner, OFM Conv.* In 2016, the Mariological Society of America bestowed upon Fr. Peter its highest accolade, *The Cardinal Wright Award.*

Fr. Peter's last months were full of suffering. Eventually, he lost his ability to communicate. For someone whose life had been one of the mind, this was a tremendous trial. He died from a fall on his head on May 8, 2018.

Fr. James McCurry, Minister Provincial of the Order of Friars Minor Conventual, gave the homily at his funeral. He said that **Fr. Peter was a "scholar, theologian, and…genuinely a true genius, one of the greatest scholars in the 800-year history of the Franciscan Order."** Here are some links to his homily,

https://airmaria.com/2018/05/18/funeral-homily-for-fr-peter-damian-fehlner/ (Video)

https://www.olaprovince.org/2018/05/09/fr-peter-damian-fehlner-ofm-conv/ (Text)

Testimony of Fr. James Bruse

Fr. James Bruse was the first spiritual director of the Secretary, the mystic of the Jesus King of All Nations Devotion.

He said, "Through the practice of the Jesus King of All Nations Devotion, we will grow spiritually and experience the reality of His Kingship. We will not fear or doubt. Jesus King of All Nations destroys doubt. We will experience His presence with us now as real and alive. He is the Son of the living God and this Devotion is a gift of His love and mercy for us to prepare us and challenge us to the extreme to reject Satan and the ways of the world and to choose Christ and to live His teachings because His Reign is coming through the Triumph of the Immaculate Heart of Mary!"

The Coming Great Chastisement and The Great Renewal

"I believe that Dan Lynch has done us a great service in linking historical facts and prophetic revelations over the past two centuries with the teachings of the Holy Scriptures and of the Roman Pontiffs about what is being manifested in our own era. He illustrates very well that the teaching of Pius XI in *Quas Primas (On the Feast of Christ the King)*, his great Encyclical of 1925 on the Kingship of Christ, is more highly relevant than ever and that it accords remarkably with the (private) revelations on Jesus King of All Nations. Because of the indissoluble bond between Jesus and Mary, His Kingship is intimately related to her Queenship and her maternal mission as the channel and Mediatrix of all the graces that flow from Him as their source. **The Church's solemn and authoritative recognition of these realities lived by her faithful can bring blazing light out of the darkness that presently threatens to snuff out the remains of Christian civilization.** Ultimately, this is an urgent appeal for each of us to cooperate in allowing Jesus to be the King of our hearts, the King of All Nations.

"**It seems impossible to me to escape the conclusion that we are at a very crucial stage in the Church and in the United States and in the world. The Devotion to Jesus King of All Nations certainly seems to be a divinely-ordained remedy for our present chaotic situation.**"

Monsignor Arthur Calkins
Mariologist and former official of the Pontifical Commission "Ecclesia Dei", Vatican City, assumed into the service of the Apostolic See and named Chaplain of His Holiness and Prelate of Honor of His Holiness

"Pope Pius XI prophesied that 'When once men recognize, both in private and in public life, that Christ is King, society will at last receive the great blessings of real liberty, well-ordered discipline, peace, and harmony....' (Pope Pius XI, *Quas Primas (On the Feast of Christ the King)*, 8, 19, 12). The Devotion to Jesus King of All Nations can't help but bring about this Era of Peace so long anticipated, not only by the popes, but the Scriptures themselves. **Dan Lynch has done a masterful job to summarize not only the critical times we are living, but the even more critical *response* needed. One way or another, the world *will* acknowledge that Jesus is Lord."**

Mark Mallett
Evangelist and Author, *The Final Confrontation*

Medjugorje's Ten Secrets: How to Prepare

"I praise Dan Lynch for his work at articulating an understanding of the Ten Secrets of Medjugorje. I also appreciate his use of favorable comments from persons of authority in the Church in assisting people to 'Not Be Afraid.'"

Fr. Charles Becker
Leader of pilgrims to Medjugorje

"In the days of Fatima, no one would have believed what has come of the world today. Our Lady's message in 1917 and 93 years later in Medjugorje has not changed. The message of Our Lady is the eternal message of the Gospels—prayer, fasting, conversion, Penance, confession, Eucharist. **Dan Lynch reminds us of the many apparitions of Our Lady and her heartfelt warning to 'turn away from sin and be faithful to the Gospel.' Only in embracing Our Lady's call will the world be saved from the road of self-destruction.** In his book, Dan gives a concise presentation of Our Lady's messages and how we can practically respond in today's world. I pray that all who come in contact with this book will take seriously the warning of our Heavenly Mother, embrace her messages, and find true peace within their souls."

Fr. Jay Finelli
The iPadre Catholic Podcast & Videocast

"Dan Lynch has done a masterful job conveying the messages of the Queen of Peace in a simple and readable style for people of all ages.

"Medjugorje is the extension of the messages of Fatima, and what Dan has written are the keys to peace of mind and soul and will provide people answers in the midst of any storm."

Ted Flynn, Author

"AWAKE, MY PEOPLE, NOW!"

See Who and What Is Coming!

Pray and Prepare
for
The Warning; The Great Chastisement;
The Triumph of the Immaculate Heart of Mary;
The Reign of Jesus King of All Nations;
The Era of Peace;
and
The Great Renewal of All Creation

Dan Lynch

Published by:
John Paul Press
144 Sheldon Road
St. Albans, VT 05478
www.JKMI.com

ISBN: 978-0-9884980-6-8 (Paperback)

ISBN: 978-0-9884980-7-5 (Hardcover)

Printed in the United States

Contents

Author's Prayer

Lord, as the author of this book, I pray with your psalmist that I might "discourse of the glory of your Kingdom and speak of your might, making known to man your might and the glorious splendor of your Kingdom. Your Kingdom is a Kingdom for all ages, and your dominion endures through all generations. May my mouth speak the praise of the Lord, and may all flesh bless His holy name forever." (Psalms 145:10–13, 21).

Author's Editorial Notes

This book contains many revelations from Jesus and the Blessed Virgin Mary through apparitions, visions, and locutions. "Apparitions" mean the interventions of a heavenly being, experienced by the external senses. "Visions" are perceived internally either as "imaginative" visions through the imagination, as "intellectual" visions through thoughts, or as external visions through the eyes. "Locutions" are supernatural messages received internally in words. They are not heard audibly.

The Church calls revelations received through apparitions, visions, or locutions "private revelations." The *Catechism of the Catholic Church* says, "Throughout the ages, there have been so-called 'private' revelations, some of which have been recognized by the authority of the Church. They do not belong, however, to the deposit of faith. It is not their role to 'improve' or 'complete' Christ's definitive Revelation, but to help live more fully by it in a certain period of history....Christian faith cannot accept 'revelations' that claim to surpass or correct the Revelation of which Christ is the fulfilment, as is the case in certain non-Christian religions and also in certain recent sects which base themselves on such 'revelations.'" (*Catechism of the Catholic Church* 67). [Hereinafter, it will be referred to as the *Catholic Catechism* and citations to it will be abbreviated as CCC.]

The term "private revelations" is unfortunate and misleading. Perhaps a better term would be "prophetic revelations" since there is usually nothing private about them and many of them are revealed for the entire Church. They are prophetic just like the messages of the Old Testament prophets who spoke the Word of God, not to teach the people anything new, but to remind them of teachings that they had forgotten. Nothing has changed since the full Revelation of Jesus Christ, but God has used His Mother, since 1830, in a powerful way as the prophetess of chastisements, of the Triumph of the Immaculate Heart of Mary, and of an Era of Peace.

Pope Urban VIII said, to help doubters, "In cases which concern private revelations, it is better to believe than not to believe, for if you believe, and it is proven true, you will be happy that you have believed, because our holy Mother asked it. If you believe, and it should be proven false, you will receive all blessings as if it had been true, because you believed it to be true."

None of the revelations contained in this book have been condemned by the Church and many of them have been approved. So, we may piously believe them merely with *human faith*.

Citations

There are various citations in this book to the book *I Will Sing of Mercy: The Journal of the Secretary of the Jesus King of All Nations Devotion*, such as this: (*Journal* 247). All of Jesus' revelations to His Secretary are contained in the *Journal*. These revelations are continuing in 2023. The number refers to the paragraph number in that book. That book may be obtained from:

John Paul Press
144 Sheldon Road
St. Albans, VT 05478
www.JKMI.com

These messages must always be interpreted in accordance with the teachings of the Catholic Church and never contrary to them. The *Journal* contains a *Nihil Obstat* that states that, as of August 15, 1993, "There is nothing contrary to faith or morals." Since that date, there have been other messages that have been submitted for approval to the appropriate bishops.

There are also various citations in this book to the book *To the Priests*, such as this: (*To the Priests* 47). The number refers to the message number in that book. That book may be obtained from,

The Marian Movement of Priests
PO Box 8
St. Francis, ME 04774
mmp-usa.net

To the Priests is a compilation of messages that Fr. Stefano Gobbi said that he had received from the Blessed Virgin Mary. Fr. Gobbi was the founder of the Marian Movement of Priests that tens of thousands of priests followed. He died on June 29, 2011. *To the*

Priests contains an *Imprimatur* that states, "There is nothing contrary to faith or morals in this manuscript."

None of the revelations contained in the book *To The Priests* have been condemned by the Church and many of them have been approved. So, we may piously believe them merely with *human faith*.

Citations to Church documents refer to the name of the author, the name of the document, and the paragraph number, if any, and look like this: (Pope John Paul II, *That They May Be One*, 40).

Scriptural citations refer to the name of the document in the Bible and the chapter and verse and look like this: (John 3:17). The scriptural citations are from various translations. I selected from various translations the best that I thought fit the particular context in which the citation was quoted. However, because of the variety, none of the particular translations are added to the citation. Some of the Psalms citations may differ by one number from another Bible translation depending on what translation of the Bible you may read.

Some of the books and other sources I cite are not readily available or are out-of-print. Some of them also have different editions with different page numbers. So, in the interest of simplicity, in most cases, I have cited only the name of the source and the author.

Every precaution has been taken to verify the accuracy of the information contained in this book. However, the author and publisher assume no responsibility for any errors or omissions. No liability is assumed for damages that may result from the use of the information contained within.

I conclude these Editorial Notes with a grateful acknowledgment and thanks to Randy Pratt who edited and formatted this book. Without his help, the book would still be stored in my computer!

Foreword by Fr. Peter Damian Fehlner, O.F.M Conv., S.T.D.

The Jesus King of All Nations Devotion has a profoundly theological character and has its roots in Sacred Scripture, both Old and New Testaments. The Devotion as such may be of recent origin, but the mystery at its core, to be enthroned in the hearts of its practitioners by its practice, is nothing less than the acceptance of and living the Kingship of Jesus everywhere in the world.

The image central to the Jesus King of All Nations Devotion, one drawing heavily on the Book of Esther, but adapted to the conditions of the Church in our times, is precisely the Kingship of Jesus dwelling in our hearts, adored and worshiped, foundation of that unity and communion of the faithful for which Jesus prayed before His Crucifixion. (See John 17:22).

From this arises the importance of prominent public enthronement of this Image in cathedrals and churches throughout the world and in all nations and the exercise of the Devotion not only by individuals, but by the entire Church and the desire of Our Lord for public approval for the practice of this Devotion publicly as well as privately. He has made this the condition for dispensing a stupendous number of blessings as fruits of the practice of this Devotion at a moment when **the world is threatened by catastrophic disasters because the Kingship of Jesus has been rejected by so many.**

The contempt for the enthronement of Jesus as King in our hearts is the root of that catastrophic future looming over the world today and particularly over the United States. And it is this contempt for the Kingship of Jesus that the practice of the Jesus King of All Nations Devotion strives to replace with that humble fear of the Lord as preface for obtaining the mercy of the King. Like the Tax Collector in the parable of the Tax Collector and the Pharisee (see Luke 18:9-14), we can begin to enjoy the peace which only the Kingship of Jesus can provide.

Precisely in view of the terrorism of the times looming everywhere, Jesus says that this Devotion is necessary because the recognition of Christ's Kingship, publicly by all, is the indispensable condition for dealing successfully with these evils

which are not willed by Jesus, but are a fruit of our refusal of His merciful Kingship.

According to **Jesus**, the decline of the world explains the need for the Devotion. He **said**, "Let it be known clearly and without question; **the poor state of the world shall decline yet further, indeed from day to day, so long as my Image and Devotion of Jesus King of All Nations remain hidden from the eyes of my Church and of the world.**" (*Journal* 380).

It also **provides the context for** correctly understanding references to **chastisements as instruments of Jesus to awaken in the nations the need to welcome in the lives of all the King of All Nations, to rejoice in His presence via the enthronement, and so avoid a definitive catastrophe.**

The principal exercise of this Devotion is the practice of virtue and loving obedience to the commandments of Jesus, precisely because we love Him as our King and lawgiver, where the central commandment is love of God the Father and love of neighbor as ourselves as Jesus does in the sacrifice of the Cross and Eucharist.

Tributary prayers designed by Jesus provide a way of linking this exercise to specific needs of our neighbors and to the comfort of God. Among these prayers are the *Novena in Honor of Jesus as True King;* **the** *Chaplet of Unity;* **the** *Novena of Holy Communions;* **the** *Litany in Honor of Jesus King of All Nations;* **and the** *Consecration to Mary, Mediatrix of All Graces,* **in view of the Triumph of the Immaculate Heart of Mary as the final realization of the Kingdom of God in the Church.**

Please see Appendix, B, The Prayers and Promises of the Devotion, on pg. 245.

Finally, there is the Medal to be carried, in one way or another, by those exercising the Devotion as a reminder of the great mercy our King has shown us in forgiving our indifference to and rejection of His Kingship that otherwise would have ended in our just condemnation.

Jesus tells us, "This Devotion to me as Jesus King of All Nations is to be a companion devotion to that of my mercy as given to my beloved daughter [St.] Faustina and to that of my Sacred Heart as given to my beloved daughter [St.] Margaret Mary." "*the saints*" (2 Corinthians 9:12). (*Journal* 165).

Jesus exhorts us, **"Take up my Devotion of Jesus King of All Nations, for in its practice you shall find for yourselves a haven of grace, mercy, and protection. Enthrone this my Image everywhere for I shall be powerfully present there and the power of my sovereign Kingship shall surely shield you from my just judgment."**

In light of the above, if the Devotion is practiced only privately, but not publicly, throughout the Church, lack of approval for public practice withholds the marvelous gifts and graces Jesus has guaranteed if the Devotion is practiced only privately, but not publicly, throughout the Church.

Jesus Himself said, "The promised graces and mercy stand at the ready, waiting to be poured out upon my Church, individual souls, religious communities, all nations, and, indeed, truly upon the entirety of creation and yet are being withheld due to the absence of recognition and approval by my holy Church." (*Journal* 381).

In conclusion, let us entrust ourselves to Jesus' Mother, and ours, as Jesus Himself said, **"All is coming to fulfillment. Be at peace. Trust in my mercy and love. Pray to my holy Mother. Entrust your lives to her. Receive the sacraments worthily and frequently. Obey my holy Spouse, the Church. Remain faithful. I love you. I bless you."**

Fr. Peter Damian Fehlner, O.F.M Conv., S.T.D.
Theologian and Spiritual Director of the
Secretary of Jesus King of All Nations

Preface by Fr. Peter Damian Fehlner, O.F.M Conv., S.T.D.

The Jesus King of All Nations Devotion is much needed by us and it is a devotion much desired by Jesus.

In a letter to his younger brother, St. Maximillian Kolbe spoke much of religious indifferentism as the central problem facing the Church in our times, the greatest obstacle to a fruitful new evangelization, to the conversion and sanctification of souls.

At the psychological level, it is often hidden under the equivocal term "personal autonomy" and at the sociological under that of "secularization". At the moral or "ethical" level, this boredom, this total disinterest in things divine poses as the final arbiter of conduct, including that of Christians. In religious matters, it is known as "private judgement" and, in one secularized formula for protection of the Sexual Revolution, it reappears as the slogan "pro-choice".

With the logical rigidity of Kantian-inspired thought, the indifferentist will claim that not even God has the last word in forming consciences. Hence, this mentality, whether that of individuals or of groups, cannot tolerate any community, such as the Catholic Church or families, which strive to be faithful to the Lord and which refuse to accept and obey laws of the State contrary to those of God or to be judged according to the opinions of private persons or groups in contradiction to the teachings of Christ. For, to the secularist, Christ is simply another obnoxious human being, not the Savior King of all nations and the final judge of all the living and the dead. In a word, indifferentism, under this or any other name, is a term indicating absence of love and devotion to Christ the King and lack of enthusiasm for the Kingdom of His Sacred Heart. Indifference to that Kingdom is indifference at once to justice and mercy for mankind.

There is no doubt about the sad fact that many believers, as well as non-believers, in the once-Christian West, have been much affected for the worse by this tragic vice of Secularism. This is surely one of the primary reasons so many of these persons are not inclined to defend the Pope against scurrile attacks presently being made on his person and on the papacy itself as the secure rock on which the Church is founded; indeed, the indifferentism and sins of Christians is, in part, a cause of such attacks.

Without the demise or, at least, effective defamation of the Pope, the promoters of ever more secularization, license, and religious indifference cannot reach their desired goal of total control. Behind this movement stands the prince of this world. We know the gates of hell will not prevail. In the meantime, however, Our Lord expects us to do our part, if for no other reason than to help these wandering sheep once again, in the fellowship of the Church, to "believe in their hearts and confess with their lips" (see Romans 10:9) the Kingship or absolute primacy of Jesus and Mary and so to root out of their souls that indifference corrosive of hope in the heavenly.

Not many years after the letter of St. Maximillian Kolbe referred to above was written, at the time of the Mexican Civil War that was so much about the Kingship of Christ and its acceptance or rejection, Pope Pius XI issued the Encyclical *Quas Primus* (*On the Feast of Christ the King*) *(1925)*. This Encyclical dealt with the urgent need to reaffirm devotion to our Savior under this title in order to deal effectively with the revolutionary secular movements emerging in the aftermath of an almost total breakdown of a once-Christian culture and civilization. The message of the Encyclical touches not only those nations affected by Communism and Nazi movements, but also by those even more insidious forms of materialism becoming almost universal throughout the world. Without this materialism, the more violent manifestations of this Secularism, which are dehumanizing as well as irreligious toward the Church and mankind, could hardly have been so successful.

Shortly before these efforts of the papal Magisterium to draw out the practical, pastoral, and spiritual implications of devotion to the Sacred Heart, there occurred, between May 13 and October 13, 1917, the apparitions and revelations of Our Lady to the shepherds at Fatima, Portugal, and, on October 17, 1917, the foundation of the Militia of Mary Immaculate by St. Maximillian Kolbe.

Both these events had, as their primary goal, the realization of the Kingdom of the Sacred Heart of Jesus through the Triumph of the Immaculate Heart of Mary: first of all in the souls of every human being by means of prayer and penance rather than politics and war.

Characteristic of these and many other divine and Marian interventions in the Church is the insistence on the inseparability of Jesus and Mary — a mystery so much insisted on by St. Francis of Assisi as the basis for the repair of a Church appearing on the verge of collapse. We might say that, in response to that petition of the prayer Our Lord taught us — "thy Kingdom come, thy Will be done on earth as it is in heaven" (see Matthew 6:10) — devotion to the Immaculate and Sacred Hearts has been given to the Church and to all believers, actual and potential.

However, now there has been given to us by Our Lord Himself a Devotion specific to His Kingship, as it were, as a direct remedy for that denial of devotion known as religious indifferentism. This Devotion is a complement to that of the two Hearts and of divine mercy. It clearly recognizes the unique place of Mary, Co-Redemptrix and Mediatrix of All Graces, in the divine plan for implementing the Kingship of Jesus in the hearts of all men and of all peoples. Who more than Jesus Himself knows precisely how to cultivate that true love of Himself known as devotion? Without such devotion directly structured by Jesus Himself, it will simply be impossible to overcome that spiritual lethargy, that boredom which is indifferentism, the greatest obstacle to the conversion, sanctification, and salvation of souls.

How important is this? Very important, for, without it, the great message of salvation fails to find its full resonance in the lives of those caught in the web of an idolatrous secularization. Pope Benedict XVI, in the first volume of his *Jesus of Nazareth*, chapter 3, discusses the place Proclamation of the Kingdom occupies in the public ministry of Jesus. The Proclamation of the Kingdom is the good news of salvation, the Gospel, not just any salvation such as the emperors of old and the secular politicians of today offer, provided we put all our hope in politics and economics.

Rather, authentic salvation is Jesus alone. Hence, only He can give this. Definitively realized in us, this salvation consists in His ruling our thoughts and desires, words and works. Effectively, He is Savior and Salvation, King and Kingdom. His Lordship is in history, yet transcends it, being the beginning of eternal life. His Kingdom is fully established in the Church when He reigns from the Cross, when He is exalted on the Cross and reigns in our hearts as we embrace the Cross, nowhere more so than in the Eucharistic mystery to be consummated in our own death and life in Jesus.

We urge you to read *The Story of the Devotion to Jesus King of All Nations,* by Dan Lynch, and *The Journal of the Secretary of the Jesus King of All Nations Devotion* and see if they do not reflect profoundly the great truths of faith just sketched. In the Devotion itself, both the wonderful promises of Jesus and the biblical references, the more pondered and lived, the more one will observe in oneself and in others who practice the various forms of this Devotion, a marvelous restoration of their interior life.

Introduction

We are living in very perilous times. Most people can sense that there is something very wrong with our culture. We are in the end-times battle between the Kingdom of God and the Kingdom of Satan that began with Adam and Eve in the Garden of Eden. (See Pope Leo XIII, *Humanum Genus (The Race of Man)*, 1–2).

On March 18, 2020, **Jesus King of All Nations said,** "Once more I appeal to my holy Church to rapidly approve **my Devotion of Jesus King of All Nations** and allow the public practice of my Devotion and the enthronement of my Image. This **is the remedy for the ills of the world; the re-acclamation of my sovereign Kingship over all mankind, over all nations.**"

Victory in this battle will only come through the recognition of the Reign of Jesus King of All Nations on earth, as it was during the period of Christendom. Jesus King of All Nations said, "In these times only one thing will be given as a remedy. I myself AM that remedy!" (*Journal* 159).

I use the term Christendom to mean a state of existence and harmony between the Catholic Church and the kings of states when Christian belief and practice prevailed in what is now generally the geographic area of Western Europe. During Christendom, culture, economics, political, and social life were inspired by Christian principles.

After the fall of the Western Roman Empire and the conversion of the barbarians to Christianity, the baptism of King Clovis of France, in 508 AD, ultimately led to the conversion of the Germanic tribes and the founding of Christendom. It ended in 1789 with the murderous beheading of French King Louis XVI during the French Revolution and the end of the line of its kings.

In Christendom, the king did not rule the Church, but protected it. Likewise, the Church did not rule the kingdom, but served as its conscience. The king acknowledged that he was subject to Jesus King of All Nations and recognized His Reign on earth.

Much of Christendom was invisible because the Kingdom of God, the Catholic Church, is not of this world. However, much of it was public and historical. **When men and women of faith recognized**

Christ as their King and proclaimed Him, Christendom appeared as a religious, social, cultural, and political presence in the world. It grew with faith, faded through apostasy, and ended with the Secularism of the French Revolution.

The kings of Christendom recognized that all authority was from God and passed through the kings to the people. The State operated from authority under God and not by power like the modern State. Jesus was the King of kings (see Revelation 19:16) and the State conformed its laws and institutions to the natural law and the divine positive law. The natural law is self-evident from reason, such as that we should do good and avoid evil. The divine positive law is revealed by God, such as the Ten Commandments.

Jesus Christ reigned in the minds and hearts of the kings and peoples for almost 13 centuries and they developed Western Civilization. **In Christendom, the temporal order with its society, culture, and politics was Christian. Today, the effects of Christendom have been overshadowed by Secularism. That is why Jesus King of All Nations appeared to two American women in 1988, and thereafter, so that His Reign will once again be recognized on earth.**

Jesus appeared in the Image that is shown on the front cover. He appeared as the King of All Nations with His red mantel enveloping the earth, holding out His scepter of mercy with the prayer around Him, "O JESUS, KING OF ALL NATIONS, MAY YOUR REIGN BE RECOGNIZED ON EARTH." He revealed prayers and promises to help us recognize His Reign on earth. These became known as the Jesus King of All Nations Devotion.

Jesus King of All Nations promises us His protection, but He pleads with each one of us to change our hearts and to embrace His gift of His Devotion. However, He respects our free will and leaves the choice to us to accept or reject both His admonition and the gift of His Devotion. **He revealed the following,**

Until the heart of man changes, the world will not and cannot change. Greater and greater will be the catastrophes in nature which itself rebels against the sinfulness of the children of men. The earth itself writhes in horror at the weight of corruption and uncleanness it supports. It cries out for justice against its inhabitants.

Embrace my Devotion of Jesus King of All Nations for it is a great mercy given by your God for these most perilous times.

Yours is the choice. I leave you free to accept or reject both my admonition and my gift. (*Journal* 372, 376, 379).

On March 18, 2020, **Jesus King of All Nations** revealed a message to His Secretary. He said that what we were seeing happening around us was the beginning of the chastisements that He has prophesied to correct the conscience of mankind. In my opinion, He was referring to the COVID–19 pandemic. He also gave us what He described as "the remedy in these most sinful times."

He **said, "Let it be known clearly and by all that the progress of the enemy, the great progress of evil, is a direct result of the obstinacy of mankind in his sinfulness and the outright denial of my sovereign Kingship and divine rights over him. This is why I have given the remedy of my Devotion of Jesus King of All Nations in these most sinful times.** I have pleaded again and again with my children to repent and be converted, many times sending my Immaculate Mother herself who is the Mother of All Mankind." (*Journal* 757–758).

Even though the Coming Great Chastisement is imminent, we are called to have hope in the promise of Jesus King of All Nations for the Great Renewal of the Holy Church, of Mankind, and of All Creation. He said,

Therefore, **let it also be known that a Great Renewal of my Holy Church, of Mankind, and, indeed, of All Creation will follow the cleansing action of my justice.** How greatly I love my people! It is for your good, O mankind, that I allow my justice to be poured out in order to awaken your conscience and correct your sinful behavior. **Yet you see how dearly I love you in that I continually warn you and even seek to comfort you in the pain of the cleansing which is almost upon you.** (*Journal* 414).

From the time of Creation, Jesus Christ has been and is now the King of All Nations. This title is not limited to geographic nations but applies to all peoples as well, as is evident in Scripture. However, this title was not explicitly revealed by Jesus until His revelations of the Jesus King of All Nations Devotion.

Nevertheless, this title will be applied to Jesus Christ in this book throughout the ages. The Roman Church has been singing this title in the "O" Antiphons since at least the eighth century. They are the antiphons that accompany the *Magnificat* canticle of Evening Prayer from December 17–23; one of those antiphons is "O King of all nations and keystone of the Church: come and save man, whom you formed from the dust!"

Jesus King is the warrior Messiah, riding into battle on a white horse with a full calvary of angels behind Him. On His head are many diadems, many crowns, symbolizing the plenitude of His royal authority. On His robe, and on His thigh, He has a name inscribed: "King of kings and Lord of lords." (See Revelation 19:11-16).

Jesus King of All Nations revealed that His Image "is a sign that I rule heaven and earth, and my Kingdom, my Reign, is near at hand. I give this Image to mankind as a source of graces and of peace. My most holy Mother is preparing the great triumph. The Triumph of her Immaculate Heart ushers in the Reign of my love and mercy. This Image, my child, must become known." (*Journal* 7, 14).

Pope Pius XI prophesied, "When once men recognize, both in private and in public life, that Christ is King, society will at last receive the great blessings of real liberty, well-ordered discipline, peace, and harmony." (Pope Pius XI, *Quas Primas (On the Feast of Christ the King)*, 19).

Because of the Original Sin of Adam and Eve, God chastised them with death and the loss of eternal life. After that, throughout history, humans have continued their rebellions against God, resulting in many chastisements from God as acts of His justice and mercy to bring humanity back to a relationship of love with Him.

Jesus King of All Nations warned us to repent or to suffer from His perfect justice. With His scriptural confirmations below, He said,

> Hear Me, O peoples of the earth! My Reign is at hand. *"….lift up your eyes and behold that the fields are already white for the harvest."* (John 4:35). Turn from your perverse and evil ways! *"….for there is no truth, and there is no mercy, and there is no knowledge of God in the land."* (Hosea 4:1). **I tell you,**

unless you turn back to me and repent, I will strike you in my most perfect justice. *"Because I know your manifold crimes, and your grievous sins...."* (Amos 5:12). Children of men, your God loves you! *"....with unquenchable fire."* (Luke 3:17). Why must you be so hard of heart so as not to reflect upon yourselves and hear the anguished cry of your God? *"Jesus cried out with a loud voice...."* (Matthew 27:46).

My children, your God appeals to you. *"I have not come to call the just, but sinners, to repentance."* (Luke 5:32). Now is the time of great mercy. *"I will show mercies to you...."* (Jeremiah 42:12). Take heed and benefit from it. *"....let him who reads understand...."* (Mark 13:14). If you do not, a most grievous chastisement will suddenly fall upon you. *"....for in one hour has thy judgment come!"* (Revelation 18:10). *(Journal 22–23).*

Because of the great evil of our times, Jesus King of All Nations has prophesied a Great Chastisement as an act of His justice and mercy to bring humanity back to a relationship of love with Him. **The remnant who will survive the Great Chastisement will be blessed with the Triumph of the Immaculate Heart of Mary, the New Pentecost, the Era of Peace, and the Great Renewal of the Holy Church, of Mankind, and of All Creation.**

So, what are the great evils of our times and who is committing them to deserve a Great Chastisement? The evils begin with the denial of the existence of the one true God of love by those who live as if He does not exist. I call these people "Secularists," derived from the Latin word *"saeculum"* (worldly), because their reality is only this material world and nothing that is transcendent or supernatural.

Many Secularists deny the self-evident truths set forth in the Declaration of Independence of the United States of America that human beings are "endowed by their Creator with certain inalienable rights" and have denied that there are "laws of nature and of nature's God." They deny God's Creation of an ordered world of nature and of human beings who are endowed by Him to know this world and to love and to serve Him with inalienable rights, such as the free exercise of religion. Moreover, they deny that God created human beings as male and female and that He instituted marriage as only between a man and a woman and the family as the foundation for all societies.

Secularists claim that human beings have the liberty to choose anything that they want, by their own power, rather than to choose what they ought. This is not true liberty, but libertinism and enslavement to sin. By their actions, they proclaim their personal autonomy to follow their own desires against the goodness and love of God and His law. Based upon their denials of a Creator God and His laws of nature, they believe that they are free to make up their own laws to support and act upon their desires.

Secularist courts and legislatures have created so-called "rights" that have been evils throughout all of history. They created rights for mothers to kill their own pre-born children; rights for homosexuals and lesbians to practice their evil sexual acts with one another and in a same-sex false marriage; and rights for human beings to attempt to change the sex that God created for them to the opposite sex in false transgenderism.

Notwithstanding that God has created human beings as male and female, they claim that you can choose to be your opposite sex. In denial of a true human marriage instituted by God between a man and a woman, they claim that you can choose to marry someone of the same sex.

To remedy these evils, Jesus King of All Nations revealed His Devotion to two American women mystics. The elements of the Devotion are the praying of His revealed prayers; wearing His revealed Medal; venerating and enthroning His revealed Image; and receiving His revealed promises of conversions, healings, and protection. He confirmed His revelations with His signs and wonders. Jesus King of All Nations said that He Himself, the public practice of His Devotion, and the enthronement of His Image are the remedies against His prophesied Great Chastisement.

Jesus is a King because kings have all authority. Jesus said, "All authority in heaven and on earth has been given to me." (Matthew 28:18). The incarnation of Jesus King of All Nations fulfilled the Old Testament prophecies of the Messiah King in the line of King David. Jesus King of All Nations established His Kingdom on earth, that is, the one, holy, catholic, and apostolic Church.

He wants His Kingdom and His Reign to be recognized on earth and in our minds and hearts. **These two aspects of His Reign are known as His Social Reign over all nations and His Individual Reign over all minds and hearts, both of which He wants to be recognized on earth.**

If souls only knew His Kingship for what it is, they would submit to Him in an instant, and He, in response, would fill them with happiness. So, we should love Him and allow Him to love us with His Sacred Heart. **It is a great thing to be loved by the Heart of a King, and He is the King of all that is, that was, and that will be.** His Heart is ours and we should give Him our hearts in return. This will seal our friendship with Him on earth and in heaven, and the Reign of Jesus King of All Nations will continue "until He has put all His enemies under His feet." (1 Corinthians 15:25).

The Catholic kings of France recognized the Reign of Jesus King of All Nations for almost 1300 years. However, the revolutionaries ended that in 1789 with the French Revolution and the beheading of their last king, King Louis XVI. This was the beginning of the rise of the Secularists who are the enemies of Christ and who include Freemasons, Socialists, Communists, and, by extension, all revolutionaries.

In 1847, Jesus King of All Nations revealed to Sr. Mary of St. Peter, a Carmelite nun in Tours, France, that these were His enemies because they denied Him, blasphemed Him, and attacked His Kingdom—the one, holy, catholic, and apostolic Church.

The enemies of Jesus King of All Nations have manufactured a Secular Culture of Death. We must battle and defeat this Culture of Death by practicing the Jesus King of All Nations Devotion, receiving the sacraments, and living a life of virtue in accordance with God's meaning and purpose for our lives, with those inalienable rights that He has endowed us with: life, true marriage and family, and the free exercise of religion.

Because of the evils of His Secularist enemies, God will intervene in human history. In His mercy, He will give a universal Warning to all humanity through an illumination of all consciences. In this illumination, we will see ourselves and our sins as God sees them, with an opportunity to repent and reform our lives.

This will be followed by a Great Chastisement upon all humanity. Many people think that a God of love does not chastise. But what human father does not punish his children in order to correct them and to set them on the right path? So, God, our Heavenly Father, will do that out of love for us.

God does chastise us. His biblical chastisements, such as the Great Flood and the destruction of Sodom and Gomorrah, were punishments for the horrendous sins of humanity.

In the modern world, God has sent His Mother Mary as a prophetess of chastisements. She has warned us many times of chastisements, since 1830, at Paris, France, when she appeared to St. Catherine Labouré and revealed the Miraculous Medal.

Some of Mary's prophecies have been fulfilled, while some are still unfulfilled, particularly those revealed at Medjugorje, Bosnia-Herzegovina. However, as Jesus said, "Fear is useless, what is needed is trust." (Luke 8:50). So, **we should trust in the promises of Jesus King of All Nations for the aversion and mitigation of chastisements and learn how to be protected from them.**

Because all previous warnings have been spurned by modern people and the evils have become so great, Jesus warned us of His coming judgment or chastisement upon all of humanity.

Jesus said, "No, my beloved, sin and the evils committed by mankind are too great, no longer will I spare my judgment to correct the conscience of mankind as a whole, but this [Jesus King of All Nations] Devotion and *Chaplet [of Unity]*, prayed with repentance, confidence, and love, will heal, save, and unite souls to my mercy who otherwise would be lost." (*Journal* 55).

Later, He warned us more severely and said, **"Awake! Lift up your heads, my people! Do you not see the signs all around you?! A great catastrophe is about to befall you!"** (*Journal* 664). **"Great is the chastisement that is ready to descend upon this sinful world to correct the consciences of individuals and the conscience of mankind as a whole!"** (*Journal* 366).

Are *You* ready?

"Stay awake and be ready! For you do not know on what day your Lord will come. " (Matthew 24:42).

"Be careful, or your hearts will be weighed down with carousing, drunkenness, and the anxieties of life, and that day will close on you suddenly like a trap. For it will come on all those who live on the face of the whole earth. Be always on the watch, and pray that you may be able to escape all that is about to happen, and that you may be able to stand before the Son of Man." (Luke 21:34–36).

This coming of the Lord will be a day of terror for the wicked, but a day of joy for the righteous. So, we should pray and wait in hope for our redemption by Jesus Christ and look forward to the day when we receive our reward of eternal life from Him.

Finally , Jesus warned us, "Hear me at last or the state of the world will continue to decline yet further until one day the Great Chastisement will fall upon you and you shall cry, 'Blessed is He who comes in the name of the Lord!'" (*Journal* 734).

However, there is hope for the world. Jesus King of All Nations also said, for those who embrace His Devotion, "I will cover them with my kingly mantle that my perfect justice may not reach them as it will reach those who abandon my law." (*Journal* 318). "My children, dear children, do not despair. There is always hope." (*Journal* 319). "I have told you of the remedy. That of the public practice of my Devotion and veneration of my Image." (*Journal* 671).

SO, AS JESUS REQUESTS OF US, LET US NOT DESPAIR, BUT RATHER LET US ACCEPT HIS REMEDY OF THE PUBLIC PRACTICE OF HIS DEVOTION AND THE VENERATION OF HIS IMAGE.

AS GOD SAID, "STAND UP! WHAT ARE YOU DOING DOWN ON YOUR FACE?...SANCTIFY THE PEOPLE SO THAT THEY WILL BE FORTIFIED FOR THE BATTLE!" (Joshua 7:10, 13).

Jesus King of All Nations said, "My Kingdom, my Reign, is near at hand. My most holy Mother is preparing the great triumph. The Triumph of her Immaculate Heart ushers in the Reign of my love and mercy." (*Journal* 7, 14). "My Spirit shall once more descend in a New Pentecost; a New Pentecost replete with the cleansing fire of His love. A fire ablaze with the love and justice of God." (*Journal* 496). "Let it also be known that a Great Renewal of my Holy Church, of Mankind, and, indeed, of All Creation will follow the cleansing action of my justice." (*Journal* 414). This will be brought by the public practice of the Jesus King of All Nations Devotion, as He has requested.

Many people are suffering through an epidemic of anxiety, depression, and drug use. Some of them are violent and many of them are suicidal. Many of them have no faith in the one true God and they are without hope.

However, Jesus said, "Be strong and do not lose hope. I AM with you to save you." (*Journal* 419). "Do not lose hope, my children. Though it seems all is lost, it is not so. I AM the Lord and Master of History and the times ever unfold on the power of my almighty hand." (*Journal* 798).

Jesus is coming soon! What is coming will not be the end of the world — it will be a new beginning. It will not be the Second Coming of Jesus Christ and the general judgement of the living and the dead. It will be Jesus King of All Nations coming through chastisements and through grace.

Many of the Old Testament prophecies will be fulfilled and the prophecies of Jesus and those of His Mother in the New Covenant will be fulfilled through a universal Warning; a Great Chastisement; the Triumph of the Immaculate Heart of Mary; the Reign of love and mercy of Jesus King of All Nations; an Era of Peace with a New Pentecost; and the Great Renewal of the Holy Church, of Mankind, and of All Creation.

"The earth shall be renewed. The blight of sin eradicated. This will result from the Triumph of the Immaculate Heart of Mary. Stand firm in the holy faith." (*Journal* 349–350). "So greatly does this world require divine cleansing that only by means of the purifying fire shall it be renewed, and its soil, the soil of the heart of man, emerge rich and fertile, ready to receive the seed of the divine Word and thus produce a harvest of holiness and virtue. A good and holy people shall the remnant be." (*Journal* 455).

The Catholic Encyclopedia of 1914 contained the following in its section on Chief Particular Prophecies,

The more noteworthy of the prophecies bearing upon "latter times" seem to have one common end, to announce great calamities impending over mankind, the triumph of the Church, and the renovation of the world. All the seers agree on two leading features as outlined by E.H. Thompson in his *The Life of the Venerable Anna Maria Taigi: the Roman Matron* (ch. 18): "First they all point to some terrible convulsion, to a revolution springing from most deep-rooted impiety, consisting in a formal opposition to God and His truth, and resulting in the most formidable persecution to which the Church has ever been subject. Secondly, they all promise for the Church a victory more splendid than she has ever achieved here below. We may add another point in which there is a remarkable agreement in the catena of modern prophecies, and that is the peculiar connection between the fortunes of France and those of the Church and the Holy See, and also the large part which that country has still to play in the history of the Church and of the world, and will continue to play to the end of time."

The primary reason for the Jesus King of All Nations Devotion is to bring the world to recognize the Kingship of Christ and His supreme authority over all creation, including His Social Reign now over all peoples and nations, as taught by Pope Pius XI in his Encyclical *Quas Primas (On the Feast of Christ the King).* That is why Jesus gave us the ejaculation, "O Jesus, King of All Nations, may your Reign be recognized on earth."

As the *Catholic Catechism* teaches, "The duty of offering God genuine worship concerns man both individually and socially. This is 'the traditional Catholic teaching on the moral duty of individuals and societies toward the true religion and the one Church of Christ.' By constantly evangelizing men, the Church works toward enabling them 'to infuse the Christian spirit into the mentality and mores, laws and structures of the communities in which [they] live.' The social duty of Christians is to respect and awaken in each man the love of the true and the good. It requires them to make known the worship of the one true religion which subsists in the one, holy, catholic, and apostolic Church. Christians are called to be the light of the world. Thus, the Church shows forth the Kingship of Christ over all creation and in particular over human societies." (CCC 2105).

Jesus King of All Nations explained why He wants the approval of His Devotion,

> **This work is eternal for it is the proclamation of my sovereign and divine Kingship; the acknowledgment of my supreme authority over all creation;** it is the song of praise sung by the Heavenly Court, by the angels who continually cry, 'Holy, holy, holy!' as they claim my divine sovereignty.
>
> **Contained within it is the totality of all of the devotions to my sacred and divine person, for it is the crowning glory of all others;** the absolute and supreme authority granted me by my Father. This authority which must be recognized by all and re-acclaimed by my holy Church. (*Journal* 706, 708).

A monumental struggle of the Kingdom of God against the Kingdom of Satan pervades the whole history of humanity, making the drama of life a spiritual battle against the powers of evil. (See CCC 409).

There are no neutral parties in this great and terrible battle against the forces of evil which have joined together against God and against His Christ. We are either for Jesus King of All Nations or against Him, for the Kingdom of God or against it.

We cannot serve two kingdoms opposed to each other. There are ultimately only two universal kingdoms which stand in opposition to one another: the Kingdom of God, a kingdom of light, love, truth, and obedience to God; and the Kingdom of Satan, a kingdom of darkness, lies, hate, and disobedience to God. There is no gray kingdom, only the Kingdom of Light and the Kingdom of Darkness, and each soul will spend eternity in one or the other. The choice is up to each individual.

Our Lady told the late Fr. Gobbi, Founder of the Marian Movement of Priests,

> **I am the great sign which appeared in the sky: I am the Woman Clothed with the Sun,** with the moon beneath my

feet, and with a crown of twelve stars upon my head. (See Revelation chapter 12).

Close to the great sign of the Woman Clothed with the Sun, there appears also that of the red dragon, of the ancient serpent, of Satan, who is now manifesting himself in all his extraordinary power.

It appears that the great dragon has won his victory because he has led humanity to build a civilization without God; he has spread everywhere the cult of money and pleasure; he has seduced minds with pride and with errors; he has violated souls with sin and evil; he has hardened hearts with egoism and hatred; and he has corrupted all the nations of the earth with the cup of lust and impurity. Satan has succeeded in bringing his wicked Kingdom upon the entire world.

But in the furious struggle of these last times, this struggle between heaven and earth, between the heavenly spirits and the demons, between the Woman and the dragon, I appear as a great sign of my greatest victory.

A *great sign* of the victory of God over every form of atheism, theoretical and practical; of good over every form of evil and sin; of love over every form of violence and hatred; of truth over every form of error and falsehood. (*To the Priests* 581).

Jesus King of All Nations revealed the following Prayer in Honor of Jesus as True King,

> O Lord our God, you alone are the most holy King and Ruler of all nations. We pray to you, Lord, in the great expectation of receiving from you, O Divine King, mercy, peace, justice, and all good things.
>
> Protect, O Lord our King, our families and the land of our birth. Guard us, we pray, most faithful one! Protect us from our enemies and from your just judgment.
>
> Forgive us, O sovereign King, our sins against you. Jesus, you are a King of Mercy. We have deserved your just judgment. Have mercy on us, Lord, and forgive us. We trust in your great mercy.

O most awe-inspiring King, we bow before you and pray; may your Reign, your Kingdom, be recognized on earth! Amen.

On May 22, 1992, in answer to the prayers of His Devotion, Jesus King of All Nations averted a seaquake chastisement in Puerto Rico that He had prophesied. Below is the message that He revealed, in a letter from the "Spiritual Mother" to the Author, regarding this aversion. (The Spiritual Mother was a spiritual advisor to the Secretary.)

Jesus said, with His confirmations from Scripture,

Daughter of my Father *"your Father"* (Mark 11:26), my beloved, my spouse *"He who is of God hears the words of God"* (John 8:47), tell my beloved priest sons, tell my beloved Bishop *"Now it was...Joanna...*[Author's note: the Spiritual Mother's first name was Johanna.] *who was telling these things to the apostles."* (Luke 24:10) that **in my GREAT MERCY I, yes, it is I MYSELF** *"and He interpreted to them the things...referring to Himself."* (Luke 24:27), **your sovereign Lord and God, who has mitigated this chastisement** *"But you, our God are good and true, slow to anger, and governing all with mercy."* (Wisdom 15:1) **to my people in the islands, my people of Puerto Rico!** *"that it might be an evident and manifest sign of the help of God."* (2 Maccabees 15:35).

"Why?" I will tell them, for you already know the reason my beloved. *"for we cannot but speak of what we have seen and heard."* (Acts 4:20). Because in this place, some have already received me as their Lord and King *"For even as Jonah was a sign to the Ninevites, so will also the Son of Man be to this generation...for they repented at the preaching of Jonah, and behold, a greater than Jonah is here."* (Luke 11:30, 32) in the Devotion that I have given you and [my Secretary] *"His servants"* (Luke 19:13) to give to the world, that of Jesus King of All Nations." *"It is what I desired"* (2 Maccabees 15:39).

My beloved priest sons, José and Jaime, along with my daughters, my spouses in the Order of the Virgin of the Aurora, received my message with loving hearts open to my Words, open to my love, and brought my message to my Beloved Bishop Enrique *"here we are, at your service"* (Job 38:35) who received you with an open heart, with an open soul, with open physical manifestations of charity toward you! *"The favors of the Lord I will recall, the glorious deeds of the Lord, because of all He has done for us; for He is good to the house of Israel; He has favored us according to His mercy and great kindness. He said: 'They are indeed my people, children who are not disloyal;' So He became their Savior in their every affliction."* (Isaiah 63:7–9).

This most beloved Bishop, Prince of my Church, and priest son of mine *"A wise magistrate lends stability to his people, and the government of a prudent man is well ordered. As the people's judge, so are his ministers; as the head of a city, its inhabitants. A wanton king destroys his people, but a city grows through the wisdom of its princes. Sovereignty over the earth is in the hand of God, who raises up on it the man of the hour; sovereignty over every man is in the hand of God, who imparts His majesty to the ruler."* (Sirach 10:1–5) did not receive you with scorn, indifference, mock the messages that I have sent, or refuse to listen!!! *"He will not speak on his own, but will speak only what he hears, and will announce to you the things to come. In doing this, he will give glory to me, because he will have received from me what he will announce to you."* (John 16:13-14).

As I told you last night [May 21, 1992] *"what have I been telling you"* (John 8:26), speaking about my people in Puerto Rico, **"I WILL HAVE MERCY ON WHOM I WILL HAVE MERCY!!" I have heard the prayers of my people in repentance, and my most holy Mother has interceded on their behalf, for these children recognize and honor my Mother! I have stopped the seaquake at this time, for it would have devastated the lands and the peoples,** *"Mighty are you, O Lord, and your faithfulness surrounds you. You rule over the surging of the sea; you still the swelling of its waves…yours are the heavens and the earth; the world and its fullness you have founded….Yours is a mighty arm; strong is your hand, exalted your right hand."* (Psalms 89:9–10, 12, 14) **with the merciful scepter of my Kingship I have done this! Yes, indeed! My messengers were correct that I sent to tell my people of the devastation of the chastisement that was** to occur today, the 22nd of May [1992]! In my justice, their horrible sins have justly deserved much more than this! *"Your hands are full of blood! Wash yourselves clean! Put away your misdeeds from before my eyes; cease doing evil; learn to do good. Make justice your aim: redress the wronged, hear the orphan's plea, defend the widow. Come now, let us set things right says the Lord: though your sins be like scarlet, they may become white as snow; Though they be crimson red, they may become white as wool. If you are willing, and obey, you shall eat the good things of the land; But if you refuse and resist, the sword shall consume you: for the mouth of the Lord has spoken!"* (Isaiah 1:15-20). **But my faithful souls have prayed to me and recognized me as King of All Nations, and have spread my Glory in this recognition!** *"Rise, O God; judge the earth, for yours are all the nations."* (Psalms 82:8).

No, not all are praying, but enough have prayed to mitigate, as you know so well, my beloved, that it is my PROMISE to those who honor me and have embraced me in my Devotion as King of All Nations! *"and instruction is to be sought from His mouth"* (Malachi 2:7).

Yes, chastisements will come..., but let them see, let them experience, let them bear witness to the MERCY that I have given them that they were not harmed! *"it shall not hurt them."* (Mark 16:18). I did not allow you to tell them ahead of time, for it is their Faith and Trust in me that I wish to receive! Through their prayers of imploring my merciful graces upon them through my Mother, they have prayed with a sincere heart! *"no dishonesty was found upon his lips."* (Malachi 2:6). For there are those who would not have prayed with a sincere heart to me, or not have prayed at all, both are the same to me....I do not hear this lip service! *"He has sent empty away."* (Luke 1:53).

I have shown them what my kingly mercy does! I have shown them what prayers with sincere hearts can do! *"And in His name will the Gentiles hope."* (Matthew 12:21). **I have shown them that if they turn to me, their Merciful King who desires to reign in their hearts, that I am a King of Mercy, a Father of Mercy, a Lord of Love who does not want their unnecessary deaths and condemnation of their souls because of their sins and stubbornness and pride!**

"So be on watch. Pray constantly for the strength to escape whatever is in prospect, and to stand secure before the Son of Man." (Luke 21:36).

HAVE NO DOUBT – THE THUNDER OF MY JUSTICE WAS GOING TO BE HEARD!!! As thunder comes before the rain…so, the thunder of my just judgment upon them was going to be heard first! Will my children *wake up* **and see the lightning first? The lightning of the merciful rays of my mercy that I wish to strike their hearts with!!! Will they notice me who AM?** *"named Jesus"* **(Matthew 1:25). Will my people finally see with the light of my grace so that I can reign in their hearts?!**

Yes, I wish to be the Light that comes before the Reign! The Reign of my Merciful Kingship! *"'Yes, when you seek me with all of your heart, you will find me with you,' says the Lord, 'and I will change your lot;'"* (Jeremiah 29:13–14). **Choose my people; choose how you wish to serve me!** *"And I saw that wisdom has the advantage over folly as much as light has the advantage over darkness."* (Ecclesiastes 2:13). I AM Jesus, your True High-Priest Victim, Prophet who cries out to you now, and Sovereign King who invites you to reign with me in mercy and love and unity, who wishes to acknowledge those who have prayed for all of my people, for they are most dear to my kingly Heart! *"That whole night they called upon the God of Israel for help."* (Judith 6:21).

It is you, my special little ones, who have found the fulfillment of my promises, not only for yourselves, but for your whole nation! *"My people is Israel, who cried to God and was saved. The Lord saved your people and delivered us from all these evils. God worked signs and great wonders, such as have not occurred among the nation. For this purpose, He arranged two lots: one for the people of GOD, the second for all the other nations…God remembered His people and rendered justice to His inheritance."* (Esther 10:6–9).

Remember what I HAVE DONE FOR YOU, MY PEOPLE, OF HOW I HAVE SPARED YOU THIS TIME! *"Gathering together with joy and happiness before God, they shall celebrate"* (Esther 10:10).

Honor my Mother, who has stood by the foot of your cross, like she stood at the foot of mine, and prayed and interceded and mediated to me for your sakes! She is the Mediatrix of All of my Graces! She is my Co-Redemptrix! *"You are the glory of*

Jerusalem, the surpassing joy of Israel; you are the splendid boast of our people. With your own hands you have done this; you have done good to Israel, and God is pleased with what you have wrought. May you be blessed by the Lord Almighty forever and ever! And all the people answered, 'Amen!'" (Judith 15:9–10). I bless you all my children. Remember the things that I have said to you! *"The child learns to reject the bad and choose the good."* (Isaiah 7:16).

1. The Monumental Struggle Against the Powers of Darkness

A monumental struggle against the powers of darkness pervades the whole history of man. The battle was joined from the very origins of the world and will continue until the last day, as the Lord has attested. (See Matthew 24:13; 13:24–30, 36–43). "Caught in this conflict, [humankind] is obliged to wrestle constantly if [it] is to cling to what is good, nor can [it] achieve [its] own integrity without great efforts and the help of God's grace." (Vatican II, *Gaudium et Spes (Pastoral Constitution on the Church in the Modern World)*, 37).

After the Fall of Adam and Eve, the Kingdom of God and the Kingdom of Satan were in constant conflict. Adam and Eve had three children: Cain, Abel, and Seth. Cain gave glory only to himself. Abel was righteous and gave glory to God. Both Cain and Abel offered sacrifices to God. Abel's sacrifice was accepted, but Cain's sacrifice was rejected because his deeds were evil. (See 1 John 3:12).

Cain then killed Abel out of resentment and was the first human murderer. God justly punished Cain so that the ground upon which he shed Abel's blood would bear no fruit for him and he would spend his life as a fugitive, although God still loved him and left a mark of protection upon him. (See Genesis 4:15). Nevertheless, wickedness continued in his family line.

Humans continued to glorify only themselves and continued in wickedness. So, the Lord said, "I will wipe out from the earth the men whom I have created, and not only the men, but also the beasts and the creeping things and the birds of the air, for I am sorry that I made them." (Genesis 6:7). However, Noah found favor with the Lord. Noah was righteous and God chose him and his family as a remnant to survive the chastisement of the Great Flood.

In obedience to God, Noah built an ark and he, his family, and the animals survived the 40-day Flood that destroyed the wicked. God blessed Noah and his family for their obedience and made a covenant with them and all living beings that the waters would never again become a flood to destroy all mortal beings. (See Genesis chapter 9).

Noah had descendants who continued the war between the Kingdom of God and the Kingdom of Satan. Noah had three sons: the righteous Shem, Japheth, and the wicked Ham. The descendants of Ham built the Tower of Babel as a monument to their own glory and were punished by God's chastisement of the confusion of languages and by their scattering throughout the world so that they could not complete the Tower.

The covenant with the righteous Noah continued through the covenant with the Jewish Patriarch, Abraham, and the covenant with Israel's King David until the new covenant of Jesus Christ.

Our redemption by Jesus Christ through His death on the Cross restored the possibility of the sharing in God's divine life that Adam and Eve had lost. Baptism restores us to sanctifying grace, but the inclination to sin (concupiscence,) as an effect of Adam and Eve's Original Sin, continues, and humanity continues to struggle against it. (See CCC 2520).

That is why St. Paul explained concupiscence and that Jesus Christ is the only remedy for it. He wrote, "The good thing I want to do, I never do; the evil thing which I do not want — that is what I do. But every time I do what I do not want to, then it is not myself acting, but the sin that lives in me....I see that acting on my body there is a different law which battles against the law in my mind. So, I am brought to be a prisoner of that law of sin which lives inside my body. What a wretched man I am! Who will rescue me from this body doomed to death? God — thanks be to Him — through Jesus Christ Our Lord." (Romans 7:19-20, 23-25).

Many humans today, with their concupiscence, pride, and disobedience continue to seek to glorify themselves and become like God. Because of the weakness of their concupiscence, **like Adam and Eve, in their pride and disobedience, and like those who tried to build the Tower of Babel,** they **continue their futile attempt to build their own heaven on earth without God.** Many humans still do not trust God and would like to become their own god, as Satan had tempted Adam and Eve to become in the beginning.

2

St. John Paul II said, "**The battle against the Devil, which is the principal task of St. Michael the Archangel, is still being fought today because the Devil is still alive and active in the world.** The evil that surrounds us today, the disorders that plague our society, man's inconsistency and brokenness, are not only the results of Original Sin, but also the results of Satan's pervasive and dark action." (St. John Paul II, *Visit to the Sanctuary of St. Michael the Archangel*, May 24, 1987).

God permits Satan to test us, as God tested the angels, to prove our love for Him. "Satan has obtained permission to sift all of you like wheat." (Luke 22:31). **At the same time, God gives us the necessary strength and assistance to resist and endure the assaults from Satan.** Jesus said to His disciples, "Behold, I give you power to tread upon serpents and scorpions and over all the power of the enemy." (Luke 10:19).

God also provides us with guardian angels. They are pure spirits who protect us and help us make morally good choices. "The whole life of the Church benefits from the mysterious and powerful help of angels....From its beginning until death, human life is surrounded by their watchful care and intercession. 'Beside each believer stands an angel as protector and shepherd leading him to life.'" (CCC 334, 336). Nevertheless, many people still make sinful choices.

The false idol of "choice" that many people worship today was set forth by the United States Supreme Court in 1992 in the case of *Casey vs. Planned Parenthood*. The Court declared, "At the heart of liberty is the right to define one's own concept of existence, of meaning, of the universe, and of the mystery of human life." By following this declaration, every human being becomes their own god.

Under this false idol and false ideology, nothing is true; everything is relative; and reality, cosmology, worldview, personal identity, and actions are all a matter of personal choice and personal autonomy, as it was with Adam and Eve in the Garden of Eden. **The utopian efforts of the Secularists, the Socialists, and the Revolutionaries who follow false ideologies are doomed to failure.**

The whole material universe is subject to laws such as the laws of physics, chemistry, biology, and mathematics. All of humanity is also subject to these laws, although human beings have the gift of free will to accept them or not accept them at their peril.

For example, human beings are subject to the law of gravity, but they can refuse to accept it and try to walk on air off the top of a tall building at the peril of their death. The science of biology teaches us the truth that human beings are conceived with their biological sex as a male or a female. However, some may try to disobey the truth, make a wrong choice, mutilate their bodies, take so-called transgender drugs, and declare that their sex is the opposite of their conceived sex, at the peril of living a life of delusion and unhappiness.

This delusion is a false belief, held with conviction, despite incontrovertible evidence to the contrary. Such people are living in denial of reality and truth, refusing to see and believe things as they really and truly are. They deny the reality of what others know to be truths that are self-evident, such as that men and women are distinct and different human beings who are complementary but equal in dignity and whose conceived sex cannot be changed.

The Secularist worldview wants to change the truth of humanity, of marriage, of family, and of sexual identity. They deny God's Creation and His creative intent for them as set forth in the Book of Genesis.

God created humanity in His own image as male and female in sex, not in gender, and He instituted marriage as only between a man and a woman, to unite them in love until death, and to be open to new life. This puts the lie to transgenderism and to a same-sex false marriage that is a counterfeit of the true marriage that God intended as an image of His relationship to His Church for which Jesus suffered and died.

Pope Benedict XVI described the effects of Original Sin on the Secularists. He **preached in a homily,** on December 8, 2005,

> The human being does not trust God. Tempted by the serpent, he harbors the suspicion that, in the end, God takes something away from his life, that God is a rival who curtails our freedom and that we will be fully human only

when we have cast him aside; in brief, that only in this way can we fully achieve our freedom.

The human being lives in the suspicion that God's love creates a dependency and that he must rid himself of this dependency if he is to be fully himself. Man does not want to receive his existence and the fullness of his life from God.

He himself wants to obtain from the Tree of Knowledge the power to shape the world, to make himself a god, raising himself to God's level, and to overcome death and darkness with his own efforts. He does not want to rely on love that to him seems untrustworthy; he relies solely on his own knowledge since it confers power upon him. Rather than on love, he sets his sights on power, with which he desires to take his own life autonomously in hand. And in doing so, he trusts in deceit rather than in truth and thereby sinks with his life into emptiness, into death.

"The doctrine of Original Sin, closely connected with that of redemption by Christ, provides lucid discernment of man's situation and activity in the world. By the sin of our first parents, Adam and Eve, the Devil has acquired a certain domination over man, even though man remains free. Original Sin entails 'captivity under the power of him who thenceforth had the power of death, that is, the Devil.' Ignorance of the fact that man has a wounded nature inclined to evil gives rise to serious errors in the areas of education, politics, social action, and morals." (CCC 407).

"The consequences of Original Sin and of all men's personal sins put the world as a whole in the sinful condition aptly described in St. John's expression, 'the sin of the world.' This expression can also refer to the negative influence exerted on people by communal situations and social structures that are the fruit of men's sins." (CCC 408).

Since the Fall from grace of Adam and Eve through their Original Sin, humanity has been divided into two Kingdoms: the Kingdom of God and the Kingdom of Satan.

The Kingdom of God, which is the one, holy, catholic, and apostolic Catholic Church, is marked by humility, obedience, and submission to the law of God. The Kingdom of Satan is marked

by pride, disobedience, and rebellion against the law of God through personal autonomous choices. Every person belongs to one or the other of those Kingdoms through their own free will. Those in the Kingdom of God will have their reward with eternal life in heaven. Those in the Kingdom of Satan will have their choice with eternal death in hell.

Jesus King of All Nations, Son of God, true God and true man, came into the world to overthrow the Kingdom of Satan and to inaugurate the Kingdom of God. "The reason the Son of God appeared was to destroy the works of the Devil." (1 John 3:8). Just prior to His public ministry, Jesus was led by the Holy Spirit into the desert where He was tempted by Satan, who wanted to be worshiped by Jesus. Satan offered Jesus all of the kingdoms of the world. Jesus told him, "It is written, 'You shall worship the Lord, your God, and Him alone shall you serve.'" (Luke 4:8).

When Satan had finished his temptations of Jesus, he left Him until an opportune time. (See Luke 4:13). Jesus won this victory over Satan in the desert, unlike Adam and Eve in the Garden of Eden who succumbed to Satan's temptation and disobeyed God.

As the New Adam, Jesus defeated Satan's temptation to pride and disobedience and, through His own humility and obedience, showed us how to do so as well. Throughout His lifetime, He conquered the assaults of Satan against the Kingdom of God (see Luke 22:3, 39-46) until **He totally defeated Satan by His triumph of the Cross and Resurrection, through which He was victorious over sin and death, both of which Satan had originally caused.** (See CCC 538–540, 2119).

Because of the victory of Jesus, both sanctifying grace and eternal life, that had been lost to humanity through Adam and Eve's Original Sin, were restored and **we now have the sacraments, especially of Penance and the Eucharist, by which our sins may be forgiven and we may gain eternal life with Jesus in heaven.**

We are called to follow Jesus' example and, through His grace and our own humility and obedience, to triumph over the Kingdom of Satan and his temptations, and over those of the world and the flesh, throughout our lifetime. "For we have not a high priest [Jesus] who is unable to sympathize with our weaknesses, but one who in every respect has been tested as we are, yet without sinning." (Hebrews 4:15).

As **Pope Leo XIII taught,**

> The race of man, after its miserable Fall from God, the Creator and the giver of heavenly gifts, "through the envy of the Devil," separated into two diverse and opposite parts, of which the one steadfastly contends for truth and virtue, the other for those things which are contrary to virtue and to truth.

> The one is **the Kingdom of God on earth, namely, the true Church of Jesus Christ, and those who desire from their heart to be united with it, so as to gain salvation, must of necessity serve God and His only-begotten Son with their whole mind and with an entire will.**

> **The other is the Kingdom of Satan, in whose possession and control are all whosoever follow the fatal example of their leader** and of our first parents [Adam and Eve], those who refuse to obey the divine and eternal law, and who have many aims of their own in contempt of God, and many aims also against God....At every period of time, each has been in conflict with the other. (Pope Leo XIII, *Humanum Genus (The Race of Man)*, 1–2).

Pope Leo's teaching about this conflict is reaffirmed in the *Catholic Catechism* that teaches, "The whole of man's history has been the story of dour combat with the powers of evil, stretching, so Our Lord tells us, from the very dawn of history until the last day. Finding himself in the midst of the battlefield, man has to struggle to do what is right, and it is at great cost to himself, and aided by God's grace, that he succeeds in achieving his own inner integrity." (*CCC* 409).

Today, this conflict continues in our culture with the Kingdom of Satan manifested by Secularism, a human ideology whose followers believe that humanity can establish a so-called "progressive" utopian peace and happiness on earth without God and act as if He does not exist.

Secularism is "secular" because it is only concerned with this world, in denial of anything transcendent or supernatural. Secularism is also called "liberal" because it wants freedom from the restraints of the moral teachings of the natural law and of the Catholic Church. Its followers are those who, as Pope Leo XIII wrote, "follow the fatal example of their leader and of our first parents, those who refuse to obey the divine and eternal law, and who have many aims of their own in contempt of God, and many aims also against God."

In 1925, **Pope Pius XI wrote** about Secularism and its characteristics that are still being manifested in the third millennium. He referred "to the plague of Secularism, its errors, and impious activities,"

> This evil spirit, as you are well aware, has not come into being in one day; it has long lurked beneath the surface. The empire of Christ over all nations was rejected. The right which the Church has from Christ Himself to teach mankind, to make laws, to govern people in all that pertains to their eternal salvation, that right was denied.
>
> Then, gradually the religion of Christ came to be likened to false religions and to be placed ignominiously on the same level with them. It was then put under the power of the State and tolerated more or less at the whim of princes and rulers. Some men went further, and wished to set up in place of God's religion a natural religion consisting in some instinctive affection of the heart. There were even some nations who thought that they could dispense with God, and that their religion should consist in impiety and the neglect of God. **The rebellion of individuals and of nations against the authority of Christ has produced deplorable consequences.** (Pope Pius XI, *Quas Primas (On the Feast of Christ the King)*, 24).

On the contrary, members of the Kingdom of God humbly submit to God and to the authority of Christ, who loves us with an infinite love and who only wants our eternal happiness. They obey the laws and teachings of Jesus King of All Nations and recognize His Reign on earth as members of His Kingdom of love, peace, joy, and justice. They are happy.

Many people search for happiness through power, fame, and fortune. However, Jesus said that the blessed and happy people are those who are poor in spirit; who mourn; who are meek; who hunger and thirst for righteousness; who are merciful; who are pure in heart; who are peacemakers; who are persecuted because of righteousness; and those who are insulted, persecuted, and falsely accused of all kinds of evil because of Him. (See Matthew 5:3–12).

There is no middle ground between the Kingdom of God and the Kingdom of Satan. Every human being, whether or not he or she knows it, by his or her own free choice, is a member of one or the other of the two Kingdoms. Jesus said, "He that is not with me, is against me." (Matthew 12:30).

Those who are against Jesus are His enemies, particularly the Secularists. They are those who have freely submitted to the Kingdom of Satan, the father of lies, who hates God and human beings. He is our adversary who "prowls around like a roaring lion, seeking someone to devour" (see 1 Peter 5:8) in order to bring them of their own free will to eternal damnation in hell.

After the fall of the Roman Empire and the conversion of the barbarians, the harmony that had existed in Christendom between the State and the Church for almost 13 centuries suffered from infiltrations by the Kingdom of Satan with its Secularism. It began with the Renaissance, continued with the Protestant Revolution, and culminated in the French Revolution. They were the predecessors of the secular culture of today, with its disbelief in the true meaning of human beings, male and female; their dignity and eternal destiny; true marriage between a man and a woman; and true family with a female mother and male father.

A part of the continuing battle between the Kingdom of God and the Kingdom of Satan is manifested in our culture by the worldview of Secularism, in opposition to the worldview of Greco-Roman, Judeo-Christian Traditionalism. This Traditionalism professes the truth that God exists and creates human beings with bodies and immortal souls to know the truth, do good, and avoid evil, to know Him, love Him, and serve Him in this world, and to share eternal happiness with Him in heaven.

Traditionalism denies the false belief of Secularism that human beings are simply random products by chance of a material universe in a world without meaning or purpose, free to do whatever they want.

In the continuing struggle between the Kingdom of God and the Kingdom of Satan, modern Secularists proclaim their personal autonomy, enlightenment, licentious choices, and so-called progress, all of which, in spite of their apparent victory, are truly a regression to the personal autonomy, original choice, and Original Sin of Adam and Eve.

On October 24, 2020, at the Catholic Identity Conference, Archbishop Carlo Maria Viganò, former Apostolic Nuncio to the United States, said,

> We know that **the New World Order project consists in the establishment of tyranny by Freemasonry: a project that dates back to the French Revolution, the Age of Enlightenment, the end of the Catholic Monarchies, and the declaration of war on the Church. We can say that the New World Order is the antithesis of Christian society**, it would be the realization of the diabolical Civitas Diaboli — *City of the Devil* — opposed to the Civitas Dei — *City of God* — **in the eternal struggle between Light and Darkness, Good and Evil, God and Satan.**

Our Lady told Fr. Gobbi, of the Marian Movement of Priests, that it appears that Satan has won his victory, "because he has led humanity to build a civilization without God; he has spread everywhere the cult of money and pleasure; he has seduced minds with pride and with errors; he has violated souls with sin and evil; he has hardened hearts with egoism and hatred; he has corrupted all the nations of the earth with the cup of lust and impurity. Satan has succeeded in bringing his wicked Kingdom upon the entire world.

"But in the furious struggle of these last times, the struggle between heaven and earth, between the heavenly spirits and the demons, between the woman and the dragon [see Revelation chapter 12], I appear as a great sign of my greatest victory. A *great sign* of the victory of God over every form of atheism, theoretical and practical, of good over every form of evil and sin, of love over every form of violence and hatred, of truth over every form of error and falsehood." (*To the Priests* 581).

This "furious struggle" will continue with the Blessed Virgin Mary, under the Kingship of Jesus Christ, the King of All Nations and the ruler of the kings of the earth. (See Revelation 1:5). He "must reign until God has put all enemies under His feet." (1 Corinthians 15:25). Then all nations shall come and worship in His presence (see Revelation 15:4) and victory will finally come with "the salvation and the power and the Kingdom of our God and the authority of His Christ." (Revelation 12:10).

God's final warnings to humanity are that this world will surely end and judgment will be eternal: heaven for the righteous and eternal damnation for the wicked, each by their own choice. The struggle with Christ and the Kingdom of God (the Catholic Church) against the Kingdom of Satan and his fallen angels will continue, but Christ has won the victory.

Jesus' victory over Satan will usher in the everlasting Reign of God. In the face of apparently insuperable evil, we are called to trust that Jesus is with us. Those who remain steadfast in their faith and confident in the risen Christ need have no fear "because perfect love casts out all fear." (1 John 4:18).

"The Son of God came to destroy the works of the Devil." (1 John 3:8). Jesus King of All Nations is unconquerable and the victor over all of His enemies who live as if God does not exist. In 1847, Jesus revealed His enemies to Sr. Mary of St. Peter, who lived in the aftermath of the French Revolution and the collapse of the monarchy. He said that His enemies included Freemasons, Communists, and, by extension, "revolutionary men," which would include Socialists, the revolutionary Secularists of the third millennium, and militant jihadist Muslims.

We should remember Christ's promise, "And so I say to you, you are Peter, and upon this rock I will build my Church and the gates of hell shall not prevail against it." (Matthew 16:18). Jesus referred to the "hell" of the damned, His enemies in the Kingdom of Satan, and He promised that Satan's Kingdom would not conquer His Church, the Kingdom of God, that was committed to the care of St. Peter and his successor popes.

This is the interpretation of **Pope Leo XIII, who wrote,** "The meaning of this divine utterance is, that, **notwithstanding the wiles and intrigues which they bring to bear against the Church, it can never be that the Church committed to the care of Peter shall succumb or in any wise fail. For the Church, as the edifice**

11

of Christ who has wisely built 'His house upon a rock,' cannot be conquered by the gates of hell, which may prevail over any man who shall be off the rock and outside the Church, but shall be powerless against it. Therefore, God confided His Church to Peter so that He might safely guard it with His unconquerable power." (Pope Leo XIII, *Satis Cognitum (On the Unity of the Church)*, 12).

Suffering, persecution, even death by martyrdom, though remaining part of the mystery of iniquity, are not the end. No matter what sufferings we may endure, **in the end, the Kingdom of God will triumph over the Kingdom of Satan because of our fidelity to Jesus Christ, the unconquerable victor over His enemies.**

The Lord of hosts says, "Then you will again distinguish between the just and the wicked, between the person who serves God, and the one who does not. **For the day is coming, blazing like an oven, when all the arrogant and all evildoers will be stubble. And the day that is coming will set them on fire, leaving them neither root nor branch, says the Lord of hosts. But for you who fear my name, the sun of justice will arise with healing in its wings and you will go out leaping like calves from the stall and tread down the wicked.** They will become dust under the soles of your feet, on the day when I take action, says the Lord of hosts." (Malachi 3:18–21).

Jesus is the sovereign Lord of history. **The righteous people will survive the final fire that the wicked will face for eternity with Satan and his fallen angels. The righteous people will live forever and ever with Jesus King of All Nations in the New Jerusalem, the everlasting Kingdom of God.**

In the Kingdom of God, Jesus Christ is King by birthright as the Son of God. The angel Gabriel announced to His Mother Mary that He would inherit the throne of King David, that His Reign would be forever, that His Kingdom would have no end, and that He would be called Son of God. (See Luke 1:32–35).

Jesus acknowledged to Pontius Pilate that He is a King (see John 18:37), but said that His Kingdom is not of this world. (See John 18:36). He said that He would come in glory to judge all the nations that will be assembled before Him sitting upon His royal throne. (See Matthew 25:31–32). He solemnly proclaimed that "full authority has been given to me both in heaven and on earth; go therefore, and make disciples of all the nations." (Matthew 28:18-19). Therefore, Jesus is indeed the King of All Nations.

The denial that Jesus is the King of All Nations leads to the culture of Secularism and the suppression of all that is sacred. Things will be sacred again when Jesus Christ reassumes His rightful place as King of all men, of all states, and of all nations.

Pope Benedict XVI said, in a homily on November 20, 2005,

> Since the announcement of His birth, the only-begotten Son of the Father, born of the Virgin Mary, was described as "King" in the Messianic sense, that is, heir to the throne of David in accordance with the prophets' promise, for a Kingdom that would have no end. (See Luke 1:32–33).

> The Kingship of Christ remained completely hidden until He was 30 years old, years spent in an ordinary life in Nazareth. Then, during His public life, Jesus inaugurated the new Kingdom, which "does not belong to this world" (John 18:36), and finally, with His death and Resurrection, He fully established it.

> Appearing to the apostles after He had risen, He said, "Full authority has been given to me both in heaven and on earth." (Matthew 28:18). This power flows from the love that God manifested in its fullness in the sacrifice of His Son. The Kingdom of God is a gift offered to the people of every epoch so that those who believe in the incarnate Word "may not die but [may] have eternal life." (John 3:16). Therefore, He proclaimed precisely in the Book of Revelation, the last book of the Bible, "I am the Alpha and the Omega,...the beginning and the end." (Revelation 22:13).

> "Christ: Alpha and Omega" is the title of the closing paragraph of Part I of *Gaudium et Spes (Pastoral Constitution on the Church in the Modern World)* from the Second Vatican Council, promulgated 40 years ago [1965].

> In that beautiful passage, which borrows some words from the Servant of God [now St.] Pope Paul VI, we read, **"The Lord is the goal of human history, the focal point of the desires of history and civilization, the center of**

mankind, the joy of all hearts, and the fulfilment of all aspirations. It is He whom the Father raised from the dead, exalted and placed at His right hand, constituting Him judge of the living and the dead. Animated and drawn together in His Spirit, we press onwards on our journey toward the consummation of history which fully corresponds to the plan of His love 'to unite all things in Him, things in heaven and things on earth.'" (Vatican II, *Gaudium et Spes (Pastoral Constitution on the Church in the Modern World)*, 45)....

May the Virgin Mary, whom God uniquely associated with the Kingship of His Son, obtain that we welcome Him as the Lord of our lives, in order to cooperate faithfully with the coming of His Kingdom of love, justice, and peace.

We can help to bring about His Kingdom of love, justice, and peace by recognizing the Kingdom of Jesus King of All Nations on earth and allowing Him to reign in our minds and hearts through the practice of the Devotion to Jesus King of All Nations.

Please see Appendix J, *How to Practice the Devotion*, on pg. 298.

Let us pray that Jesus King of All Nations will protect, defend, and guide us through the events that He has prophesied: the warnings and preliminary chastisements that will increase in severity up to The Universal Warning to correct the conscience of mankind as a whole. These events will be followed by the Great Chastisement, the Triumph of the Immaculate Heart of Mary, the New Pentecost, and the New Era of Peace, and will culminate in the Great Renewal of the Holy Church, of Mankind, and of All Creation.

2. The Mystics and the Origins of the Devotion to Jesus King of All Nations

Beginning in 1988, two American women received apparitions from Jesus. He revealed His title as "Jesus King of All Nations" in apparitions to them in the State of Virginia in the United States of America. Most of the revelations were made to the younger woman who called herself "His servant." Jesus called her "His Secretary." The older woman called herself "His Secretary's Spiritual Mother." Each will be referred to hereafter by these respective titles.

After the death of her Spiritual Mother, His Secretary has continued to receive the revelations of Jesus King of All Nations.

Jesus revealed that He wants His Reign to be recognized on earth. He also revealed His Image and an ejaculation to help us to recognize His Reign, "O Jesus, King of All Nations, may your Reign be recognized on earth!" These words are engraved on a Medal that Jesus requested be struck for us to keep in reverence.

The revelations of Jesus King of All Nations are recorded in *I Will Sing of Mercy: The Journal of the Secretary of the Jesus King of All Nations Devotion*, hereafter referred to as the *Journal*. The revelations are written in a style that may seem to be interrupted by scriptural quotations. However, these are definitely *not* interruptions. They were given by Jesus Himself.

Jesus appeared to His Secretary at random and would dictate His messages. The messages were normally given to her through interior intellectual locutions and were audible to her ears only occasionally. At different points in His dictation, Jesus would tell her to open Scripture. She would do so and write down what He specified. Jesus would then continue His dictation. These scriptural quotations are shown in italics in the *Journal* and in this book. Amazingly, they fit the context of the dictation and show that God's Word in Scripture is still living today. The dictations and the scriptural quotations make a harmonious whole.

In reading the *Journal,* we should not skip the scriptural quotations to make what we might think is easier reading. Jesus wants them to be read integrally with His dictations as confirmations of them. Remember that His Secretary took His dictations, obediently went where He led her to His Word in Scripture, wrote it down, and then continued to take His dictation so that we would have His living Word take root in our hearts. On our part, we should read it as He intends.

In His great love for us, Jesus revealed Images of Himself; of Mary, Mediatrix of All Graces; and of St. Michael the Archangel. He requested that a Medal be struck of Himself and St. Michael. He also revealed prayers and promises of healings, conversions, protection, and the peace, love, and joy of His Kingdom so that we may be one in Him with unity in one flock with one shepherd in the one, holy, catholic, and apostolic Church.

Jesus called these revelations the "Jesus King of All Nations Devotion." He wants to reign in all hearts and nations and He wants His Reign to be recognized on earth. He wants us to practice His revealed Devotion; to enthrone and venerate His revealed Image; to wear His revealed Medal; to pray the Rosary and His revealed prayers; to receive the sacraments of Penance and the Eucharist; to recognize St. Michael the Archangel as the Protector of the Blessed Sacrament; and to recognize His Mother as the Mediatrix of All Graces.

Jesus wants His Church to proclaim the dogma and title that His Mother is "Mary, Mediatrix of All Graces." He wants to grant us graces of forgiveness, conversion, healing, protection, and peace through the mediation of His Mother.

In His mercy, Jesus gives us an opportunity to recognize His Reign now, before He reclaims it in His justice. We should accept this opportunity and "approach the throne of grace to receive mercy..." (Hebrews 4:16).

Jesus told His Secretary, "I have come to entrust to you a message of great importance for the world. I tell you, my very little one, **the days are coming when mankind will cry out to me for mercy. I tell you, my child, that in these times only one thing will be given as a remedy. I myself AM that remedy! Let souls give devotion to me, through my most holy Mother, as Jesus King of All Nations."** (*Journal* 159–160).

Jesus said, "I want to reign in all hearts!" (*Journal* 233). "My throne on this earth remains in the hearts of all men. I most particularly reign in the most Holy Eucharist, and in loving hearts…that believe in me, that speak with me, and I tell you, my daughter, that I do speak in the hearts of all men." (*Journal* 197).

The Reign of Jesus King of All Nations is recognized by our acceptance of His sovereignty, by our submission to His Reign, authority, rule, and law through faith and conversion, by obedience to His commandments, by sacramental receptions, and by a virtuous life. His Reign is established in our hearts by our consecration to Mary, Mediatrix of All Graces, in which we pray, "I give and consecrate myself to you, Mary, Mediatrix of All Graces, that Jesus, our one true mediator, who is the King of All Nations, may reign in every heart." (*Journal* 244).

Jesus revealed, "This Devotion to me as Jesus King of All Nations is to be a companion devotion to that of my mercy as given to my beloved daughter, [St.] Faustina, and to that of my Sacred Heart as given to my beloved daughter, [St.] Margaret Mary." (*Journal* 165).

Pope Pius XII wrote, with reference to the devotion to the Sacred Heart of Jesus, "It demands the full and absolute determination of surrendering and consecrating oneself to the love of the divine Redeemer. The wounded Heart of the Savior is the living sign and symbol of that love. [Author's note: This wounded Heart is shown in the Image of Jesus King of All Nations.] It is likewise clear, even to a greater degree, that this devotion especially declares that we must repay divine love with our own love." (Pope Pius XII, *Haurietis Aquas (You Will Draw Water)*, 6).

Jesus promised His Secretary, "I shall unite all mankind, even unto the end of time, under my divine Reign of Kingship." (*Journal* 53). "…the merciful Reign of my Kingdom will be proclaimed everywhere among the nations through which shall come the end-time salvation of mankind by unity in my holy Catholic Church!" (*Journal* 155).

In this manner, Jesus, our Victim-High Priest, True Prophet, and Sovereign King, expressed His desire to be recognized as the King of All Nations on earth, to reign in all hearts, and to bring unity.

Jesus revealed that He wants His Church to approve the Jesus King of All Nations Devotion as a remedy for the evil state of the world.

The state of the world is that its evil is worse now than at the time of Noah. The evils of that time brought on God's chastisement of the Great Flood. Because of the evils of our time, Jesus King of All Nations has prophesied a Great Chastisement and the Triumph of the Immaculate Heart of Mary that will usher in the Reign of His love and mercy with the Great Renewal of the Holy Church, of Mankind, and of All Creation.

Jesus said that His Jesus King of All Nations Devotion is the remedy for the evils of our times. We should practice His Devotion for protection from the Great Chastisement and hope that we will be a part of the remnant that will live in the Era of Peace with the Great Renewal.

Please see Appendix J, *How to Practice the Devotion*, on pg. 298.

The Secretary's Theologian Spiritual Director, Fr. Peter Damian Fehlner

The Secretary's spiritual director was **theologian Fr. Peter Damian Fehlner, O.F.M Conv., S.T.D.** Fr. Peter believed, without any doubt, all of the revelations of the Jesus King of All Nations Devotion.

Fr. Peter remained anonymous as her spiritual director until his death. He also advised the Secretary to remain anonymous because he didn't want her to be unnecessarily subject to public scrutiny but wanted, rather, that the focus remain solely on the Devotion itself.

He studied all of the revelations of the Devotion and **wrote that he believed in "the authenticity of these revelations as revelations directly dictated by Jesus to His Secretary and the truth of their content."**

He wrote that the revelations were **"a remedy for the imminent chastisement under way."**

He concluded that promoters of the Devotion will **"realize the love of Jesus for all those assisting Him in its revelation and promotion among the faithful."**

Fr. Peter's Spiritual Director was Fr. George Kosicki, a promoter of the Divine Mercy Devotion that Jesus revealed was a companion devotion to the Jesus King of All Nations Devotion. Fr. Kosicki explained, "The Divine Mercy message is a call for a global consciousness. It's a prayer for the whole world. And if you don't realize the world is in bad shape, you are really in bad shape. The world, more than anything, needs mercy — mercy from one another and mercy from God."

Fr. Kosicki was the author of such books as *Faustina, Saint for Our Times: A Personal Look at Her Life, Spirituality, and Legacy; Now is the Time for Mercy; John Paul II: The Great Mercy Pope Beatification Edition;* and *Divine Mercy Minutes with Jesus: Praying Daily on Jesus' Words from the Diary of St. Faustina.*

Fr. Peter sent the Jesus King of All Nations devotional materials to Fr. Kosicki, who became enthusiastic about the Devotion. He saw the link between it and the Divine Mercy Devotion. Fr. Kosicki approved Fr. Peter's Testimonials of the Devotion. He died on August 11, 2014.

On August 12, 1951, Fr. Peter entered the Franciscan Friars Conventual Novitiate in Middleburg, New York. He was ordained to the priesthood, on July 14, 1957, at the Basilica of St. Alessio in Rome, Italy. He was an avid scholar and received a Doctoral Degree in Sacred Theology (S.T.D.) from the Seraphicum in Rome in 1959. He was one of the world's leading experts on the writings and theology of St. Bonaventure.

Fr. Peter taught dogmatic theology at St. Anthony-on-Hudson Theological Seminary in Rensselaer, New York, for over 25 years. During his tenure, the theological library became a world-class collection. Through the years, he also held a position on the Pontifical Faculty of St. Bonaventure in the Seraphicum in Rome. In 1984, he moved to Casa Kolbe, in Rome, where he became the Assistant International Director of the Militia Immaculata and editor of its publication, *Miles Immaculatae*. In this position, he became renowned worldwide as a speaker at conferences, retreats, symposia, and media events.

From 2008 to 2014, Fr. Peter served as Rector of the Shrine of Our Lady of Guadalupe in La Crosse, Wisconsin. In 2015, Fr. Peter's scholarly genius was recognized by academics at Notre Dame

University at a symposium dedicated to his theological writings, including the 6-volume critical edition of the *Collected Writings of Father Peter Damian Fehlner, OFM Conv.* In 2016, the Mariological Society of America bestowed upon Fr. Peter its highest accolade, *The Cardinal Wright Award.*

Fr. Peter's last months were full of suffering. Eventually, he lost his ability to communicate. For someone whose life was one of the mind, this was a tremendous trial. He died from a fall on his head on May 8, 2018.

Fr. James McCurry, Minister Provincial of the Order of Friars Minor Conventual, gave the homily at his funeral. He said that Fr. Peter was a "scholar, theologian, and...genuinely a true genius, one of the greatest scholars in the 800-year history of the Franciscan Order."

Here is a link to the video of his homily,

https://airmaria.com/2018/05/18/funeral-homily-for-fr-peter-damian-fehlner/

Devotions

Jesus told His Secretary, "My child, I would have my faithful ones know that the end-goal of this [Jesus King of All Nations] Devotion, and indeed of all devotions, is that of true love and worship of me, their God. To enable my children, who are feeble, to come to me the more easily, I give them 'reminders,' images of myself, in one form or another. The Image of myself as Jesus King of All Nations is a gift of love from my Heart to my children, intended to put before their minds the remembrance of me and therefore help them to hold me close in their hearts as my most holy Mother did so perfectly when she was on earth.

"When in mind, the 'Image' remains but an idea, but once the soul allows it to take root and grow in the heart, it becomes a living faith, a living reality, a living love. And this 'living faith' becomes 'faith in action.' This was my Mother's perfect response to the Will of God; her 'faith in action.' Thus, my little one, **this is the end-goal of this and of all devotions given by me as gifts to my children; that of the sanctification and resulting salvation of their souls."** (*Journal* Preface).

Devotion means to show love, honor, and dedication for another person. Devotions of the Catholic Church are ways of showing our love for the Holy Trinity (Father, Son, and Holy Spirit), the Blessed Virgin Mary, and the angels and saints. Authentic popular devotions are an invaluable means of promoting an increased love of God.

Devotions are a form of popular piety whereby the religious sense of the faithful is expressed outside of the liturgy from which they have their source and to which they lead. The liturgy includes, above all, the Eucharist, and the other six sacraments, but also other actions of the Church, such as the daily prayer of the Liturgy of the Hours, the rites of Christian burial, and the rites for the dedication of a church or for those making a religious profession.

Devotions include the following: adoration of the Blessed Sacrament; veneration of images; wearing of medals; holy hours of prayer; consecrations; rosaries; novenas; and litanies. Images can be signs of Jesus, Mary, the angels, or the saints, or the mysteries of our faith, a means of reminding us of them, and vehicles of God's graces.

Devotions to the Blessed Virgin Mary, the angels, and the saints differ from devotion to the Holy Trinity. We worship and adore only the Holy Trinity. We honor and give special devotion to the Blessed Virgin Mary, the angels, and the saints. We do not adore them. "This very special devotion...differs essentially from the adoration which is given to the incarnate Word and equally to the Father and the Holy Spirit, and greatly fosters this adoration." (CCC 971).

The Second Vatican Council pointed out that the spiritual life "is not limited solely to participation in the liturgy." St. Paul said that we must pray without ceasing. Popular devotional practices play a crucial role in helping to foster this ceaseless prayer. (Vatican II, *The Constitution on the Sacred Liturgy*, 12; see 1 Thessalonians 5:17).

"Besides sacramental liturgy and sacramentals, catechesis must take into account the forms of piety and popular devotions among the faithful. The religious sense of the Christian people has always found expression in various forms of piety surrounding the Church's sacramental life, such as the veneration of relics, visits to sanctuaries, pilgrimages, processions, the Stations of the Cross, the Rosary, medals, etc." (CCC 1674).

The United States Conference of Catholic Bishops asserted that an increase in popular piety is evidence of the Church's influence on society. In a document issued on November 12, 2003, they **wrote,**

> **First of all, by introducing the Catholic faith, the Church transforms the culture, leaving the imprint of the faith on the culture.**
>
> At the same time, however, the Church assimilates certain aspects of the culture, as some elements of the culture become absorbed and integrated into the life of the Church. This twofold process can be seen in the development of popular devotional practices.
>
> **While this inculturation of the faith takes place in the liturgy, popular devotions carry the faith a step deeper into the everyday life of a particular culture.** When properly ordered to the liturgy, popular devotions perform an irreplaceable function of bringing worship into daily life for people of various cultures and times. (United States Conference of Catholic Bishops, *Popular Devotional Practices: Basic Questions and Answers*).

In summary, both the liturgy and popular piety have a role in this transformation.

Popular devotions can lead to conversion, communion, and solidarity and to an increase of virtue and holiness to confront our modern secular culture. **Devotion to Christ the King conforms to Sacred Scripture and the Teaching Authority of the Church. It did not begin with private revelations. The faithful have always recognized and honored Christ as their King. So, the revelations of the Jesus King of All Nations Devotion add nothing new to Catholic doctrine.**

The significance of these revelations is that Jesus Christ, King of All Nations, willed in an extraordinary way to call the minds of humanity at this time to His scriptural title (see Psalms 47:8–9) **and to His Reign without end.** (See Luke 1:33). Jesus Christ is our Victim-High Priest, True Prophet, and Sovereign King of all. (See CCC 1546; *Journal* 561, 236).

In the Scriptures, we find many references to Jesus as the King of All Nations, to His Reign, and to His Kingdom, including the following,

The Lord shall become King over the whole earth; on that day the Lord shall be the only One, and His name the only One. (Zechariah 14:9). He comes to rule the world with justice and the peoples with equity. (Psalms 98:9).

The Lord reigns; let the earth rejoice. (Psalms 97:1). Say among the nations, "The Lord reigns! Yea, the world is established, it shall never be moved; He will judge the peoples with equity." (Psalms 96:10).

Who would dare refuse you honor, or the glory due your name, Lord? Since you alone are holy, all nations shall come and worship in your presence. (Revelation 15:4). For King of all the earth is God; sing hymns of praise. God reigns over the nations, God sits upon His holy throne. (Psalms 47:8-9).

The Lord is King, in splendor robed; robed is the Lord and girt about with strength; and He has made the world firm, not to be moved. Your throne stands firm from of old; from everlasting you are, Lord. (Psalms 93:1-2). His splendor spreads like the light; rays shine forth from beside Him, where His power is concealed.

The Lord God will give Him the throne of David, His Father. He will rule over the house of Jacob forever and His Reign will be without end. (Luke 1:32-33).

His dominion is vast and forever peaceful, from David's throne, and over His Kingdom, which He confirms and sustains by judgment and justice, both now and forever. (Isaiah 9:6).

This is the time of fulfillment. The Reign of God is at hand! Reform your lives and believe in the Gospel! (Mark 1:15). Full authority has been given to me both in heaven and on earth; go, therefore, and make disciples of all the nations. (Matthew 28:18-19).

Jesus Christ [is] the faithful witness, the first-born from the dead and ruler of the kings of the earth. (Revelation 1:5). Christ must reign until God has put all enemies under His feet. (1 Corinthians 15:25). So that at Jesus' name every knee must bend in the heavens, on the earth, and under the earth, and every tongue proclaim to the glory of God the Father: Jesus Christ is Lord! (Philippians 2:10–11).

The Kingdom of God is…of justice, peace, and the joy that is given by the Holy Spirit. (Romans 14:17). So, let us constantly approach the throne of grace to receive mercy and favor and help in time of need. (Hebrews 4:16).

Now have come salvation and the power and the Kingdom of our God and the authority of His Christ. (Revelation 12:10).

"Embrace My Devotion of Jesus King of All Nations for It Is a Great Mercy"

Jesus told St. Faustina, "Before the Day of Justice I am sending the Day of Mercy." (*Diary* 1588). **"He who refuses to pass through the door of my mercy must pass through the door of my justice…."** (*Diary* 1146). Are we passing from the Day of Mercy to the Day of His Justice?

We are living in what Jesus King of All Nations called "most perilous times." With wars, worldwide terror, mass murders, mayhem, and natural disasters, we can see that these times are certainly "most perilous!" These may be chastisements allowed by Jesus to bring us to repentance and to hope in His protection.

Jesus said, "Fear is useless, what is needed is trust!" (Luke 8:50). He promises us His protection, but He pleads with each one of us to change our hearts and to embrace His gift of the Jesus King of All Nations Devotion. However, He respects our free will and leaves the choice to us to accept or reject both His admonition and the gift of His Devotion. **He revealed the following,**

Until the heart of man changes, the world will not and cannot change. Greater and greater will be the catastrophes in nature which itself rebels against the sinfulness of the children of men. The earth itself writhes in horror at the weight of corruption and uncleanness it supports. It cries out for justice against its inhabitants.

Embrace my Devotion of Jesus King of All Nations for it is a great mercy given by your God for these most perilous times. Contained within it are gems of all-manner of grace given through the mediation of my Immaculate Mother: graces of forgiveness, healing, and renewal of minds and hearts. Why are my people not taking advantage of this gift of mine?

[Please see Appendix J, *How to Practice the Devotion,* on pg. 298.]

Let this be done. Let my gift be accepted with faith and great confidence in my kingly mercy and divine generosity. Where is your faith, oh my people? You bind my hands through your lack of faith.

Yours is the choice. I leave you free to accept or reject both my admonition and my gift. (*Journal* 372, 376–379).

Likewise, Pope Benedict XVI said in an *Address,* on November 25, 2008, that each individual person has to make the choice, "whether to practice justice or wickedness, to embrace love and forgiveness or revenge and homicidal hatred. On this depends [not only] our personal salvation but also the salvation of the world. This is why Jesus wishes to associate us with His Kingship; this is why He invites us to collaborate in the coming of His Kingdom of love, justice, and peace."

He also said, "We, and we alone, can prevent Him from reigning over us and hence hinder His Kingship over the world: over the family, over society, over history. We men and women have the faculty to choose whose side we wish to be on: with Christ and His angels or with the Devil and his followers, to use the same language as the Gospel." (Pope Benedict XVI, *Papal Address,* November 25, 2008).

The Pope emphasized, "Historical kingship does not matter to God; but He wants to reign in people's hearts, and from there, over the world: He is King of the whole universe but, the critical point, the zone in which His Kingdom is at risk, is our heart, for it is there that God encounters our freedom."

So, in response to the pleas of Jesus and Pope Benedict, we should not prevent Jesus from reigning over us, but should choose to recognize His Jesus King of All Nations Devotion as

His "**great mercy given by your God for these most perilous times.**"

We should accept this gift from Jesus and embrace His Devotion to prevent His prophesied chastisements from nature, from man, and from heaven itself. Jesus promised that, for each time that we say His Novena prayers, "I will mitigate the severity of the chastisements upon your country." (*Journal* 41). He also promised us His protection for wearing His Medal and enthroning His Image.

The original revelations were granted the *Nihil Obstat*, on August 15, 1993, declaring that they are free from doctrinal and moral error. Bishop Enrique Rivera D.D. of Caguas, Puerto Rico, granted the *Nihil Obstat* and wrote that he recognized "the need to foster more devotion to Our Lord and Savior, Jesus the Christ, True King of All Nations."

Jesus Himself said that the messages were from heaven. He said, "Let it be known and made perfectly clear that these revelations, the Devotion of Jesus King of All Nations and the related messages, are indeed from heaven. There is a tremendous lack of faith and trust on the part of many of my ministers regarding any private revelation." (*Journal* 431).

Jesus also said, "**You see the great seriousness of these times. The very downfall of society and of the moral order and the corruption within my very Church are themselves great signs of the authenticity of my Devotion and my messages.**" (*Journal* 768).

The late Fr. Albert J. Hebert said, "These revelations are very important. America is honored by their being given here because they not only apply to us, our nation, but to all the world. They are aimed at the universal restoration of Christ as King of All Nations and, more proximately, to prepare the way for His welcome at His Second Coming. **I urge all to secure the publications of the Jesus King of All Nations Devotion and to respond to and spread the messages.**"

He continued, "One must read the full account of the *Journal* to have a comprehensive view of them and insight concerning the rich spiritual treasures therein and the vital apostolate outlined there for our times, NOW TIMES! And get the Medal!"

The Devotion has several elements:

The Images are of Jesus King of All Nations; Jesus, Mediator, Our Lady, Mediatrix of All Graces; and St. Michael the Archangel;

The Medal manifests Jesus King of All Nations on the front side with the images of Jesus, our Eucharistic King, and St. Michael the Archangel, Protector of the Kingdom of God on Earth, on the reverse side;

Adoration of the Most Blessed Sacrament with emphasis on reverence for the real presence of Jesus Christ;

The Prayers are the *Chaplet of Unity*; the *Novena of Chaplets of Unity*; the *Novena in Honor of Jesus as True King*; the *Novena of Holy Communions*; the *Litany in Honor of Jesus King of All Nations*; the *Consecration to Mary, Mediatrix of All Graces*; and the *Special Blessing*;

The Promises are the graces of conversion, healing, final perseverance, unity, peace in hearts and homes; a special grace emanating from the Sacred and Immaculate Hearts; the gifts of the Holy Spirit; protection from harm and natural disasters; and mitigation of chastisements and all forms of God's justice; and

The Practice of the Devotion consists of living the Word of Scripture; veneration of the images and the enthronement of the Image of Jesus; wearing the Medal; recitation of the prayers; the reception of the Sacrament of Penance; and the reverent reception and adoration of the Eucharist.

The elements of the Jesus King of All Nations Devotion were primarily revealed to Jesus' Secretary and secondarily to her Spiritual Mother. Each of them had visions of Jesus King of All Nations and of St. Michael the Archangel.

Jesus' Secretary received the name of the Devotion; the request for the Medal; the *Novena of Holy Communions* and the *Novena Prayer in Honor of Jesus Christ True King*; the *Consecration to Mary, Mediatrix of All Graces*; the *Litany in Honor of Jesus King of All Nations*; and the request for the enthronement of the Image.

Her Spiritual Mother received the *Chaplet of Unity* and the request for *Novenas of Chaplets of Unity*; the Image of Jesus, Mediator, Our Lady, Mediatrix of All Graces; and the *Special Blessing*.

The Importance of the Jesus King of All Nations Devotion

Jesus said, "My child, you do not yet fully perceive the great importance of this Devotion of mine. It is to be no less significant than that to my Most Sacred Heart or that to my Divine Mercy. Indeed, it is the culmination of these two as they are both found within the one crowned by the sacred truth of my supreme and sovereign Kingship." (*Journal* 550). "When one venerates this Image [of Jesus King of All Nations], my Sacred Heart and my Divine Mercy are also venerated." (*Journal* 554).

Jesus also said, "This Devotion to me as Jesus King of All Nations is to be a companion Devotion to that of my mercy as given to my beloved daughter, [St.] Faustina, and to that of my Sacred Heart as given to my beloved daughter, [St.] Margaret Mary." (*Journal* 165).

Jesus appeared to St. Margaret Mary in the Burgundian French village of Paray-le-Monial, on December 27, 1673, the Feast of St. John the Evangelist, and thereafter over the next 18 months. He revealed to her the devotion to His Sacred Heart and asked for the receptions of Holy Communions on the first Friday of each of nine consecutive months in reparation for the offenses against Him. He also asked for a "Holy Hour" on Thursday nights to meditate on His Agony in the Garden of Gethsemane.

St. Margaret Mary wrote, "He showed me that it was His great desire of being loved by men and of withdrawing them from the path of ruin into which Satan hurls such crowds of them that made Him form the design of manifesting His Heart to men, with all the treasures of love, of mercy, of grace, of sanctification, and of salvation which it contains, in order that those who desire to render to Him and procure for Him all the honor and love possible might themselves be abundantly enriched with those divine treasures of which this Heart is the source."

Later, Jesus said to her, "Behold the Heart that has so loved men that it has spared nothing, even to exhausting and consuming itself, in order to testify to its love; and, in return, I receive from the greater part only ingratitude, by their irreverence and sacrilege, and by the coldness and contempt they have for me in this Sacrament of Love. But what I feel most keenly is that it is hearts which are consecrated to me that treat me thus." The Solemnity of the Sacred Heart was instituted in 1856 and Sr. Margaret Mary was declared a saint in 1920.

When Jesus' Secretary was working on her *Journal* of the Jesus King of All Nations Devotion, she had a vision of St. Margaret Mary coming to her, carrying in her hand a very large Heart, alive, with flames issuing from the top. St. Margaret Mary said, "I bring you the Master's Heart; go and set the world on fire with it." Our cold world needs to be set on fire with the love of the Sacred Heart of Jesus and His mercy that are shown in His Image of Jesus King of All Nations.

The message and devotion to Jesus as the Divine Mercy is based on the revelations of Jesus to St. Faustina Kowalska, an uneducated Polish nun, in the 1930s. She wrote a *Diary* about the mercy of Jesus. Jesus revealed an image of Himself; the *Chaplet of Divine Mercy*; and a novena for us to appreciate His unfathomable mercy and for us to plead for mercy on us and on the whole world. He asked that we remember His mercy at 3 PM, the hour of great mercy, the hour at which He died on the Cross. He asked for the institution of a Feast of Divine Mercy.

St. John Paul II wrote, "This was precisely the time when those ideologies of evil, Nazism, and Communism were taking shape. Sr. Faustina became the herald of the one message capable of offsetting the evil of those ideologies, that fact that God is mercy — the truth of the merciful Christ. And for this reason, when I was called to the See of Peter, I felt impelled to pass on those experiences of a fellow Pole that deserve a place in the treasury of the universal Church." (Pope John Paul II, *Memory and Identity*).

St. John Paul II canonized Sr. Faustina and instituted The Feast of Divine Mercy. He also entrusted the world to Divine Mercy when he dedicated a shrine erected in a suburb of Krakow, Poland, on August 18, 2002. During his homily, the Pope preached, "In this shrine, I wish solemnly to entrust the world to Divine Mercy. I do so with the burning desire that the message of God's merciful love, proclaimed here through St. Faustina, may be made known to all the peoples of the earth and fill their hearts with hope.

"How greatly today's world needs God's mercy! In every continent, from the depth of human suffering, a cry of mercy seems to rise up," the Holy Father exclaimed.

"Where hatred and the thirst for revenge dominate, where war brings suffering and death to the innocent, there the grace of mercy is needed in order to settle human minds and hearts and to bring about peace," the Pope continued.

"Wherever respect for life and human dignity are lacking, there is need of God's merciful love, in whose light we see the inexpressible value of every human being," he added. "Mercy is needed in order to ensure that every injustice in the world will come to an end in the splendor of truth."

At the end, the Pope quoted Jesus' words as recorded in St. Faustina's *Diary*, "From here, there must go forth 'the spark which will prepare the world for His final Coming.'" (*Diary* 1732).

"This spark needs to be lighted by the grace of God," the Holy Father stressed. "This fire of mercy needs to be passed on to the world. In the mercy of God, the world will find peace and mankind will find happiness!"

St. John Paul II died on the Vigil of the Feast of Divine Mercy, April 2, 2005. His last message to the world was about Divine Mercy. It was read the day after his death on Divine Mercy Sunday. The Pope wrote,

> To humanity, which at times seems to be lost and dominated by the power of evil, egoism, and fear, the risen Lord offers as a gift His love that forgives, reconciles, and reopens the spirit to hope.

> It is love that converts hearts and gives peace. How much need the world has to understand and accept Divine Mercy! Lord, who with your death and Resurrection reveal the love of the Father, we believe in you and with confidence repeat to you today: Jesus, I trust in you, have mercy on us and on the whole world.

In his last book, he wrote, "The limit imposed upon evil is ultimately Divine Mercy."

In the Image of Divine Mercy, Jesus is standing with His left hand pointed to His Heart, from which red and pale rays emanate. They symbolize the blood and water that gushed forth from His Heart at His Crucifixion and His merciful sacraments of the Eucharist and Baptism. The words, "Jesus, I trust in you!" are at the bottom of the Image.

Jesus appeared to St. Faustina, as He did to His apostles in the Upper Room, as the risen Christ who bears the great message of Divine Mercy. Jesus said to His apostles, "Peace be with you. As the Father has sent me, even so I send you....Receive the Holy Spirit. If you forgive the sins of any, they are forgiven; if you retain the sins of any, they are retained." (John 20:21–23).

On February 22, 1931, Jesus appeared to St. Faustina and told her, "Paint an image according to the pattern you see, with the signature: Jesus, I trust in you! I desire that this Image be venerated, first in your chapel, and [then] throughout the world." (*Diary* 47).

Jesus King of All Nations made a similar request to the Secretary of His Devotion. He asked her to have an image painted of Him that contained His Sacred Heart and the wounds in His wrists, from both of which emanated rays similar to those in the Divine Mercy image.

Jesus King of All Nations said, "This Devotion of Jesus King of All Nations is truly a most wondrous gift from my Most Sacred Heart to my holy Church and to the entire world." (*Journal* 594). "My great mercy has compelled me to once more intervene in the history of mankind in these gravely sinful and truly perilous times." (*Journal* 596). "This Devotion is the crowning glory of all devotions to me. Let this be known....This revelation today regarding this truth is a keystone holding the others together." (*Journal* 556).

In a private message to His Secretary, Jesus said that there is a "great link between my three devotions, the crowning glory of which is that to my sovereign Kingship for in this Devotion the other two are present, that to my Most Sacred Heart and to my Divine Mercy."

This Devotion is the culmination of the three-in-one great devotions to Jesus of His love (the Sacred Heart Devotion); His mercy (the Divine Mercy Devotion); and His Kingship, justice, and protection (the Jesus King of All Nations Devotion).

In the Image of Jesus King of All Nations, we see Him crowned as King, with His arms spread wide, His wounded Sacred Heart exposed, and manifesting His mercy by pouring His merciful blood and water onto our cold, violent, and heartsick world. His mercy is primarily represented in His Image by the colored rays of light emanating from the wounds in His hands. Just as in the Divine Mercy image, it is this divine light that symbolizes His greatest attribute: His mercy. He pleads for us to recognize His Reign.

Jesus King revealed the prayer, "O Jesus, King of All Nations, may your Reign be recognized on earth!" We can help His Reign be recognized on earth by giving Him the love of our childlike hearts and allowing Him to reign in our hearts and our minds.

Jesus said,

> **This work is eternal for it is the proclamation of my sovereign and divine Kingship; the acknowledgment of my supreme authority over all creation;** it is the song of praise sung by the Heavenly Court, by the angels who continually cry, 'Holy, holy, holy!' as they claim my divine sovereignty. (*Journal* 706).

> **Contained within it is the totality of all of the devotions to my sacred and divine person, for it is the crowning glory of all others;** the absolute and supreme authority granted me by my Father. This authority which must be recognized by all and re-acclaimed by my holy Church. (*Journal* 708).

In a message to His Secretary, on October 6, 2015, **Jesus said,**

> Let the work for the approval of my [Jesus King of All Nations] Devotion go forward. This must be accomplished. Time is of the essence. Do not grow lax in this great work. It must be the focus of your lives. All those whom I have called to this are responsible for their particular part. Never give up. Never let up. This Devotion is vital for these times.

Mankind has forgotten its God, *"they became proud of heart and forgot me."* (Hosea 13:6), and **by means of this Devotion I wish to renew in the hearts of man belief in me and true worship of me.** No, never relent. This is the work of God.

"Only, conduct yourselves in a way worthy of the Gospel of Christ, so that, whether I come and see you or am absent, I may hear news of you, that you are standing firm in one spirit, with one mind struggling together for the faith of the Gospel, not intimidated by your opponents. This is proof to them not of destruction, but of your salvation. And this is God's doing." (Philippians 1:27–28).

Yes, let this message be given to those I have called to this work.

"God is faithful, and by Him you were called" (1 Corinthians 1:9).

"for the favoring hand of our God was upon us" (Ezra 8:18).

Abandoning this work is greatly displeasing to me. Where is your faith? Where is your trust? Why do obstacles deter you? Have I not forewarned you of these? Does this not accompany all of my works? Has not the evil one opposed my work from the beginning? Never give up. Continue your efforts even when all seems lost. Am I not the Lord, the Almighty? It shall be as I so will it to be. Courage!"

"Be careful, then, that what was said in the prophets not come about: 'Look on, you scoffers, be amazed and disappear. For I am doing a work in your days, a work that you will never believe even if someone tells you.'" (Acts 13:40–41). (*Journal* 641-650).

Yes, as Jesus said, "It shall be as I so will it to be," because He is the King of All Nations.

3. The Act of Entrustment of the United States of America to Jesus King of All Nations

On November 21, 2021, on the Solemnity of Jesus Christ, King of the Universe, in his Cathedral of St. Francis Xavier, Bishop David Ricken of the Diocese of Green Bay, Wisconsin, entrusted the United States of America to Jesus King of All Nations. His priests and pastoral leaders joined Bishop Ricken in reciting a Special Litany for Christ to reign.

The photo below shows Bishop Ricken in the Entrance Procession.

Bishop Ricken preached in his homily,

We must remember that the Kingdom of God is just what it says it is, God's Kingdom. And that means that God is Sovereign Lord of all of creation, of the universe, of each and every nation.

The good news is that God's Reign is not about ruling with an iron fist. No, God is the best ruler we could possibly have and, when He returns to earth, He will fully establish His Kingdom of love, respect, peace, joy, and fullness of life.

In the meantime, we must entrust ourselves to Him and ask for the grace to be faithful to Him in difficult times, which it seems are on the horizon more and more. We must be ready every day, brothers and sisters, for trials and sufferings and sacrifices, unlike anything we have faced in our lives previously.

We must persevere through these trials and keep our eyes focused on Jesus. It is obvious that our nation is under great trial now with the aftereffect of the pandemic, as well as social, economic, and political divisions that seem to grow each day. Countries with great antipathy to the United States are beating the drums of domination as they flex their muscles in many ways. There are even divisions in the Church about fundamental moral questions, which are creating stress in the Body of Christ. In the midst of all this upheaval, brothers and sisters, we must remember that Jesus is our King.

Friends, this is a time for fervent prayer and fasting, for calling one another back to Jesus, for committing or recommitting ourselves to living as disciples of Christ. Let us not delay, for we know not the day nor the hour of the Lord's coming. I urge each of you to join me in entrusting your life to Christ the King and praying for our diocese, our state, and our nation. With God as our King, we know that no evil can overcome us!

Please see Appendix H, *The Act of Entrustment of the United States of America to Jesus King of All Nations*, on pg. 290

4. The Divine Plan of Jesus King of All Nations for the Great Renewal of His Holy Church, the United States of America, and All Nations.

Only 5 days after the Entrustment of the United States of America to Jesus King of All Nations, made on November 21, 2021, the Feast of Christ the King, by Bishop David Ricken of the Diocese of Green Bay, Wisconsin, in his Cathedral of St. Francis Xavier, Jesus revealed His Divine Plan to His Secretary, the mystic of His Devotion, on November 26, 2021.

Jesus revealed that, from the state of Wisconsin, USA, shall come bounteous graces for the renewal of His holy Church, of this nation [the USA,] and, indeed, of all the nations of the world.

I believe that this Divine Plan is a fruit of the Entrustment of the USA to Jesus King of All Nations made only 5 days before.

Jesus King of All Nations revealed,

> Go forward now and honor me as Jesus King of All Nations in my Devotion; that which I revealed from heaven to help my poor children in the dangerous and truly sinful, evil times in which they live.
>
> This Devotion is a sign from heaven that these are the end-times and the eternal plan of the Father for mankind continues to unfold. Once more I proclaim: this Devotion is the crowning glory of all devotions to my sacred person.

On December 8, 2021, Jesus King of All Nations revealed, with His scriptural confirmations (see *Journal* 849 and following),

> I send my daughter, my servant, my Secretary once more with my message, my Devotion of Jesus King of All Nations. *"Behold, I am sending my messenger ahead of you; he will prepare your way. A voice of one crying out in the desert: 'Prepare the way of the Lord, make straight His paths.'"* (Mark 1:2–3).

It is the keen desire of my most Sacred Heart that my Devotion, as I have revealed it, be embraced and fully employed first by my holy Church and then spread throughout the entire world. *"for the king's order was urgent."* (Daniel 3:22).

You see time grows very short. These are the times for my sovereign Kingship, my Divine Reign, my Eternal Rule to be boldly and unabashedly proclaimed. *"This shall be to the Lord's renown, an everlasting imperishable sign."* (Isaiah 55:13).

Wake up, my people! Come to the foot of my throne to receive mercy, peace, and forgiveness. Come to receive protection from what is soon to come upon the world. *"Because you have kept my message of endurance, I will keep you safe in the time of trial that is going to come to the whole world to test the inhabitants of the earth. I am coming quickly. Hold fast to what you have, so that no one may take your crown."* (Revelation 3:10–11).

Once more do all that is possible to you to bring about my Reign, my sovereign Kingship in all souls, in all nations!

I plead with you now to employ my full Devotion to include my Image which I myself have designed. This Image in particular moves my Sacred Heart with pity for my children. *"For our God is a consuming fire."* (Hebrews 12:29).

It draws down my graces, mercy, and protection. This Image must be solemnly enthroned. This is my divine desire. My holy plan. Let it be so. Let it be done. *"The Lord is here."* (Ezekiel 48:35). *"He answered, "You have said so."* (Matthew 26:25).

On the same day, Our Lady revealed to His Secretary,

I am the Immaculate Queen of Heaven and earth! Mary, the Immaculate, sinless one, the most holy Mother of God.

I was sent here to this wild land [Wisconsin], to usher in the Reign of my Divine Son who is Jesus King of All Nations. I have come to prepare this chosen land in this vast country for the coming of Jesus Christ, the Sovereign Lord and King of all.

Blessed is this land by the Almighty Lord for it is chosen, it is consecrated by the Lord and marked as His by my appearance here.

My Divine Son sends me to precede Him, to make straight His path, to announce His coming.

Do not miss the time of His visitation but make way for the coming of the Sovereign Lord, the King of All Nations!

You are blessed, Wisconsin, you are blessed, land of Green Bay. For the Lord has chosen you as the particular dwelling place of His Throne,...

...the land from which His Kingship shall be acclaimed anew! A bright light shining forth for the conversion of the nations!"

Our Lady apparently referred to her apparition as Our Lady of Good Help to Adele Brise in Wisconsin in October of 1859. Bishop David Ricken of the Diocese of Green Bay, Wisconsin, who made the Entrustment of the United States of America to Jesus King of All Nations, also approved that apparition — the only approved apparition in the United States of America.

Signs and Wonders of a Visitation of the Image of Jesus King of All Nations

Susanne Malestic, Guardian of the life-sized Visitation Image of Jesus King of All Nations, hosted an extended Visitation with the Image in the state of Wisconsin in 2022.

One evening, Susanne hosted the Image in her home. A former-Catholic friend of hers approached the Image to venerate it. Susanne said that as he stood very close to the Image, he began shaking, with his muscles doing all sorts of rippling and contracting — she had never seen anything like it.

She said that he "went into ecstasy." It lasted for about 20 minutes, and his eyes filled with tears. The man said that Jesus had given him a Scripture in his mind regarding Moses and the burning bush. He was told, "Take off your shoes for the ground on which you stand is holy ground." This was the very same thing that God had told Moses as he stood before the burning bush on Mount Sinai! (See Exodus 3:5).

On another occasion, a Deacon from St. Andrew's Parish in Delavan, Wisconsin, met with Susanne at her home to venerate the Image. She explained the Devotion to the Deacon and read him messages from the *Journal*. Then she explained the promises of Jesus King of All Nations, especially those of protection. The Deacon asked her, "Why haven't I ever heard about this!"

After their discussion, Susanne left him alone with the Image for some time. When she returned, she said that the Deacon had tears in his eyes and explained to her what had happened to him.

He said that while he was venerating the Image, he was drawn to focus on the feet of Jesus in the Image. As he did so, he heard Jesus say to him, "Be my feet; bring me to St. Andrew's church."

It was as if the Visitation fulfilled the Scripture, "Jesus went around to all the towns and villages, teaching in their synagogues, proclaiming the Gospel of the Kingdom, and curing every disease and illness. At the sight of the crowds, His Heart was moved with pity for them because they were troubled and abandoned, like sheep without a shepherd." (Matthew 9:35-36).

So, Susanne and the Deacon began to schedule the date for a Visitation. The Deacon said that Jesus wished it to be on August 1st. Jesus had probably chosen that date because it is the anniversary of His revelation of His Medal to His Secretary, the mystic of the Devotion.

Susanne also reported that a woman made the nine-day *Novena in Honor of Jesus as True King* and, on the ninth day, she was surrounded with the fragrance of roses!

She also said that "holy glitter" frequently appears on the Image. It comes and goes and moves to different areas. Susanne said it most often appears as she prays before the Image. People have also felt heat and pulsating from Jesus' Sacred Heart and wounds, and some venerators have seen His Heart beating and His eyes change color.

A woman doctor told Susanne that she was partially blind from macular degeneration of her left eye. She said that she approached the Image and placed her hand on the Sacred Heart

The Divine Plan of Jesus King of All Nations for the Great
Renewal of His Holy Church, the United States of America, and
All Nations.

of Jesus. As she did so, she felt heat running through her hand and arm and into her left eye and said that she could see!

Susanne took the Image to La Salette Shrine in Twin Lakes, Wisconsin. It is the very modest shrine of a Polish community out in the countryside. Susanne described it as a beautifully peaceful evening. They had time for Eucharistic adoration, confessions, veneration of the Image, and the prayers of the Devotion with the pastor, Fr. Andrew, leading. People prostrated themselves before the Image.

5. Secularism

Jesus King of All Nations wants us to recognize His Reign on earth; to have confidence in His gifts; to implore His protection, especially from His enemies and our enemies and from His chastisements; to ask for His forgiveness; to trust in His mercy; and to implore Him for the recognition of His Kingdom on earth by others.

To help us to obtain these promises, Jesus King of All Nations revealed to us the following prayer, *The Novena in Honor of Jesus as True King,*

> O Lord our God, you alone are the most holy King and ruler of all nations. We pray to you, Lord, in the great expectation of receiving from you, O divine King, mercy, peace, justice, and all good things.

> Protect, O Lord our King, our families and the land of our birth. Guard us, we pray, most faithful one! Protect us from our enemies and from your just judgment.

> Forgive us, O sovereign King, our sins against you. Jesus, you are a King of mercy. We have deserved your just judgment. Have mercy on us, Lord, and forgive us. We trust in your great mercy.

> O most awe-inspiring King, we bow before you and pray; may your Reign, your Kingdom, be recognized on earth! Amen.

Please see *The Novena in Honor of Jesus as True King* on pg. 245.

This Novena prayer summarizes how Jesus wants us to recognize Him and how He wants us to petition Him in order to receive His protection from Secularism, His enemy and our

enemy, and its Culture of Death. The following italicized parts of the prayer exemplify this.

O Lord our God, you alone are the most holy King and ruler of all nations. This statement shows how Jesus wants us to recognize Him as God and King and Ruler of all nations.

We pray to you, Lord, in the great expectation of receiving from you, O divine King, mercy, peace, justice, and all good things. This prayer of petition shows our confidence in the divine mercy of Jesus King of All Nations.

Protect, O Lord our King, our families and the land of our birth. This prayer is a petition for protection of our families and our country.

Protect us from our enemies and from your just judgment. This is a prayer of petition for His protection from His chastisements and from His enemies and our enemies, including the Secularists, their Culture of Death, and militant jihadist Muslims.

Forgive us, O sovereign King, our sins against you. This is a prayer of contrition for our sins against Jesus King of All Nations.

We bow before you and pray; may your Reign, your Kingdom, be recognized on earth! Amen. This is a prayer of petition that the Reign and Kingdom of Jesus King of All Nations will be recognized on earth.

Regarding His Jesus King of All Nations Devotion, Jesus said, "Contained within it is the totality of all of the devotions to my sacred and divine person for it is the crowning glory of all others; the absolute and supreme authority granted me by my Father. This authority which must be recognized by all and re-acclaimed by my holy Church." (*Journal* 708).

If we pray His Novena prayer with sincerity, wear His Medal, and enthrone His Image, we can have confidence that He will grant the petitions contained in the prayer. Let us not be like King Louis XVI of France, who did not respond to Jesus' requests to consecrate himself to His Sacred Heart and to enthrone the Image of His Sacred Heart. The King's failure to do so led to His beheading and the French Revolution.

The greatest obstacle to the recognition of the Social Reign of Jesus King of All Nations on earth are the Secularists. Their culture is a culture of worldliness, peopled by those who live as if God does not exist and who have not come to know the love of the one true God. They have brought us a Culture of Death.

Human societies have cultures that are formed by their values. These include judgments of good or evil that people make about certain human behaviors or the actions of the State. Today, many cultural values are upside down. What was once judged as unquestionably evil is now judged as socially good, to the extent that some politicians can say, "Abortion is not just a legal right, it is a social good."

St. John Paul II wrote, "We need now more than ever to have the courage to look the truth in the eye and to call things by their proper name, without yielding to convenient compromises or to the temptation of self-deception. In this regard, the reproach of the prophet is extremely straightforward, **'Woe to those who call evil good and good evil, who put darkness for light and light for darkness.'**" (Isaiah 5:20). (Pope John Paul II, *Evangelium Vitae (The Gospel of Life)*, 58).

T.S. Eliot wrote, "The world is trying the experiment of attempting to form a civilized but non-Christian mentality. The experiment will fail; but we must be very patient in awaiting its collapse; meanwhile redeeming the time: so that the faith may be preserved alive through the dark ages before us; to renew and rebuild civilization, and save the world from suicide." (T. S. Eliot, *Thoughts After Lambeth*, 1931).

Historian Arnold Toynbee also commented on civilization's suicide. He said, "Civilizations die from suicide, not by murder," by which he meant that they are not killed by outsiders but by themselves through the death of their culture. They no longer see any meaning to life and do not follow a moral code, but simply make their own choices according to their own individual, personal desires. **The sure sign of Secularism's Culture of Death is its exaltation of personal autonomy and the choice to do whatever one wills.**

Modern Secularism is the end result of humanity's increasing confidence in human capabilities without God. It began with the

Italian Renaissance, in the 14ᵗʰ century, with the humanistic belief that man was the center of his own universe. It continued with the rebellion against the Teaching Authority of the Catholic Church in the Protestant Revolution in the 16ᵗʰ century. It was established in the 18ᵗʰ century in the Enlightenment and it was institutionalized with the Goddess of Reason, without God or faith, during the French Revolution.

Secularism is the ideology that the meaning of human life and the principles of social organization should be derived only from the material world, without recourse to God. It promotes the ideas that there should be a complete separation between Church and State and that humanity should live in this world, using reason alone without faith in God, who they believe either does not exist or cannot be known. They believe that there is no eternal life in heaven or eternal damnation in hell.

The believers in Secularism are known as Secularists, Liberals, or Leftists. They also call themselves "Progressives," because they falsely believe that they are promoting the progress of humanity in this world.

The essential belief of Secularists is that happiness and good can only be sought and found in the material world, with freedom from any restraint, in order to exercise their own personal choices. Secularism denies the essential meaning, purpose, nature, design, and dignity of humanity and our need for redemption by God and His plan for our eternal destiny of happiness with Him.

Many Secularists are revolutionaries because they promote the overthrow of traditional governments and the establishment of new ones by revolution, especially Socialism and Communism. In 1847, Sr. Mary of St. Peter of Tours, France, revealed that Freemasons, Communists, and, by extension, all revolutionaries are enemies of Jesus Christ and of His Church, which they have tried to overthrow by revolution since the French Revolution.

The terminology of the political spectrum of Left and Right (Liberal and Conservative) originated during the French Revolution from the place where the deputies in the French National Assembly sat. The Royalists favored the traditional monarchy and sat on the right. The Jacobins favored the revolutionaries and sat on the left. And so it is today, when the traditionalists (Conservatives) are said to be on the Right and the revolutionaries (Liberals) are said to be on the Left.

Eventually, after the French Revolution, as Marxism in various forms came to dominate the politics of self-styled reformers, it began to define the political spectrum. The Left's followers of Marx became the people in power and replaced the Right's monarchists and their traditionalist followers. However, this dichotomy became less defined as more and more people opposed traditional Conservatives and became the revolutionary Leftists of Communism and Secularism.

Today, many Secularists are Cultural Marxists. Marxism calls for violent revolution by the so-called oppressed workers, ironically, through a dictatorship over them called the Dictatorship of the Proletariat.

Cultural Marxism seeks to influence the culture and thereby gain influence and power in society. In that way, their power is gained indirectly as it comes from the culture and not from violent revolution.

Its goals are not economic, as in Marxism, but cultural. Cultural Marxism seeks to eliminate the so-called "oppression" of many groups of people, such as women, minority races, and sexually deviant groups such as practicing homosexuals and so-called transgenders. They feel "oppressed" by those who deny the biological reality of transgenderism and those who believe in the truth of the immorality of homosexuality.

Cultural Marxists exhibit irrationality in promoting their many causes for supposed social justice. Their latest cause is to deny the reality of God's creation of human beings as male and female and to promote the revolutionary cause of so-called transgenderism, whereby people can identify themselves not by the sex in which they were created, but, rather, as the opposite sex by their own irrational choice.

Generally, the revolutionary causes of the Cultural Marxists are not founded on reason, truth, or facts but, rather, on propaganda. Most attempts to reason with them or discuss the basis of their revolutionary causes are met with personal name-calling or *ad hominem* arguments that attack the person of the inquirer.

Cultural Marxism, including Black Lives Matter, wants to eliminate the nuclear family. It attacks the foundations of traditional cultures that practice true marriage, true nuclear families, patriotism, and traditional morality.

The people in our culture today are now divided generally between those who are Secularists and act as if God does not exist and the rest of the people who are traditional Conservatives and have a foundational belief in God and the Greco-Roman, Judeo-Christian tradition. This is the modern manifestation of the primeval battle between the Kingdom of Satan and the Kingdom of God.

The revolutions of Secularists have caused millions of deaths, especially through the French Revolution, the Russian Revolution, the Mexican Revolution, the Spanish Civil War, the Chinese Revolution, and the Cuban Revolution.

Many of the characteristics of Secularists and their beliefs are set forth in the three Humanist Manifestos published in 1933, 1973, and 2003, and in *A Secular Humanist Declaration* published in 1980. Most Secularists share the following beliefs (in alphabetical order):

Atheism, Agnosticism, or so-called *"Spiritualism"* whereby there is no God or they don't know if He exists or they believe that they are "spiritual," but without reference to God;

Communism whereby there will be a classless society, after the State has withered away, where all people share all property in common and the burdens and profits of labor. However, this has never happened;

Egalitarianism whereby there will be the removal of all inequality among people;

Humanism whereby human reason and efforts alone, without God's help, will solve humanity's problems;

Liberalism whereby they will be freed from the restraints of objectively good moral values and from family, community, the Catholic Church, and any other groups that restrain them from choosing to do the evil that they want to do. This is license, not liberty, and destroys the social fabric that produces citizens capable of self-government;

Materialism whereby only the material world exists with no transcendent or spiritual realm and no human soul, whose destiny is to eternal life in heaven or eternal damnation in hell;

Personal autonomy whereby they can exercise their personal choices and desires without reference to the objective moral good;

Progressivism whereby they can bring so-called "progress" to communities and nations only through secular humanistic efforts;

Rationalism whereby only reason can bring about good in humanity without the necessity of faith;

Scientism whereby science is the only source of human knowledge;

Socialism whereby they deprive people of their private property with a dictatorship State that owns and administers the means of production and distribution of goods;

Statism whereby there will be separation of Church and State in which Church members should simply have the right to worship in their own buildings, but not to freely exercise their religion in public. They believe that human problems should be solved only by the State without any reference to the Church or intermediary private associations and that the State should have substantial centralized control over social and economic affairs. Statism may also become idolatry. "Idolatry not only refers to false pagan worship. It remains a constant temptation to faith....Man commits idolatry whenever he honors and reveres a creature in place of God, whether this be gods or demons...[or]...the State...." (CCC 2113); and

Tolerance whereby they say that they are tolerant, but, in fact, they are very intolerant of those who disagree with their beliefs and, rather than dialogue with them, they simply say that they are hateful and call them names, such as bigots, racists, or homophobes.

Many Secularists share many disbeliefs:

They disbelieve that God created human beings as male and female and believe that humans may "transgender" and choose their own sex, regardless of how God created them;

They disbelieve that marriage is instituted by God whereby a male and female are united for life in an indissoluble relationship that is open to new life. So they believe that human beings may enter into a false marriage with another person of the same sex;

They disbelieve that humans have a tendency to sin because of Original Sin and believe that humans need no redemption and may obtain goodness, happiness, and peace on earth, without God, through human reason and human efforts alone;

They disbelieve in the creation of the world by an intelligent God with an orderly design and believe only in the evolution of life through chance; and

They disbelieve that human beings are in need of salvation from sin and death and think that they can save themselves. They believe that peace on earth can be established through a worldwide society of equality through mutually cooperative human efforts alone.

Life is meant to be more than the secular goals of a utopian society of liberty and equality with freedom for libertinism and freedom from restraint of vices. In truth, technology, production, and economic growth are only relative goals that should be subordinated to the love of God, family, and neighbors. We should also pursue truth, goodness, and beauty through study, the practice of virtues, and appreciation of the creative arts.

God has endowed us with the faculty of the imagination: to guide our intellects and wills toward their proper ends of truth, goodness, beauty, and love. With the proper use of our imaginations, we can envision these ends and, through our words and actions, create and perform works of truth, goodness, beauty, and love in science, engineering, literature, history, art, architecture, and music.

However, we must constantly be alert, subject to reason, and dismiss from our imaginations Satan's attempts to influence them to produce the opposites of these proper ends, which are lies, evil, ugliness, and hate. As Jesus said, "For from within, out of the heart of man, come evil thoughts…" (Mark 7:21).

In our secular culture, it is very important to be alert for musical lyrics that attempt to influence us to imagine lies in order to lead us to produce a utopian world without God. One example of this that sums up the belief of Secularists is the song *Imagine*, by John Lennon. He sang that we can bring peace on earth without concern for our true destinies to either eternal heaven or to hell and without having to live a virtuous life or having to do good, but simply by imagining it and the world will become one!

Fr. Peter Damian Fehlner, the spiritual director of the Secretary of the Jesus King of All Nations Devotion, believed that the practice of the Devotion will conquer Secularism.

He wrote, "For the vast majority, the practice of the Devotion is the only way in which a profound practical truth such as that of Jesus King of All Nations can be incorporated into each and all. Without this, Secularism will quickly produce an unheard-of disaster. With it, Secularism will be stopped dead, and the new evangelization will begin to produce stupendous fruits, particularly in the order of sanctity and of respect for the laws of God so basic to a social order truly humane and religious rather than that of the concentration camp."

One example of "an unheard-of disaster" produced by Secularism was the Sexual Revolution.

The Sexual Revolution

Sr. Mary of St. Peter said that Jesus called all revolutionaries His enemies. These include the sexual revolutionaries who promote contraception, abortion, infanticide, same-sex false marriage, and so-called transgenderism.

"In the 1960s, an egregious event occurred, on a scale unprecedented in history. It could be said that in the 20 years from

1960 to 1980, the previously normative standards regarding sexuality collapsed entirely and a new normalcy arose that has by now been the subject of laborious attempts at disruption....Among the freedoms that the [Sexual] Revolution sought to fight for was this all-out sexual freedom, one which no longer conceded any norms." (Pope Emeritus Benedict XVI, *The Church and the Scandal of Sexual Abuse*).

The pioneers of the 1960s Sexual Revolution were sexual anthropologist Margaret Mead and birth control advocate Margaret Sanger, founder of what is today Planned Parenthood. In 1961, they paved the way for the beginning of the American Sexual Revolution. It was also the year that the Federal Drug Administration gave its approval to the first birth control pill.

I completed college and law school in the 1960s when slogans fostered the development of the Sexual Revolution. The sloganeers told us, "Don't trust anyone over 30; Do your own thing; If it feels good, do it; Make love not war; and Turn on, tune in, and drop out [with drugs]." Many young adults practiced the slogans, rebelled against their parents' formation, and joined the Sexual Revolution that was further encouraged by the decisions of the United States Supreme Court that legalized the sales of contraceptives and the anti-life business of abortion.

The foundational false ideology of the Sexual Revolution was the same as all of the other revolutions—the false idea that we can live as if God does not exist, that there is no objective good and evil but that moral values are personal, relative, and whatever one chooses them to be, even if they are objectively evil, such as fornication, adultery, contraception, and abortion.

Margaret Mead promoted the false ideology that moral laws were merely social inventions made by humans that could then be changed by humans. This false ideology was a revolutionary attempt to overthrow the traditional truth of almost two millennia that moral laws were instituted by God in the Ten Commandments. This false ideology allowed people to make their own personal choices to do sexually whatever they wanted.

That false ideology also led to the false ideology of Margaret Sanger that contraception was a moral good and that ideology led to the approval of the birth control pill and, ultimately, to the *Casey vs Planned Parenthood* decision of the United States Supreme Court that allows the choice and freedom to engage in whatever sexual acts one may choose. That false ideology led to the Secularist's Culture of Death with legalized homosexuality, same-sex false marriage, and false transgenderism. Youth who are pro-life emphatically reject these false ideologies and believe that life is precious.

In January 2019, **Jewish truth teller Ben Shapiro addressed the Legatus Catholic Leadership Conference of business executives. He said, "Young people are not looking for pizza, guitars, and a vague spirituality. They are looking for a sense of meaning. They are looking for rules, they are looking for duty. They are looking for a reason to live. That is what young people want."**

Our Lady of America gave young people a reason to live. She asked them to be pure and wanted them to study and live the spirituality of the divine indwelling in which we recognize the indwelling of the living Holy Trinity in our souls. **She said that the youth of America would bring conversion to the world as Torchbearers of the Queen.**

One of those Torchbearers was a homeschooled high school young lady who worked part-time at our apostolic center. 15-year-old Lily Yandow attended the 2019 March for Life as part of the Diocese of Vermont's *Life Is Precious Pilgrimage*. She wrote about it for you. Please take a vicarious armchair pilgrimage with her in Washington, DC: on the bus, in the March, at an assisted living home, at the Basilica of the National Shrine of the Immaculate Conception, and at the Memorial shrines, when reading what she wrote,

> *After 12 hours overnight on a bus, we arrived in DC at around 7:30 Friday morning. We started off at the youth rally at Mason University. There, Mass was said and there were multiple speakers, including Sr. Bethany Madonna of the Sisters of Life. After this, everyone was provided with a free lunch by Chick-fil-A. Next, we marched.*
>
> *We marched for those who couldn't defend themselves. We marched because women deserve better. We marched to end*

abortion. We marched for life. It was an incredible atmosphere, hundreds of thousands of people united in one noble, heroic, and vital goal to express the truth: Life Is Precious.

There were so many creative and meaningful signs held by those who marched. We marched to the Supreme Court, where women were giving their testimonies, holding posters that read, "I regret my abortion." This is where the Vermont group regrouped. We all knew where to go, because our group leader had a tiger stuffed-animal tied to a pole hoisted in the air, which was quite funny but also functional; it was much easier to keep track of the group.

After this, we met up with the bus and went to the local high school where we would be sleeping. This trip was to proclaim the value of all life, not just the unborn, so the next morning we visited an assisted living home. We visited with the elderly, who all seemed to enjoy our company. I spent most of my time there playing cards with a fantastic old man who could not speak, but sure knew how to smile, and, instead of shaking hands, he fist-bumped!

We departed from the assisted living and headed to the city. Our first stop was the Holocaust Memorial. The Holocaust was a horrible thing, and there was so much at the Memorial about "not letting it happen again." This struck many of us on the trip, because it is happening, and so many people don't even care. Millions of unborn children thoughtlessly murdered, and the number continues to rise. The Holocaust was a terrible event, but in a way it gives me hope. The Holocaust ended, and so can abortion.

Our next stop was at the Basilica of the National Shrine of the Immaculate Conception. I had been there once before, but this time we had a guided tour. It was very interesting and the meaning behind all of the art was explained to us. The Basilica is a beautiful and incredible place.

At the Shrine, Fr. Jon Schnobrich celebrated Mass for us. Before Mass, we were able to pray in front of the heart of St. John Vianney, which was on pilgrimage throughout America. This was a wonderful surprise for us because none of us knew about it beforehand.

Next, we went to the St. John Paul II National Shrine. It was interesting to go to this place and the Holocaust Memorial, *because St. John Paul II was a light in the darkness during the Holocaust. Both St. John Paul II and St. Mother Teresa were on my mind a lot throughout the trip, and it dawned on me that, although they did great things, they were nothing more than ordinary people who loved in an extraordinary way. How much better would the world be if we could just learn to love.*

We finished off the day with visits to the Lincoln Memorial, the Washington Monument, and the Vietnam Veterans Memorial. A friend that I had made on the trip had some family friends and relatives that died in Vietnam. We searched for their names on the Wall and found them!

We picked up pizza from Costco for the second night in a row and headed back to the high school. We had originally planned to leave the next day, Sunday morning, but were delayed by a snowstorm. As result, we had a whole extra day in DC, so we went to the Franciscan Monastery of the Holy Land in America. I absolutely loved the outside area at the monastery: stone walkways, gardens, and grottos. We left early the next morning, around 6:30, and we arrived in Burlington that evening

Overall, it was a meaningful pilgrimage that I am thankful I was able to experience.

Contrary to this "meaningful pilgrimage" of young Lily Yandow, the Sexual Revolution ultimately decimated the unity of families through no-fault divorce. It has left in its wake many narcissistic individuals who do not have an understanding of the meaning of life, why they exist, who they are, and where they are going. They were often not properly formed in good families and search today for substitute families, such as in the so-called LGBT communities and in identity politics.

Only the truth, goodness, and beauty of the Catholic Church's teachings on human sexuality, marriage, and the family and the practice of them can save people from the horrific consequences of the Sexual Revolution and the Culture of Death.

We should believe that God's Will for sex is for bonding and for babies. The purpose of sexual intercourse is to unite a married man and woman in love with an openness to the creation and acceptance of new life.

The Sexual Revolution left us with rampant fornication, adultery, contraception, fatherless children, broken families, and broken children; abortion, sodomy, sexually transmitted diseases, such as AIDS; and same-sex false marriages. It brought widespread pornography addiction, sexual harassment, sexual abuse of minors, and the denial of a person's biological sex that has now culminated in false transgenderism and transhumanism.

The Revolution of Transgenderism and Transhumanism

Pope Francis said, while meeting with the bishops of Poland, in July 2016, "Today, in schools they are teaching this to children — to children! — that everyone can choose their gender."

Referring to a meeting that he had with Pope Emeritus Benedict XVI, Pope Francis told the bishops, "Speaking with Pope Benedict, who is well, and has a clear mind, he was telling me, 'Holiness, this is the epoch of sin against God the creator.' He's intelligent! **God created man and woman, God created the world this way, this way, this way, and we are doing the opposite."**

"God created man in His image; in the divine image He created him; male and female He created them." (Genesis 1:27). "*Man and woman have been created*, which is to say, *willed* by God: on the one hand, in perfect equality as human persons; on the other, in their respective beings as man and woman. 'Being man' or 'being woman' is a reality which is good and willed by God:...." (CCC 369).

The science of genetics teaches us that male cells (which contain XY chromosomes) differ, from the very moment of conception, from female cells (with their XX chromosomes). Men and women are two different kinds of human beings and being either of them is good and willed by God.

Historically, gender and biological sex were commonly understood to be the same so that a female was understood to be of the female gender and of the female sex. Now, some people differentiate between gender and sex through a false gender ideology commonly called "gender theory." They teach that sexual identity is more of a social construct than a given natural or biological fact. They teach that gender is not the same as biological sex and that people may choose to be the opposite sex of their biological sex.

They call this "transgenderism," whereby a person, through free choice, drugs, and the mutilation of his or her body, may claim to be the opposite sex of his or her biological sex. We should have compassion for these people who suffer from gender dysphoria, a disorder in which they do not accept their biological sexual identity, which has been willed by God and is, therefore, good.

However, **the cure for sexual identity disorder for these suffering people is not to mutilate their bodies in an attempt to appear as a member of the opposite biological sex, but to care for them so that they may accept the biological sex that God created for them. Human beings have a nature that must be respected and may not be manipulated at will.**

On June 10, 2019, **the Vatican's Congregation for Catholic Education issued its document,** *Male and Female He Created Them.* **They wrote, "'Gender theory' denies the difference and reciprocity in nature of a man and a woman and envisages a society without sexual differences, thereby eliminating the anthropological basis of the family.** This ideology leads to educational programs and legislative enactments that promote a personal identity and emotional intimacy radically separated from the biological difference between male and female. Consequently, human identity becomes the choice of the individual, one which can change over time."

The National Catholic Bioethics Center stated in its "Brief Statement on Transgenderism,"

> **Taking up or engaging in behavioral changes, including mannerisms, social cues, clothing, or modes of speaking those social mores ascribe to the opposite sex, does not alter the innate sexual identity of the embodied spirit, which is the human person.** Hormonal interventions, to block the body's sex-specific hormones or provide the sex-specific hormones of the opposite sex, likewise alter nothing of a person's innate sexual identity....So-called sex reassignment surgeries of any kind, designed to give the body an appearance with more of the culturally-expected qualities of the opposite sex, also cannot modify the true

sexual identity of the person, who was created male or female.

Directly intending to transition one's given bodily [created] sex into a "new" one (even though this may be perceived as the "real" and "true" one) means intending to alter what is unalterable, to establish a false identity in place of one's true identity, and so to deny and contradict one's own authentic human existence as a male or female body–soul unity. Such an action cannot be consonant with the good of the whole person.

The lie of transgenderism that people, even minors, can change their God-given sex is a rejection of God's Creation, of human nature, and of the natural law. The acceptance of that lie has now led to the lie of "transhumanism" that not only can people choose their own sex, but that they can also choose to try to live forever as transhumans in a new body.

Martin Rothblatt, the male founder of Sirius Satellite Radio, chose to undergo radical sex-reassignment surgery in 1994. His name is now Martine Rothblatt and he calls himself a female. He is the author of *From Transgender to Transhuman.*

He believes that software advances will make it technologically possible to separate our minds from our bodies and merge the resultant "file" and call it "mindware." He claims that he is on the threshold of creating humanity outside of DNA-driven flesh bodies.

However, we must always be mindful that we are male and female creatures who are created by an immortal, omnipotent God who loves us. **We should not rebel against our Creator and manipulate His creation of human beings as male and female with the illusion that human beings can attain immortality.**

Pope Benedict XVI said, "When the freedom to be creative becomes the freedom to create oneself, then necessarily the Maker Himself is denied and ultimately man too is stripped of his dignity as a creature of God, as the image of God at the core of his being…when God is denied, human dignity also disappears." (Pope Benedict XVI, *Christmas Address to the Roman Curia,* December 21, 2012).

The 2002 Vatican statement of the International Theological Commission, *Communion and Stewardship: Human Persons Created in the Image of God*, stated that "changing the genetic identity of man as a human person through the production of an infrahuman being is radically immoral," implying that "man has full right of disposal over his own biological nature." The statement also argues that creation of a superhuman or spiritually superior being is "unthinkable," since true improvement can come only through religious experience and "realizing more fully the image of God."

The Church insists on the rights of the Church, the family, and of Catholic educators to defend authentic teaching and understanding of the dignity of the human person in the face of an increasingly exclusivist approach to education in line with Secularism's so-called progressive principles.

The Secularists' Culture of Death

French philosopher Jean Jacques Rousseau wrote, "Man is naturally good and that it is by our institutions alone that men become wicked." (Jean Jacques Rousseau, *Rousseau's Confessions*). This is directly contrary to the truth that **man is not naturally good but is predisposed toward evil because of Original Sin and its consequences from which we may be saved by the redemption of Jesus Christ.**

Secularists are not naturally good but are really libertines who want to destroy any laws and customs that might prevent them from doing all that they desire to do. For example, they want to destroy any law or regulation that would limit the choice for abortion.

Moreover, they're not drawn to true humanism, but to emotional humanitarianism. They teach how to do social good in the abstract, but, hypocritically, they do not practice it in the concrete. For example, Jean Jacques Rousseau also wrote *Emile, or On Education*, a book on how to raise and educate children. However, he sent all of his own children to the Paris Foundling Hospital immediately upon their birth. He never knew or even saw them!

Catholic teachings on faith and morals have the potential to inform cultures through the conversion and transformation of consciences. On May 23, 1999, **the Pontifical Council for Culture issued its document,** *Toward a Pastoral Approach to Culture.* **Its paragraph numbers are cited in parentheses below. The document reminds us that "it is one of the properties of the human person that he can achieve true and full humanity only by means of culture."** (1). "Culture only exists through man, by man, and for man. It is the whole of human activity, human intelligence, and emotions, the human quest for meaning, human customs, and ethics." (2).

"The first and fundamental dimension of culture, as St. John Paul II stressed to UNESCO, is healthy morality, moral culture." (2).

A culture of life and love can transmit moral values to a nation, such as the recognition of the dignity of every human being created in the image and likeness of God; the meaning and purpose of life; salvation through the forgiveness of sins; and the destiny of eternal life with God with a resurrected body. The witness of the good news of the Gospel can transform the culture from a Culture of Death to a Culture of Life.

When there is no shared commitment in a culture to certain moral truths about the human person and his life and dignity, there is no moral consensus of the people regarding the good or evil of certain fundamental human behaviors or actions by the State and there is a division in the culture.

Cultures are not formed by the State or by local governments. They should be formed by individual human beings in community with one another who are virtuous and share moral truths about the human person, his life and his dignity. They should form a moral consensus in society regarding the good or evil of human behaviors and actions. However, many modern cultures are personally autonomous, narcissistic, ignorant of history and philosophy, nonreflective, materialistic, and consumeristic.

A moral social order is founded upon individual virtuous human beings who must resolve the conflicts between good and evil within their own consciences, either by following the goodness, truth, and beauty of the natural law infused by God or by following the temptations of Satan, away from all of that into social disorder.

Many modern cultures do not respect the dignity and life of every human person, especially the unborn. So, they are not fulfilling what St. John Paul II called, "the condition for the survival of America [which] is to respect every human person, especially the weakest and most defenseless ones, those as yet unborn." (Pope John Paul II, *Address*, September 19, 1987).

Instead, he called our culture a Culture of Death. Unrestrained courts and legislatures have enabled the killing of the unborn by legalized contraception with its abortifacient drugs and by legalized abortion. They have destroyed true marriage and the family through no-fault divorce and legalized same-sex false marriage. They have enabled death by so-called "physician-assisted suicide." They have destroyed the meaning of being created male or female by honoring the choices of deluded persons to try to change their God-created sex and to self-proclaim their sexual identity.

Sins committed by individual men and women are at the heart of this Culture of Death. The normalization of these immoral choices results in the creation of sinful structures that impose the will of the powerful on the weak in both domestic and international affairs. For example, the imposition of the will of President Obama's administration to coerce Catholic charities, such as the Little Sisters of the Poor, against their consciences, to insure their employees for coverage for contraceptives and abortifacients that cause abortions.

St. John Paul II wrote, "In this way, democracy, contradicting its own principles, effectively moves toward a form of totalitarianism. The State is no longer the 'common home' where all can live together on the basis of principles of fundamental equality, but is transformed into a tyrant State." (Pope John Paul II, *Evangelium Vitae (The Gospel of Life)*, 20).

St. John Paul II also wrote, "When people think they possess the secret of a perfect social organization which makes evil impossible, they also think that they can use any means, including violence and deceit, in order to bring that organization into being. Politics then becomes a 'secular religion' which operates under the illusion of creating paradise in this world. But **no political society—which possesses its own autonomy and laws—can ever be confused**

with the Kingdom of God." (Pope John Paul II, *Centesimus Annus*, 25).

Because of this, it is extremely urgent to recognize the Social Reign of Jesus King of All Nations over all societies and states and to obey the natural law and God's revealed moral law that are binding upon the consciences of all peoples, societies, states, and nations.

In 1929, **Hilaire Belloc wrote in his book,** *Europe and the Faith,*

> **We have reached at last a state of society which cannot endure, and a dissolution of standards, a melting of the spiritual framework such that the body politic fails.** Men everywhere feel that an attempt to continue down this endless and ever-darkening road is like the piling up of debt. We go further and further from a settlement.
>
> Our various forms of knowledge diverge more and more. Authority, the very principle of life, loses its meaning, and this awful edifice of civilization which we have inherited, and which is still our trust, trembles and threatens to crash down. It is clearly insecure. It may fall in any moment. We who still live may see the ruin. But ruin when it comes is not only a sudden, it is also a final, thing.
>
> In such a crux there remains the historical truth: that this our European structure, built upon the noble foundations of classical antiquity, was formed through, exists by, is consonant to, and will stand only in the mold of the Catholic Church.

Jesus King of All Nations and His Church are the only remedies for the Secularists' Culture of Death. He revealed in His *Litany in Honor of Jesus King of All Nations* **the invocation, "Jesus King of All Nations, the only remedy for a world so ill, may we serve you."**

Our prevalent culture is "secular" because it recognizes only this material world, without the transcendent recognition of God and His truth, and because it recognizes personal autonomy, by which people may choose to live as if God does not exist and do whatever they will.

Those who support our Culture of Death make their own worldly choices, particularly sexual choices, and seek to have those choices legalized or supported by the State, even by those who do not agree with them. They follow self, sexual "liberation," and Secularism and see their salvation in the State and science (Statism and Scientism) through modern technology.

In *America the Beautiful*, we sing, "America! America! God mend thine every flaw, Confirm thy soul in self-control, Thy liberty in law!" However, **Secularists do not want to mend America's flaws with laws. They do not want to confirm their souls in self-control or their liberties in law, they simply want to be libertines**, able to follow their desires and do whatever they want, especially with recreational sex and the avoidance of its consequences of pregnancy through an abortion.

One example of their libertinism is that, in 2018, with fear that the United States Supreme Court might overrule legalized abortion, Planned Parenthood of New York City launched a fundraising campaign, which they named "#FreedomtoFck."

Planned Parenthood NYC Action touted, "New Yorkers have more sex than the rest of America (Woo! We did it!)." The message at the conclusion of their video is, "Protect our right to safely f**k whoever the f**k we want. Donate to Planned Parenthood."

Secularists also place great hope in modern technology. This has led to the attempts to create "Artificial Intelligence." Truly, **intelligence can be created only by God. However, the Artificial Intelligence that humans will attempt to make (since we cannot create anything) will be like a false god.**

Engineer Anthony Levandowski helped to develop the self-driving car. Now he is forming the first church of Artificial Intelligence. The new religion of Artificial Intelligence is called Way of the Future. The corporate formation documents state that its activities will focus on "the realization, acceptance, and worship of a godhead based on Artificial Intelligence (AI) developed through computer hardware and software."

Mr. Levandowski said, "What is going to be created will effectively be a god. It's not a god in the sense that it makes lightning or causes hurricanes. But if there is something a billion times smarter than the smartest human, what else are you going to call it?"

However, in January 2018, **Pope Francis warned about the threat to humanity of Artificial Intelligence.** At the World Economic Forum Meeting at Davos, he said, "Artificial intelligence, robotics, and other technological innovations must be so employed that they contribute to the service of humanity and to the protection of our common home, rather than to the contrary, as some assessments unfortunately foresee."

Jesus King of All Nations said that modern technology can be an idol. He said, "Children of men, you are blinded by sin! You are blinded by pride! Never in the history of the world has mankind been so laden down with sin. Noise is everywhere. Confusion abounds. **The idolatry of modern technology is a tool of the enemy with which he withdraws hearts and minds from hearing the gentle, loving voice of God.**" (*Journal* 339).

We must confront the Secularists' Culture of Death with the Culture of Life for which St. John Paul II always prayed. We need to let Jesus King of All Nations reign in our minds and hearts so that we can be Jesus to others and see Jesus in them. In turn, they will see Jesus in us and be attracted to Him by the witness of our virtuous lives, especially through the practice of chastity, patience, humility, peace, and the presence of Jesus King of All Nations in our hearts. They will say of us, as did the pagan Romans of the early Christians, "See how those Christians love one another and us!"

And we will see, as did the Christians of pagan Rome, a change in the Secularists' Culture of Death, one person at a time, toward the end of its transformation to a Culture of Life.

The Sins of the Secularists

After the rebellion and fall of the bad angels, our human parents, Adam and Eve, rebelled against the will of God's commandment to eat only of His Tree of Life and not of the Tree of the Knowledge of Good and Evil. They exercised their free will, following the lies of Satan, in opposition to God's perfect Will for them, turned from the Tree of Life to the Tree of the Knowledge of Good and Evil, and ate of it.

This was *the* Original Sin and caused the chastisement to the human race of arduous work, painful births, sin, death, and the loss of sanctifying grace and eternal life. They were the first Secularists who, by their own free will, exercised their personal autonomy in opposition to God, as if He did not exist. They did it their way and not God's way.

The sins of the Secularists are the consequence of their pride and, like Adam and Eve, they follow the lies of Satan so that they can act as their own gods and disobey the one true God.

Secularists say that they are "tolerant" and "non-judgmental" of the beliefs and practices of others, but in reality, they are intolerant and judgmental of those who oppose their beliefs and practices. This leads to discrimination against their opponents and their rights of free speech, free assembly, and free exercise of their religion. This is what happened during the 18th century French Revolution with the beheading of the legitimate King, Louis XVI, ending the rule of the French Catholic monarchs who had reigned for over 1300 years. This was followed by the revolutionaries' Reign of Terror against their peaceful opponents that included the genocide of the Catholics of the Vendée region of France that killed approximately a half million people and the beheading of over 2000 people in Paris.

Tolerance means recognizing and respecting other people's opinions and beliefs and their right to hold them, even if you disagree with them. However, Secularists are intolerant and disrespectful of many opinions and beliefs that are contrary to their core beliefs, such as free choices for evil practices, mostly based upon unnatural sex and sexuality, including fornication, abortion, same-sex sexual acts, same-sex false marriages, and false transgenderism.

The intolerance of the Secularists can be seen as evidenced by their bullying tactics of bringing harassing lawsuits against their critics, "canceling" them, boycotting them, threatening them and confronting them in public, and pressuring corporations to withhold advertising that supports their critics.

Secularists act as if those who oppose their opinions, beliefs, and practices are evil. They call them hateful, bigots, Nazis, homophobes, etc. and try to silence them. They punish them economically through the loss of their jobs, attacks with public exposure, and ridicule in the media.

Recent laws, court decisions, and punishments in educational institutions, the workplace, and the business world have affected the rights of many people to use free speech and the free exercise of their religion to oppose Secularists. These are fundamental rights enshrined in the Constitution of the United States. It is hypocritical for Secularists to interfere with them while proclaiming that they are tolerant when, in fact, they are often intolerant. Ironically, it is precisely those rights that allow the Secularists to pursue their intolerance: free speech, freedom of the press, etc.

In the Soviet Union, everyone had to toe the "party line." That term meant the dictates, ideologies, and propaganda of the Communist Party. People had no freedom of thought, speech, or press for any idea that deviated from the party line. Anyone who dissented committed a crime and was called a "dissident." By this means, the Communist Party totally controlled politics and society.

Dissidents were either imprisoned or punished economically through denial of the Communist Party's perks, such as a nice apartment or a good job. Many dissidents, such as Alexander Solzhenitsyn, were sent to the Gulag, a chain of Soviet forced-labor concentration camps. He told the story in his 1973 book, *The Gulag Archipelago*.

In 1966, Mao Zedong, Chairman of the Communist Party of China began his Chinese Cultural Revolution. He began to purge the so-called "anti-revolutionary enemies" of his Communist State. He started with the capitalists, intellectuals, religious believers, and traditionalists. He used his youthful Red Guards to "purify" the culture.

They spread throughout the land, spouting their slogans, such as "to rebel is justified," and their propaganda against the so-called "Four Olds": old customs, old culture, old habits, and old ideas. The country went mad: Mao's enemies were publicly paraded and humiliated, many were imprisoned and tortured in forced-labor camps, and over 1 million were killed or died in the famine caused by the Revolution.

Our modern "Cancel Culture" movement seeks to abolish all history and religious faith and any memorials to them. Students

and others destroy churches, statues, and other memorials of our traditions just like the revolutionary iconoclasts of the Byzantine Empire, the revolutionaries of the French Revolution, the revolutionary Red Guards of the Chinese Cultural Revolution, and the revolutionary Islamic Taliban. Revolutionaries always try to destroy tradition, history, and memorials to the past.

In a manner similar to the Communist Soviet Union and Communist China, many Secularists today demand "political correctness," which is their "party line," and denounce old customs, culture, habits, and ideas. They attack freedom of thought, speech, or press for any idea that deviates from the ideologies of their "political correctness."

Dissidents against the Secularist Culture of Death are called "haters," and pro-life and pro-family groups are called "hate groups" who communicate "hateful things" and commit "hateful acts," such as exercising their freedom of conscience and refusing to create a wedding cake for a same-sex false marriage. Because of these false accusations, they are subject to harassing lawsuits, criminal investigations, and "hearings" without jury trials before so-called Civil Rights Commissions. These investigations and hearings often violate the United States Constitution's First Amendment rights to the free exercise of religion, press, and speech.

Secularists believe in creating their own utopian heaven on earth without reference to God. They want to marginalize God to the privacy of homes and churches and keep Him out of public life. They promote what Pope Benedict XVI called "a dictatorship of relativism" where there is no objective truth, and they are intolerant of anything contrary to their beliefs and practices.

In sociologist Christian Smith's in-depth survey of "emerging adults" (18 to 24-year-olds), 60 percent said that morality is a personal choice, entirely a matter of individual decision. Forty-seven percent of America's emerging adults agreed that "morals are relative, there are no definite rights and wrongs for everybody."

Many of these "emerging adults" are embracing Wokeism. This title was derived from the slang word "woke" and now refers to people supposedly waking up to the secular political ideology of a new reality. This is a Secularist social philosophy and movement that embraces neo-Marxism and cultural Marxism imbued with social justice, identity politics, and the teaching of Critical Theory that criticizes society and culture in order to reveal and challenge so-called "power structures."

Beyond Marxism, which called for the freedom of the so-called oppressed workers, Wokeism has broadened the so-called oppressed to include practicing lesbians, gays, bisexuals, transgenders, and Blacks. The "oppressors" are those who believe in Western civilization, and, in particular, those whom they call "White Supremacists," who use the evil "racist power" of "systemic white supremacy" to maintain their power.

The Woke teach those who follow them that "the system" is evil, beyond redemption, and can only be saved by people who Stay Woke. They think that they have the truth and the special knowledge to liberate humanity from their "oppressors" and bring happiness on earth to the "oppressed." Most of them do not believe in God, His judgment of eternal happiness with Him in heaven, or their eternal damnation in hell from their rejection of Him.

The Woke believe that the existing hierarchies of power must be torn down and, as they say, "built back better." However, they do not say how it will be built back, especially when **their real goal is the total destruction and remaking of Western civilization. Wokeism has infiltrated the fields of education, medicine, media, entertainment, sports, the military, and the corporate culture.**

The Woke use the means of false education, propaganda, and, eventually, like all revolutionaries, such violent people as the Nazi brownshirts, the young Chinese Red Guard, and, now, Antifa on the streets of America. Like all revolutionaries, the logical conclusion of their beliefs is that the "oppressor" class must be eliminated by violence, if necessary, as the French revolutionaries tried to do with their beheading guillotines that resulted in the near-destruction of the French culture and the Catholic Church in France.

Secularist beliefs form an ideology for how to supposedly be happy in this world and create a society without God — without consideration of the meaning and purpose of human beings and their innate dignity, eternal destiny, and immortal souls, made in the image of their creator God — with only the natural rights and liberties that must be protected by the State.

Modern Secularism will fall just like Communism because it is a false ideology that is contrary to human nature. Secularism cannot satisfy the innate hunger of human beings to know, love, and serve the one true God because, as St. Augustine wrote, "Our hearts were made for you alone, O Lord, and will not be satisfied until they rest in you."

The Secularists' idea that they are leading the world to a so-called "progressive" future is a lie. They are truly leading a regression back to the Garden of Eden. Many Secularists have fallen to Satan's temptation of Adam and Eve in the Garden of Eden that they would become like God. But, like Adam and Eve, they and their ideology will fall.

The *Catholic Catechism* teaches us,

> The supreme religious deception is that of the Antichrist, a pseudo-messianism by which man glorifies himself in place of God and of His Messiah come in the flesh.

> The Antichrist's deception already begins to take shape in the world every time the claim is made to realize within history that messianic hope [such as Secularism] which can only be realized beyond history through the eschatological judgment. The Church has rejected…the "intrinsically perverse" political form of a secular messianism. (CCC 675-676).

St. John Paul II summed up the sins of the Secularists. He referred to Europe and wrote, "[They] attempt to promote a vision of man apart from God and apart from Christ. This sort of thinking has led to man being considered as 'the absolute center of reality which makes him occupy — falsely — the place of God and which forgets that it is not man who creates God, but rather God who creates man. Forgetfulness of God led to the abandonment of man.' It is therefore no wonder that, in this context, a vast field has opened for the unrestrained development of nihilism in philosophy, of relativism in values and morality, and of pragmatism — and even cynical hedonism — in daily life. [A secular] culture gives the impression of 'silent apostasy' on the part of people who have all that they need and who live as if God does not exist." (Pope John Paul II, *Ecclesia in Europa (The Church in Europe)*, 9).

Europeans had started to live as if God does not exist from the time of the French Revolution. Since then, France, so-called the Eldest Daughter of the Church has continued its Secularist sins. As the third millennium began, the French Secularists sought to eliminate any reference to God in the proposed European Union Constitution. They did not want to acknowledge the one true God who had providentially protected France for over a thousand years.

In response, St. John Paul II gave a series of Sunday Angelus addresses. He taught that God, not the State, should be acknowledged in the Constitution as the source of all inalienable human rights.

On July 20, 2003, he said, "It can be said that the Christian faith has shaped the culture of Europe constituting a whole with its history and, notwithstanding the painful division between East and West, Christianity has become the religion of the European peoples. Despite the strong and widespread phenomenon of secularization, the new Europe must be helped to build herself by revitalizing her original Christian roots."

French Secularist President, Jacques Chirac, responded in September 2003, "France is a lay state, and as such she does not have a habit of calling for insertions of a religious nature into constitutional texts."

That is why, as of 2019, only four percent of French Catholics attend Sunday Mass on a regular basis; more tourists visited the Cathedral of Notre Dame, owned by the State, than Catholic worshipers; civil marriages make up more than 60 percent of all marriages; and there are only 10,000 priests left in France, an 80 percent drop from the 1950 number of 50,000.

These are the consequences of the sins of the Secularists "who have lifted themselves up against God, and sought to attain their goals apart from Him." (See Vatican II, *Gaudium et Spes (Pastoral Constitution on the Church in the Modern World)*, 13).

The sins of the Secularists against life include the promotion of so-called "physician-assisted suicide"; same-sex false marriage; false transgenderism with the results of supporting the delusions of its practitioners and of ruining women's sports because of the participation of male competitors; and the promotion of abortion on demand, from conception until birth, without any restrictions whatsoever.

A case study on the sins of the Secularists is the rapid 26-year secularization of the people of Ireland, from voting to prohibit abortion in 1992 to voting to legalize it in 2018.

In 1992, a young girl became pregnant in Ireland and threatened to commit suicide unless she were allowed to have an abortion in Ireland, which had prohibited abortion. Sinead O'Connor, an Irish rock singer, took to the streets with a few hundred supporters and proclaimed, "We made the law and we can change it."

This made world-wide news and, providentially, I saw it on television. I communicated with one of my pro-life priest friends in Ireland and told him that, if he could guarantee ten thousand Rosary Processors in Dublin in reparation for the few hundred who took to the streets with Sinead O'Connor, I would come with the Missionary Image of Our Lady of Guadalupe to lead them.

I was invited and, in May of 1992, Fr. Michael O'Carroll, C.S.Sp., world-renowned Mariologist, the Missionary Image, and I led a Rosary Procession of thousands of the faithful in Dublin. It was the largest Rosary Procession in Ireland since the Eucharistic Congress of 1932. We prayed that Ireland would be kept abortion-free.

As the months passed, the movement for abortion rights raged like a forest fire across Ireland, fueled by the secular media and the government. Finally, the government proposed to the Irish people an amendment to their Constitution, which at the time prohibited abortion, only legalizing it in certain situations. A referendum vote was scheduled. Once again, Our Lady had a special mission.

We were called to come to Ireland again in November of 1992. This time, we made numerous Visitations to many churches to pray and fast against legalized abortion in Ireland. For ten days, we called upon the Irish martyrs to intercede to save Ireland from both the abortion threat and the secular enemy within, far greater threats than their British enemy in the past.

Our Irish missionary journey ended at Knock Shrine. Six thousand of the faithful filled the Shrine on a beautiful spring-like day. It was very unusual to have such fine weather so late in the

Fall, so nice that we had our closing Rosary Procession outside on the Shrine grounds.

Fr. Michael O'Carroll preached to the congregation, followed by a talk by me. I exhorted the Irish people to be true to the faith in imitation of the Irish martyrs who were beatified by St. John Paul II and to follow his teaching that no one may vote to legalize abortion under any circumstances. I said, "As the Irish martyrs died for their faith, let us live ours!"

Before the Missionary Image arrived in Ireland, the polls said that 70% of the Irish people favored legalized abortion. After the Visitation, the polls changed to 70% against legalized abortion and, soon thereafter, the proposed Constitutional amendment to legalize abortion was defeated by the Irish people. Many of the Irish faithful attributed this victory to Our Lady of Guadalupe.

However, the Secular Revolution continued in Ireland and, in 2015, the Irish voted by a huge majority to legalize same-sex false marriage. They became the first country in the world to do so by a vote of the people themselves and not by their representatives or courts.

Ireland's Secular Revolution culminated three years later, in 2018, with an overwhelming vote, again, not by their representatives or courts, but by the Irish people themselves, to legalize abortion by repealing the eighth amendment to the Irish Constitution that had prohibited it.

The Taoiseach [leader of Ireland], Leo Varadkar, celebrated Ireland's rejection of protection for its pre-born children and said, "What we have seen today is the culmination of a quiet revolution [that has been taking place] for the past 10 or 20 years."

"I'm really overwhelmed and proud," said a young woman, wiping away tears. "With the referendum on same-sex marriage and this vote to legalize abortion, we are leading the way — we are a new country. The old Ireland is gone." Yes, the old Ireland that had protected the institution of true marriage and Ireland's pre-born children was indeed gone!

Shortly after that vote, Pope Francis visited Ireland. Taoiseach Varadkar told him that Ireland had experienced far-reaching social changes since the previous papal visit by St. John Paul II in 1979.

He said that Ireland was more diverse and less religious, with modernized laws on divorce, contraception, abortion, and same-sex false marriage. He said that we understand "that marriages do not always work, that women should make their own decisions, and that families come in many different, wonderful forms, including same-sex parents." The sins of the Secularists had prevailed over Ireland's Culture of Life in only 26 years.

During the 40-year period before 2019, with a world average of over 50 million deaths by abortion annually, two billion unborn children were killed by abortion. Only one hundred years before, that was the same total as the whole world's population!

The sins of the Secularists — the killing of such a horrific number of innocent pre-born children, and the selling of the body parts of many of them — have reflected the loss of right reason for many Secularists.

For those Secularists who live as if God does not exist, something or someone must fill the emptiness in their hearts. Many of them have been chastised by God with a metaphorical veil that covers their eyes so they cannot see reality and the truth because they do not want to see reality and the truth. So, they are left with only their willfulness and their power to do what they want to do and to fill the void with various addictions and vices.

Many Secularists who believe that human beings are the highest beings also believe that human power must therefore be the highest good. So, many of them seek political power to attain and then maintain their so-called rights to do evils: commit abortions, practice sodomy, engage in same-sex false marriages, and attempt to change their biological sex. For some of them, this leads to the practice of Satanism, even in public.

It is easy to turn to Satanism to fill the void in their empty hearts and to empower them to promote their false ideologies, rather than turn to the one true God who loves them and wants them to do good and to be happy with Him forever in eternal life. Many of them are now manifesting publicly their Satanic practices to do evil to others who are obstacles to their wickedness.

For example, Satanists promoted a movement to "Bind Trump" with "Magic Resistance." They cast spells "to bind Donald Trump and all those who abet him every waning crescent moon at midnight ending when he is driven from office." The witches' spells involved lengthy incantations, calling on spirits and "demons of the infernal realms" to bind our President so that "he may fail utterly."

This is all very serious—Satan has power to wreak havoc and those who invoke him empower him. St. Paul tells us, "For we are not contending against flesh and blood, but against principalities, against the powers, against the world rulers of this present darkness, against the spiritual hosts of wickedness in the heavenly places." (Ephesians 6:10).

Jex Blackmore, a self-proclaimed Satanic feminist, said, "We are going to disrupt, distort, destroy....We are going to storm press conferences, kidnap an executive, release snakes in the governor's mansion, execute the President."

In October 2018, a coven of New York witches placed a hex on US Supreme Court Justice Brett Kavanaugh. Dakota Bracciale, one of the organizers of the event, said the hex was "aimed at exposing Brett Kavanaugh for what he truly is, to cause him harm and see him undone."

The Satanic Temple's co-founder, Lucien Greaves, said, "The Homosexual Agenda is but one front in the Satanic Revolution."

On June 7, 2019, Hemant Mehta wrote in an article in the Friendly Atheist,

> In celebrating Pride, the LGBTQ community and its allies should make no apologies and no concessions, offer no conciliation nor comfort to those who claim indignation on behalf of their superstition. Happily, we should let the stale theocratic prohibitions of the Dark Ages recede into oblivion and abandon any efforts to desperately reinterpret archaic scriptures to mean the opposite of what they clearly state.

> The Church does not want us, and we have no need of them. The so-called "Law of God" means nothing to us, we who put human dignity and personal sovereignty first. Wave the banner high, and leave the Bible behind.

> Happy Pride.
> Hail Satan.

Sr. Lucia, the Fatima visionary, said, "The final battle between the Lord and the Reign of Satan will be about marriage and the family. Don't be afraid, because anyone who operates for the sanctity of marriage and the family will always be contended and opposed in every way, because this is the decisive issue. However, Our Lady has already crushed its head."

The sins of the Secularists are now evident in our Culture of Death that is not founded on the truths of life from conception; of the meaning of human life with dignity ordered to eternal life with God; of the only sexes of male and female; of immutable, indissoluble marriage only between one man and one woman; of sexual acts only within a united monogamous marriage that is open to new life; and of only natural death.

During the 2020 presidential election, Secular Democrats urged Joe Biden to fight what they described as a "national security threat" — "Christian nationalism" and the "Trump administration's actions to advance religious freedom."

In November 2020, the Secular Democrats of America PAC presented Joe Biden with a 28-page agenda of their recommendations, including eliminating the country's official motto of "In God we trust." The group argues that the current motto is not "inclusive" of non-religious people or a secular political ideology.

Tobit prophesied, "All the nations of the world shall be converted and shall offer God true worship; all shall abandon their idols which have deceitfully led them into error." (Tobit 14:6).

May we practice the Jesus King of All Nations Devotion as Jesus requests and may the nations be converted and may Tobit's prophecy be fulfilled in our time by our culture's abandonment of "their idols which have deceitfully led them into error." (Tobit 14:6).

May our nation abandon its idol of "choice" that has brought forth the fruits of legalized contraception, abortion, sodomy, same-sex false marriages, and so-called "physician-assisted suicide," all of which are symptoms of our secular Culture of Death.

The remedy to the Secularist's Culture of Death is Jesus Christ Himself, whom we must know, love, and serve and whose Reign over all nations we must recognize in order to transform our world, which is being degraded by those human beings who live as though God does not exist.

Venerable Archbishop Fulton J. Sheen said over a half century ago,

> Our nation is too full of those who are crying "Down." Down with the police! Down with the churches! Down with teachers! Down with government!
>
> Can you build anything down? You cannot. It's certainly time in our nation to change our words. **Let's begin to use the word "Up." Up from all of this filth. Up from all of this violence. Up from this indifference of courts. Up to eternity. Up, up to God.**
>
> There's a new kind of violence that's sweeping our country, our schools, our streets which involves the destruction of everything that is in the past.
>
> The first characteristic of the new violence of our day is what we will call "Elitism." Namely, there is a dominant minority that makes a lot of noise and that uses violence to force its will on others. They only know what they are against and do not know what they are for…destroy property, burn homes, they will do anything to enforce their will.
>
> Satanism is behind it too. This is another characteristic of it. The world is built on order. There's a plan so that scientists are able to discover the laws of the universe. And in discovering the laws of the universe, men find harmony. This harmony and order had to come from somewhere. It came from God. What is the essence of Satanism? **The essence of Satanism is the destruction of that order: the order of law, the order of morality, the order of religion, the order of ethics…of anything.**
>
> Before the Flood in the book of Genesis we read, "In the days of Noah, there was violence on the earth." All of the violence that happens in our country points to a decay in our civilization. How are we going to get out?…

Moses wrote, "As the eagle stirs among the young, so God stirs among the nations."

Maybe God is stirring us, bringing us to the brink of danger in order that we might begin to examine ourselves and restore the dignity of man and belief in God.

God has warned us that if we do not obey Him and recognize the Reign of Jesus King of All Nations, we will suffer from chastisements.

Psalm 2 was originally composed for the coronations of the Davidic Kings. However, it **can be applied to Jesus King of All Nations and read as a warning from Him to His Secularist enemies,**

> **Why do the nations conspire,**
>> **and the peoples plot in vain?**
> **The kings of the earth set themselves,**
>> **and the rulers take counsel together,**
>> **against the LORD and His anointed, saying,**
> **"Let us burst their bonds asunder,**
>> **and cast their cords from us."**
> **He who sits in the heavens laughs;**
>> **the LORD has them in derision.**
> **Then He will speak to them in His wrath,**
>> **and terrify them in His fury, saying,**
> **"I have set my king**
>> **on Zion, my holy hill."**
> I will tell of the decree of the LORD:
>> He said to me, "You are my son,
>> today I have begotten you.
> Ask of me, and I will make the nations your heritage,
>> and the ends of the earth your possession.
> You shall break them with a rod of iron,
>> and dash them in pieces like a potter's vessel."
> Now therefore, O kings, be wise;
>> be warned, O rulers of the earth.
> Serve the LORD with fear,
>> with trembling kiss His feet,
> lest He be angry, and you perish in the way;
>> for His wrath is quickly kindled.
> Blessed are all who take refuge in Him! (Psalms 2).

6. Warnings

The future manifestations of God's mercy and justice will start with warnings and preliminary chastisements; increase in severity, building to the universal warning to correct all consciences; and end with the Great Chastisement. This will be followed by the Triumph of the Immaculate Heart of Mary, the New Pentecost, and the Era of Peace, culminating in the Great Renewal of the Holy Church, of Mankind, and of All Creation.

Warnings are calls from God or His prophets to obey, to change, to pray, to fast, to convert, and to repent, or to suffer from chastisements. Chastisements are also known as punishments or judgments. Adam and Eve were warned by God not to eat of the Tree of the Knowledge of Good and Evil or they would die. They disobeyed God and He chastised them with death and the loss of grace and eternal life. Noah was warned by God about a flood to come. He obeyed God, built an ark, and saved the lives of his family from the chastisement of the Great Flood. (See Hebrews 11:7).

Biblical Warnings

God's first warning was to Adam and Eve. He warned them that they could eat freely of the Tree of Life and every other tree in the Garden of Eden, but if they ate of the Tree of the Knowledge of Good and Evil, they would die. (See Genesis 2:16–17). **He gave them the warning of the chastisement of death if they did not obey, because He is a God of love and goodness and did not want them to die but to live.** This warning was prototypical of all of God's subsequent warnings to humanity from His prophets, from Him, and from His Mother. These warnings take the form of doing or not doing certain things because, if they disobeyed the warning, they would be chastised.

However, Adam and Eve deliberately ignored God's warning and they and, consequently, all of humanity, were chastised with death and the loss of eternal life.

Since the Fall of Adam and Eve, God has warned humanity, initially, through His servants, the prophets. (See Amos 3:7). **God's love for His sinful children is shown through the prophets, who issued warnings to repent and turn back to God or to suffer chastisements.**

God's warning through the prophet Jeremiah is an example of God's formula that that *if* you listen and turn from your evil ways, *then* He will not punish you; but *if* you do not listen to Him and do evil, *then* He will punish you.

Jeremiah said, "Thus says the Lord: stand in the court of the Lord's house [the Temple], and speak to all the cities of Judah which come to worship in the house of the Lord all the words that I command you to speak to them; do not hold back a word. It may be they will listen, and each one turn from his evil way, that I may repent of the evil which I intend to do to them because of their evil doings. You shall say to them, 'Thus says the Lord, if you will not listen to me, to walk in my law which I have set before you, and to heed the words of my servants the prophets whom I send to you urgently, though you have not heeded, then I will make this house [the Temple] like Shiloh [the former house of the tabernacle that was destroyed], and I will make this city a curse for all the nations of the earth.'" (Jeremiah 26:2–6).

Isaiah, Jeremiah, and Ezekiel all warned the Jews of chastisements for their sins. (See Isaiah chapter 1; Jeremiah chapter 1; Ezekiel chapter 23). These warnings were ignored and so the chastisements were fulfilled.

In the New Testament, God continued to warn the Jewish people to give up their evil ways. **Jesus gave the same warning that the prophet John the Baptist had given, "Repent, for the Kingdom of Heaven is at hand."** (Matthew 3:2; 4:17).

After the Tower of Siloam fell and killed some people, Jesus was asked if they were guiltier than all the others in Jerusalem. He warned them in a statement that still applies today, "Certainly not! But I tell you, unless you repent, you will all perish as they did." (Luke 13:5).

Finally, **Jesus warned Jerusalem of its destruction.** (See Luke 21:6, 20–24). **However, just as the Jews did not listen to the prophets before Him, the people did not listen to Jesus and**

Jerusalem was annihilated. Jesus prophesied that not a stone upon a stone would be left in Jerusalem because they did not recognize the path to peace. (See Luke 19:42–44). This prophecy was literally fulfilled in the year 70 AD by the Roman General Titus, who killed tens of thousands and razed the city.

When God's warnings are spurned, chastisements follow. The prophet Ezekiel prophesied a chastisement because all previous warnings had been spurned by the Jews. Ezekiel said, "Thus says the Lord: a sword, a sword has been sharpened, a sword, a sword has been burnished: To work slaughter has it been sharpened, to flash lightning has it been burnished. Why should I now withdraw it? You have spurned the rod and every judgment!" (Ezekiel 21:14-15).

Likewise, **Jesus King of All Nations said, "My children do not hear. They do not see. They stop their ears that they may not hear. They cover their eyes that they may not see. They are willfully blind and willfully deaf."** (*Journal* 315).

Because of this willful spurning of God's warnings, Jesus said, "I have pleaded again and again with my children to repent and be converted, many times sending my Immaculate Mother herself, who is the Mother of All Mankind. **How many have listened? How many have responded? Too few to stay the hand of divine justice which is falling upon you. You are reaping the fruit of your obstinate and sinful ways."** (*Journal* 758–759).

Modern Warnings to America

In the modern world, God has sent the Blessed Virgin Mary as a prophet, many times, and at many places, to warn us to repent.

In the 1980s, at San Nicolas, Argentina, Mary said, "You must be warned, children, the plague is big. At these moments, all humanity is hanging by a thread. My children, the senseless person is dead, even if alive, because he does not fear the justice of God, nor fears not fulfilling of His Commandments. He wants to ignore the fact that the Lord's Day and His judgment will arrive. Blessed are those who fear God's judgment."

Mary continued, "**God's warning is over the world. Those who stay in the Lord have nothing to fear, but those who deny what**

comes from Him do. Two-thirds of the world is lost and the other part must pray and make reparation for the Lord to take pity. The Devil wants to have full domination over the earth. He wants to destroy. The earth is in great danger."

St. John Paul II gave several warnings to America. In 1979, he stood in front of the United States Supreme Court justices who had legalized abortion and said, "When the sacredness of life before birth is attacked, we will stand up and proclaim that no one ever has the authority to destroy unborn life."

In 1987, he issued another warning to America when he left Detroit. **"This is the dignity of America, the reason she exists, the condition for her survival — yes, the ultimate test of her greatness: to respect every human person, especially the weakest and most defenseless ones, those as yet unborn."**

In 1993, at World Youth Day in Denver, he once again warned America. He said, "If you want equal justice for all, lasting justice and peace, America: defend life. America needs much prayer…lest it lose its soul. Do not be afraid to go out on the streets and into public places, like the first apostles. This is no time to be ashamed of the Gospel. It is the time to preach it from the rooftops. Do not be afraid to break out of comfortable and routine modes of living, in order to take up the challenge of making Christ known in the modern metropolis….America, defend life so that you may live in peace and harmony. **Woe to you if you do not succeed in defending life."**

These are the most severe prophetic warnings that America has ever received. St. John Paul II told us that the very condition for our nation's survival is to end abortion. He used the warning words of the prophets, "Woe to you…"

In 1855, President Lincoln said, "Can we, as a nation, continue together permanently–forever half slave and half free? The problem is too mighty for me. May God, in His mercy, superintend the solution."

One hundred and forty years later, St. John Paul II said, "President Lincoln's question is no less a question for the present generation of Americans. Democracy cannot be sustained without a shared commitment to certain moral truths about the human person and human community." (Pope John Paul II, *Address*,

October 1995). **Can we continue together as a nation permanently — forever half pro-abortion and half pro-life?**

Like the prophets of old, St. John Paul II called the Church in America to conversion by "a profound interior renewal through a revitalization of missionary zeal. As the tragic events of September 11, 2001, have made clear, the building of a global culture of solidarity and respect for human dignity is one of the great moral tasks confronting humanity today." (Pope John Paul II, *Address to U.S. Bishops of Boston and Hartford*, September 2, 2004).

On January 23, 2019, with no respect for human dignity, New York celebrated its legalization of abortion up to birth by lighting up its Freedom Tower, the replacement for the Twin Towers that God had allowed to be destroyed by the chastisement of the 9/11 Attack on America.

This moral task, as proposed by St. John Paul II, is confronted by a Culture of Death. From the mass media reports, **it appears that there are storm clouds of a Civil War of morals and values looming over American culture.**

The division in our culture is between the proponents of a Culture of Life and the proponents of a Culture of Death. St. John Paul II said, "This struggle parallels the apocalyptic combat described in [Revelation 11:19–12:1]. Death battles against Life: a 'Culture of Death' seeks to impose itself on our desire to live, and live to the full.... Vast sectors of society are confused about what is right and what is wrong, and are at the mercy of those with the power to 'create' opinion and impose it on others." (Pope John Paul II, World Youth Day, Homily, Denver, Colorado, 1993).

There are acts committed by the proponents of a Culture of Death that include the "canceling" of a Culture of Life, vandalism of statues, violence in the streets, boycotting, and employment and social media terminations.

A Culture of Death invites God's chastisement as an act of mercy to bring people to repentance and salvation.

St. John Paul II stressed "the importance of the evangelization of culture", especially "the new global culture which is rapidly taking shape as a result of unprecedented growth in communications and the expansion of a world economy. I am convinced that the Church in the United States can play a critical role in meeting this challenge." He said,

> For the Church in America, the evangelization of culture can thus offer a unique contribution to the Church's mission *ad gentes* (to the nations) in our day....Catholics of all ages must be helped to appreciate more fully the distinctiveness of the Christian message, its capacity to satisfy the deepest yearnings of the human heart in every age, and the beauty of its summons to a life completely centered on faith in the Triune God, obedience to His revealed Word, and loving configuration to Christ's paschal mystery, in which we see disclosed the full measure of our humanity and our supernatural call to fulfillment in love." (See Vatican II, *Gaudium et Spes (Pastoral Constitution on the Church in the Modern World)*, 22).

> **....In the end, it is in the conversion of hearts and the spiritual renewal of humanity that the hope of a better tomorrow lies, and here the witness, example, and cooperation of religious believers have a unique role to play....**

> May the Church in your country discover the sources for a profound interior renewal through a revitalization of missionary zeal, above all by promoting vocations to missionary Institutes and proposing, especially to young people, the lofty ideal of a life completely devoted to the Gospel....(Pope John Paul II, *Address to U.S. Bishops of Boston and Hartford*, September 2, 2004).

Pope Benedict XVI said, "The threat of judgment also concerns us, the Church in Europe, Europe, and the West in general...the Lord is also crying out to our ears...'If you do not repent, I will come to you and remove your lampstand from its place.'" Light can also be taken away from us and we do well to let this warning ring out with its full seriousness in our hearts, while crying to the Lord, "Help us to repent!" (Pope Benedict XVI, *Opening Homily*, Synod of Bishops, October 2, 2005).

When there is prosperity, many set aside their faith. They act as if God does not exist and they do not need His help. They think that they are self-sufficient. Faith diminishes and Secularism, materialism, and consumerism increase to no end except the fulfillment of their own choices and desires.

Humanity continually refuses to learn from God or to obey Him. They killed the prophets and ignored the warnings that God sent to prepare the world to receive His Son. Similarly, many ignore the modern prophets, especially the Mother of God and St. John Paul II, and the messages that God has sent to warn the world of chastisements.

Moses told the Jews to "choose life." He said, "I call heaven and earth today to witness against you; I have set before you life and death, the blessing and the curse. Choose life, then, that you and your descendants may live." (Deuteronomy 30:19). However, **Americans have chosen not life but death to the extent that St. John Paul II called our culture a Culture of Death.**

In 1995, **in an Encyclical Letter, Pope John Paul made the connection between contraception and abortion,**

> Contraception and abortion are often closely connected, as fruits of the same tree. The close connection which exists, in mentality, between the practice of contraception and that of abortion is becoming increasingly obvious. It is being demonstrated in an alarming way by the development of chemical products, intrauterine devices, and vaccines which really act as abortifacients in the very early stages of the development of the life of the new human being.
>
> The various techniques of artificial reproduction, which would seem to be at the service of life, actually open the door to new threats against life. They are morally unacceptable, since they separate procreation from the fully human context of the conjugal act. (Pope John Paul II, *Evangelium Vitae (The Gospel of Life)*).
>
> **To claim the right to abortion, infanticide, and euthanasia, and to recognize that right in law, means to attribute to human freedom a perverse and evil significance — that of an absolute power over others and against others. This is the death of true freedom:** "Truly, truly, I say to you, everyone who commits sin is a slave to sin." (John 8:34).

We are facing an enormous and dramatic clash between good and evil, life and death, and the "culture of life" and the "culture of death." We find ourselves not only "faced with" but necessarily "in the midst of" this conflict: we are all involved and we all share in it, with the inescapable responsibility of choosing to be unconditionally pro-life. **"Choose life, that you and your descendants may live."** (Deuteronomy 30:15, 19).

Contrary to this admonition to choose life, many Americans choose to practice the legalized evil choices created by our courts and legislatures. Many Americans commit legalized choices for contraceptive abortifacients, abortions, infertile sodomy, same-sex false marriages, and false transgenderism.

These evil choices have attacked the meaning of humanity and God's creative intent at its heart. Humans were created male and female to freely choose to enter into a lifelong marriage without divorce for the purpose of uniting them in love, with an openness to new life. Evil choices invite God's chastisements.

As the chastisements from nature and wicked humans begin, people begin to sense that something is very wrong with the world. Their only hope is to change, repent, and convert for, as Jesus said, "But I tell you, unless you repent, you will all perish as they did." (Luke 13:5).

The Great Flood, according to Jewish tradition in the Mizpah, was a chastisement brought by God because of the people's celebrations, at that time, of same-sex false marriages. **Before the Great Flood, life went on as usual. People made such evil choices and did as they pleased. Then the rains came. The waters rose. They could not control God's natural forces. It rained for 40 days. When the floods came, everything in their wake was destroyed. Nothing was spared except for the faithful remnant of Noah, his family, the animals, and seed.**

St. Peter wrote that the godless "deliberately ignore the fact that the heavens existed of old and earth was formed out of water and through water by the Word of God, and that it was through the same factors **that the world of those days was destroyed by the floodwaters. It is the same Word which is reserving the present heavens and earth for fire, keeping them until the Day of Judgment and of the destruction of sinners."** (2 Peter 3:5–7).

Jesus King of All Nations warned us. He said, "My children, I do not want to strike you in my justice! I, your God, plead with you; turn back from this dangerous road you follow! I tell you though, if you do not, my pleading will come to an end, and my justice will have to accomplish itself. Your God loves you! Why do you not recognize my warnings in nature? My children, please return to your God." (*Journal* 214).

"Until the heart of man changes, the world will not and cannot change. Greater and greater will be the catastrophes in nature which itself rebels against the sinfulness of the children of men. The earth itself writhes in horror at the weight of corruption and uncleanness it supports. It cries out for justice against its inhabitants." (*Journal* 372).

Jesus King of All Nations told His Secretary, "I tell you most solemnly, little one, that **one of the fruits of this Devotion will be the buying of more time from my mercy in order that souls may be converted before it is too late.**" (*Journal* 303). "Does not the fact that the world still exists speak volumes on the patience of your God? I AM generous, my child, I AM infinitely generous." (*Journal* 304). "**Once more my Immaculate Mother has obtained the mercy of time for my erring children. Time in which to turn from evils, be converted, and return to me, the all-powerful, all-merciful God who forgives.**" (*Journal* 360).

Divine Mercy and the Universal Warning through the Illumination of All Consciences

In the 1930s, Jesus told St. Faustina, "I am prolonging the time of mercy for the sake of [sinners]. But woe to them if they do not recognize this time of my visitation." (*Diary* 1160). In 70 AD, the Jews failed to recognize their time of His visitation and were chastised by the destruction of their Temple, as Jesus had prophesied. (See Luke 19:43–44).

"While there is still time, let them have recourse to the fount of my mercy;..." (*Diary* 848). "He who refuses to pass through the door of my mercy must pass through the door of my justice..." (*Diary* 1146).

Our Lady told Fr. Gobbi, "The Holy Spirit will come to establish the glorious Reign of Christ, and it will be a Reign of grace, holiness, love, of justice, and of peace. With His divine love, He will open the doors of hearts and illuminate all consciences. Every person will see himself in the burning fire of divine truth. It will be like a judgment in miniature. And then Jesus Christ will bring His glorious Reign in the world." (*To the Priests* 383).

This merciful warning, illumination of conscience, and judgment in miniature was experienced by St. Faustina. As she wrote,

> Once I was summoned to the judgment [seat] of God. I stood alone before the Lord. Jesus appeared such as we know Him during His Passion. After a moment, His wounds disappeared except for five, those in His hands, His feet, and His side. Suddenly, I saw the complete condition of my soul as God sees it. I could clearly see all that is displeasing to God. I did not know that even the smallest transgressions will have to be accounted for.
>
> What a moment! Who can describe it? To stand before the thrice-holy God! Jesus asked me, "Who are you?" I answered, "I am your servant, Lord." "You are guilty of one day of fire in purgatory." I wanted to throw myself immediately into the flames of purgatory, but Jesus stopped me and said, "Which do you prefer, suffer now for one day in purgatory or for a short while on earth?" I replied, "Jesus, I want to suffer in purgatory, and I want to suffer also the greatest pains on earth, even if it were until the end of the world."
>
> Jesus said, "One [of the two] is enough; you will go back to earth, and there you will suffer much, but not for long; you will accomplish my Will and my desires, and a faithful servant of mine will help you to do this. Now, rest your head on my bosom, on my Heart, and draw from it strength and power for these sufferings, because you will find neither relief nor help nor comfort anywhere else. Know that you will have much, much to suffer, but don't let this frighten you; I am with you." (*Diary* 36).

In our Secular Culture of Death, the Secularists live as if God does not exist. They have not come to know of His love for them.

They live as if only this world exists and there is nothing transcendent.

Their sins cry out to God to chastise the world. However, God is fair and, in His mercy, He will warn us before He chastises us. He will illuminate the consciences of all peoples so that they may freely choose Him or Satan.

During the illumination, they will see themselves, at that time, as if they were at their particular judgment at the time of their death. They will see their sins as God sees them and their just punishment that may be avoided by their repentance and conversion.

Because all previous warnings have been spurned by modern people and the evils are so great, Jesus King of All Nations said, "I delight not in the suffering of my children. I desire to awaken their darkened consciences that they may recognize their sinfulness and be converted so that there may be a renewal of hearts and minds thereby causing the world itself to be renewed." (*Journal* 370).

Edson Glauber, a mystic from Itapiranga, Brazil, wrote about the Warning. In 2010, his Bishop, Carillo Gritti, approved his apparitions to be of supernatural origin. Later, the Congregation for the Doctrine of the Faith said that, while it could not yet determine that the apparitions were supernatural in origin, they did not find that the apparitions were *not* supernatural; they did not condemn them or his messages; and we are free to give human belief to them. Edson wrote,

> **God will give us a [Universal] Warning. The Warning that He will give will be a great sign of His mercy to all who really believe in His presence, repent of their wrong deeds and attitudes, and decide for a holier life before the Great Chastisement comes.** The Warning can come in great proportions, according to the situation of the world at that time. This will be dependent upon whether the people accept the messages of the Virgin and put them into practice or reject them and continue to offend God with their crimes.
>
> It will be the same way with the Chastisement. It will come as a consequence of disobedience to God. Our Lady said that God does not punish us because He wants to, but He allows the torments which the world will soon have to

go through because people use their freedom improperly and badly. This is all the fault of people's own sins.

During the Warning, the world will be purified of its sins. This purification will be given wherever the people happen to be. Each one will see, in proportion, greater or not, depending on the condition of each person's soul, more or less according to each person. This will feel as if it is the strongest purification that you have ever experienced. It will be a revelation that God will give to the world according to its sins.

If this purification does not come to the world, people will never give value and honor to the holy name of God. The purification, therefore, will be a revelation of all of our sins, those that we have committed up to that moment, because those that we have already confessed to the priest, with sincerity and repentance, will not be remembered. We will see even the smallest sins, in a horrible manner, before God.

Jesus and Our Lady already made me go through this purification a long time before seeing Our Lady. I went through a year of being purified that made me suffer much. This happened in 1993. It was as if I saw all that I had committed in my life. My faults and my sins passed before me. This caused me great sorrow for the sins I had committed and I formed the intent to really amend and repent myself of them.

Generally, people fear and are horrified, but this grace of purification, for those who want to serve God, is an experience of His love and of His mercy, as has never occurred in the world, because He will give us an opportunity to know Him deeply as never before. (*Terra da Fe' (Land of Faith), Volume II*, Galileu Borsa Limo Manaus, 2004).

Jesus said, "No, my beloved, sin and the evils committed by mankind are too great, no longer will I spare my judgment to correct the conscience of mankind as a whole, but this [Jesus King of All Nations] Devotion and *Chaplet [of Unity]* prayed with repentance, confidence, and love, will heal, save, and unite souls to my mercy who otherwise would be lost." (*Journal* 55).

On December 8, 1956, **Our Lady told Blessed Elena Aiello, "The only valid means for placating divine justice is to pray and do penance, returning to God with sincere sorrow for the faults committed, and then the chastisement of divine justice will be mitigated by mercy.** Humanity will never find peace if it does not return to my Immaculate Heart as Mother of Mercy and Mediatrix of Men, and to the Heart of my Son, Jesus!"

God's patient withholding of a chastisement of divine justice is a sign of His mercy. As St. Peter wrote, "The Lord is not slow about His promise as some count slowness, but is forbearing toward you, not wishing that any should perish, but that all should reach repentance. Therefore, beloved, since you wait for these, be zealous to be found by Him without spot or blemish, and at peace." (2 Peter 3:8–14).

Jesus King of All Nations warned us to repent or to suffer from His perfect justice. With His scriptural confirmations included, He said,

> **Hear me, O peoples of the earth! My Reign is at hand.** *"....lift up your eyes and behold that the fields are already white for the harvest."* (John 4:35). **Turn from your perverse and evil ways!** *"....for there is no truth, and there is no mercy, and there is no knowledge of God in the land."* (Hosea 4:1). **I tell you, unless you turn back to me and repent, I will strike you in my most perfect justice.** *"Because I know your manifold crimes, and your grievous sins...."* (Amos 5:12). **Children of men, your God loves you!** *"....with unquenchable fire."* (Luke 3:17). **Why must you be so hard of heart so as not to reflect upon yourselves and hear the anguished cry of your God?** *"Jesus cried out with a loud voice...."* (Matthew 27:46).

> **My children, your God appeals to you.** *"I have not come to call the just, but sinners, to repentance."* (Luke 5:32). **Now is the time of great mercy.** *"I will show mercies to you...."* (Jeremiah 42:12). **Take heed and benefit from it.** *"....let him who reads understand...."* (Mark 13:14). **If you do not, a most grievous chastisement will suddenly fall upon you.** *"....for in one hour has thy judgment come!"* (Revelation 18:10).

I, in my great mercy, "....*mercy triumphs over judgment.*" (James 2:13) give to you, O mankind, a treasure, through which I will grant tremendous blessings and graces to peoples of every race and nation. "....*the gift of God's grace....in accordance with the working of His power.*" (Ephesians 3:7). **My children, come before my Image of Jesus King of All Nations and pray for your countries. Pray for your people. Pray for your families. Pray for my mercy which I will graciously grant to those peoples and nations that acknowledge me as True King!** "*And I will make a covenant of peace with them....*" (Ezekiel 35:25). **I AM your sure refuge in these most evil and truly dangerous times.** "*O Lord, my rock, my stronghold, my deliverer, my God, my rocky cliff, to which I flee for safety, my shield, the horn of my salvation, my fortification!*" (Psalms 17:3).

Children of men, your God is consumed with love for you! "*Thou shalt love the Lord thy God....*" (Matthew 22:37). Why then do you not love me? "*And Jesus wept.*" (John 11:35). **Return to me, my children; it is not yet too late. See how great is the patience and mercy of your God!** "*....because I have you in my Heart, all of you....*" (Philippians 1:7). My children, I AM your God and King! Hear me! "*If anyone has ears to hear, let him hear.*" (Mark 4:23). (*Journal* 22-25).

Divine Justice and Divine Mercy

God is love. He exercises His love through His attributes, most notably His divine justice and His divine mercy. His justice is giving us what we might deserve, eternal damnation for our sins. His mercy is giving us what we don't deserve, the forgiveness of our sins and eternal life. In His divine justice, He might condemn us for our unrepentant sins to eternal damnation in hell. In His divine mercy, He redeems us from our repented sins to eternal life with Him in heaven. God's final condemnatory justice at our particular judgment upon our death is irredeemable, but His justice during our life on earth is redeemable through our repentance.

Cardinal Joseph Ratzinger, later Pope Benedict XVI, wrote in his book, *To Look on Christ,* **"A Jesus who agrees with everything and everyone, a Jesus without His holy wrath, without the**

harshness of truth and true love is not the real Jesus as the Scripture shows but a miserable caricature. A conception of 'gospel' in which the seriousness of God's wrath is absent has nothing to do with the biblical Gospel."

Justice and mercy are two sides of the same coin of God's love. They are complimentary. St. Thomas Aquinas wrote that justice presupposes mercy and both appear in punishment. He wrote, "Thus justice must exist in all God's works. Now the work of divine justice always presupposes the work of [divine] mercy; and is founded thereupon..." (St. Thomas Aquinas, *Summa Theologica (Summary of Theology)*, I, Ques 21, Art 4).

St. Bernard of Clairvaux once remarked that when he thought of God's judgments for too long, he grew fearful. And when he thought for too long of God's mercy, he grew lax. This experience taught him to sing of not only the mercies of the Lord, and not alone His judgments, but judgment and mercy united in one embrace. (See *Life of St. Bernard*, London 1916, 232).

In the 1930's, Europe suffered from economic misery. However, on November 15, 1935, **Jesus revealed to Sr. Consolata Betrone of Turin, Italy, that the crisis was an act of mercy, not justice.**

Jesus said, "The distress which reigns in the world at the present time is not the work of my justice, but of my mercy. For fewer sins are being committed because money is scarce, and many more prayers are being raised to heaven by people in financial straits. Do not think that the sorrowful conditions on earth do not move me; but I love souls; I wish them to be saved; and in order to achieve my end, I am constrained to be severe; but believe me, I do it out of mercy! During times of abundance, souls forget me and are lost; in times of distress, they turn to me and save themselves. That is indeed the way it happens!"

It is impossible for God to be just without being merciful and to be merciful without being just. **Jesus King of All Nations said, "The cup is overflowing. My justice must be poured out. Yet my mercy is ever present even when my justice is revealed."** (*Journal* 348). "My perfect justice, however, is always tempered by my infinite mercy. It is indeed itself an act of mercy. Whenever my justice is accomplished, for I AM mercy itself, and there is no action, either within or without the divine Godhead that is not imbued with mercy, as it is part of my very nature as God. It is in fact the crowning glory of all my divine attributes." (*Journal* 367).

The *Catholic Catechism* does not define the justice of God. Fr. John Hardon defined it as "the constant and unchanging Will of God to give everyone what is due him or her. Every possible form of justice is possessed by God. He practices legal justice in that through the natural and moral law He coordinates creatures to the common good; distributive justice because He gives to His creatures everything they need to fulfill the purpose of their existence; remunerative justice because He rewards the good; and vindictive [condemnatory] justice because He punishes the wicked." (Fr. John Hardon, *Modern Catholic Dictionary*).

St. Thomas Aquinas wrote, "Justice and mercy appear in the punishment of the just in this world, since by afflictions lesser faults are cleansed in them, and they are the more raised up from earthly affections to God. As to this, Gregory says (Moral. xxvi, 9): 'The evils that press on us in this world force us to go to God.'" (St. Thomas Aquinas, *Summa Theologica (Summary of Theology)*, I, Ques 21, Art 4, Reply to Objection 3).

God chastises those He loves. He chastised the Jewish people for their sins by their exile of 70 years in the Babylonian Captivity in order to bring them to repentance and to receive His mercy with their return to their homeland in Jerusalem, to be restored in their land, and to rebuild the destroyed Temple.

In our day, Jesus King of All Nations prophesies an imminent catastrophic chastisement. With this prophecy, He reveals that the remedy is the Jesus King of All Nations Devotion which, with a universal acceptance and public practice of it in the Church, will lead to a humble acknowledgement that the chastisement is deserved in justice. Then, with such humble recognition, it will be followed by a conversion of the chastisement from being an instrument of judgment on sin and refusal, in theory and in practice, to respect the Kingship of Jesus, to being an instrument of mercy and genuine reform, specifically through the maternal mediation of Mary, Mediatrix of All Graces, and through mercy.

In this perspective, the Devotion to Jesus King of All Nations can be a marvelous way to implant in all believers the doctrinal foundations for the complementarity of divine justice and divine mercy and so be a complement to the revelations of Our Lady of Fatima and St. Faustina.

Jesus, through His mercy flowing from the goodness or justice of His Heart, rather than restrain chastisements after all other attempts to elicit repentance have failed, permits them as a last resort. He often uses His sovereign power over the natural order through natural disasters to intensify the chastisement so as to awaken and save even the most perverse.

The first purposes of a chastisement are to awaken our humility, negate our self-assurance and self-justification, and bring us to repentance and, only secondarily, to punish definitively if we reject this opportunity. **For example, for Noah and his family, the chastisement of the Great Flood was medicinal and they were saved, but for the wicked who refused to believe and hope in the promise of a redeemer, it was condemnatory and they drowned.**

Jesus King of All Nations does not abandon those for whose salvation He gave His life. Rather, He turns chastisements, as He turned death itself, into a means of repentance and redemption. Only we can prevent His justice from triumphing in the form of mercy.

Pope Benedict XVI said, "Christ's Kingship over the world can be prevented insofar as men and women refuse to let Him reign over their hearts....We, and we alone, can prevent Him from reigning over us and hence hinder His Kingship over the world: over the family, over society, over history. We men and women have the faculty to choose whose side we wish to be on: with Christ and His angels or with the Devil and his followers, to use the same language as the Gospel." (Pope Benedict XVI, *Homily*, November 22, 2008).

In an *Address*, on September 10, 2003, **St. John Paul II said,** "God, in fact, is not indifferent before good and evil; He enters mysteriously the scene of human history with His judgment which, sooner or later, will unmask evil, defend the victims, and indicate the way of justice....**The object of God's action is never ruin, pure and simple condemnation, the annihilation of the sinner." We must implore God for mercy before He enters with His justice.**

St. John Paul II also taught us about God's entry into the world and the complementarity of His divine justice and His divine mercy. He spoke of the Canticle of Habakkuk in Scripture, referring to its verses,

The Lord's entry into the world has a precise meaning. He wills to enter into human history....Then God shows His indignation (verse 3:2c) against evil. And the song makes reference to a series of inexorable divine interventions, without specifying if it is through direct or indirect actions.

Israel's Exodus is evoked, when the Pharaoh's cavalry was drowned in the sea (verse 3:15). But what is also perceived is the prospect of the work that the Lord is about to accomplish in the confrontations with the new oppressor of His people.

The divine intervention is described in an almost "visible" way through a series of agricultural images: "Though the fig tree do not blossom, nor fruit be on the vines, the produce of the olive fail and the fields yield no food, the flock will be cut off from the fold, and there will be no herd in the stalls" (verse 3:17). All signs of peace and fruitfulness are eliminated and the world appears as a desert. This is a cherished symbol of other prophets (see Jeremiah 4:19–26; 12:7–13; 14:1–10) to illustrate the Lord's judgment, who is not indifferent before evil, oppression, and injustice.

In face of the divine intervention, the man of prayer remains terrified (see Habakkuk 3:16), he shakes and feels his soul emptied and stricken by a tremor, because the God of justice is infallible, very different from earthly judges.

However, the Lord's entry has yet another function, which our song exalts with joy. Indeed, in His indignation He does not forget His compassionate mercy (verse 3:2). He goes forth from the horizon of His glory not only to destroy the arrogance of the wicked, but also to save His people and His anointed (verse 3:13), namely Israel and its King.

He also wills to be the liberator of the oppressed, to make hope arise in the hearts of victims, to open a new era of justice.

Because of this, although marked by a "tone of lament," our canticle is transformed into a hymn of joy. In fact, the anticipated calamities look toward the deliverance from oppressors (verse 3:15). Therefore, they spark joy in the righteous who exclaims: "Yet I will rejoice in the Lord, I will joy in the God of my salvation." (verse 3:18).

The same attitude is suggested by Jesus to His disciples at the time of the apocalyptic cataclysms: "Now when these things begin to take place, look up and raise your heads, because your redemption is drawing near." (Luke 21:28)....When one has the Lord beside him, one no longer fears nightmares and obstacles, but goes forward with a light step and joy on the ever harsh way of life. (Pope John Paul II, *General Audience*, May 15, 2002).

On October 17, 2013, **Fr. Peter Damian Fehlner, OFM Conv., S.T.D., the spiritual director of the Jesus King of All Nations Devotion, sent me an email concerning the theology of chastisement. He wrote, "I do not think in practice very many bishops have reflected much on this ancient theology,** particularly in its Franciscan form. Had they done so just a little, they would have recognized how profound is the theology behind the Devotion of Jesus King of All Nations. Only Our Lord could have written so simply and profoundly."

He also wrote,

> **In the minds of some American bishops, the Devotion is an example of pious terrorism and superficial emotionalism. This is a view they have succeeded in selling a large number of American bishops, or at least making them fearful about being associated with it.**

> **By pious terrorism, I mean a concept of chastisement imposed by an angry God in virtue of condemnatory justice, as it is presented so often by Protestant sects, rather than in terms of a medicinal justice, imposed in the first instance as a means to salvation of those who otherwise would have been condemned as were the angels who revolted against God.**

> **The chastisement, then, is in part an instrument of a just and merciful God, but is also a consequence of sin which makes possible redemptive salvation.** This was true after the Fall of our first parents: Satan had already received

condemnatory justice for his rebellion against God. Adam and Eve received medicinal justice with the chastisement of the loss of eternal life in Paradise that resulted from their Fall. It remains true thereafter.

Mysteriously, divine justice seems to bring on divine mercy. Baruch prophesied, "Fear not, my children; call out to God! He who brought this upon you will remember you. As your hearts have been disposed to stray from God, turn now ten times the more to seek Him; For He who has brought disaster upon you will, in saving you, bring you back enduring joy." (Baruch 4:5–12, 27–29).

Jesus said, "I came in this Image and Devotion to extend to sinful mankind the scepter of my great mercy before it becomes necessary to wield it as the rod of my justice. I AM perfectly merciful and perfectly just." (*Journal* 825). "You see that I AM infinitely merciful and accept a smaller amount than my justice requires. This is the pre-eminence of my divine mercy. It is my greatest divine attribute." (*Journal* 673).

Jesus also said in an unpublished message, on December 28, 2011,

My Kingship is a Reign of love and mercy for even in my perfect justice my love and mercy are glorified. My divine rule is a rule of love, compassion, and delicate mercy. The suaveness of the mercy of God is indeed exquisite.

"O Lord, your kindness reaches to heaven; your faithfulness, to the clouds. Your justice is like the mountains of God; your judgments, like the mighty deep; man and beast you save, O Lord. How precious is your kindness, O God! The children of men take refuge in the shadow of your wings." (Psalms 36:6–8).

My divine laws are given for the good of man. It is in his rebelling that my scepter of mercy becomes a holy rod of justice. In my Image of Jesus King of All Nations, my arms are wide open just as they were upon the Cross to receive my sinful, wounded children in order that I might forgive and heal them.

Even now my arms remain open in love and mercy but my hand has firm hold upon my scepter, the symbol of the unalterable laws of God and of His perfect justice. What a most wonderful meeting of the perfection of eternal love and justice come together under the binding mortar that is my sovereign Kingship and divine authority.

Praise and glorify your God for His mighty deeds! Give thanks to Him for calling you into the participation of His very life!

"And now, bless the God of all, who has done wondrous things on earth;" (Sirach 50:22).

Let us pray, "Blessed be God who lives forever, whose Kingdom is eternal. For He both punishes and then has mercy." (Tobit 13:1-2).

Jesus King of All Nations said, "This time of my mercy is almost completed and the time of my justice swiftly approaches wherein it will be poured out upon the world. Let souls embrace my Devotion of Jesus King of All Nations and thereby obtain for themselves all of my great promises contained therein." (*Journal* 361–362).

"You see clearly the catastrophes taking place in all aspects of human life. I AM in part leaving man to his own sinful path for he has ignored me and denied me to my very face." (*Journal* 728).

"My justice will not be restrained much longer. Already the cup is tipped and the wine of my justice drips down upon the world so great is the sinfulness and obstinacy of this generation. My warnings shall cease and the cup poured out in full so as to be completely drained. **This generation shall drink the wine of my justice. Heed me and take to yourselves the divine aid and succor offered in my Image and Devotion."** (*Journal* 401).

7. Chastisements

Introduction

The prophet Isaiah said, "When your judgment dawns upon the earth, the world's inhabitants learn justice....O Lord, oppressed by your punishment, we cried out in anguish under your chastising." (Isaiah 26:9, 16).

Jesus King of All Nations uses the terms "justice," "judgment," and "chastisement" interchangeably. **I define "chastisement" as an act of God's love, justice, and mercy to correct our consciences and to bring us to repentance, reconciliation, and peace with Him. It is not vengeance that God exacts, but a just punishment to help sinners to convert.** Chastisements are sent by God directly, such as the destruction of Sodom and Gomorrah, or indirectly through others or natural forces, and allowed by God, such as the Indian Ocean Tsunami of 2004 that killed over 230,000 people in 14 countries, one of the deadliest disasters in recorded history.

God's justice is not mean-spirited. **The purpose of God's justice is not to condemn us, but to redeem us. The greatest act of God's justice and mercy was upon Jesus Himself, the God-Man who was a totally innocent victim. He took upon Himself the punishment for all of our sins in order to redeem us, save us, and grant us the gift of eternal life through the forgiveness of our sins.**

This is how we can understand how the merciful work for our salvation could require so cruel a form of justice or satisfaction in the form of death by crucifixion. God willed to save us, not in just any way, but, in the best way, by fulfilling all justice and so attracting us most powerfully to love His mercy.

God's justice exercised through chastisements is for the purpose of bringing sinners to repentance by receiving His mercy, lest they die in their unrepentant sins and suffer eternal damnation. **It is better to suffer from God's justice and repent and receive His mercy than to suffer from the justice of His particular judgment upon death with damnation to hell.**

God's purpose for chastisements is medicinal — to bring humanity to repentance and conversion in order to live in His love and grace. Scripture says that God chastises those He loves. "Whatever is dear to me I reprove and chastise. Be honest about it, therefore. Repent!" (Revelation 3:19). **Jesus King of All Nations said, "I correct my children out of love for them."** (*Journal* 370).

Out of His love for us, God exercises His justice, during our lifetimes, through chastisements to bring us to repentance. This began with the Fall of Adam and Eve and the exercise of God's justice by the chastisement of their loss of sanctifying grace and eternal life and their banishment from Paradise. However, this chastisement was redeemable by His mercy and their repentance through the redemption of a promised Redeemer, Jesus Christ. (See Genesis chapter 3).

Since Adam and Eve's Fall from grace, chastisements from God are acts of merciful justice to redeem those who, because of their sins, are destined for hell and the loss of eternal life if they do not repent. They are an act of mercy — an attempt to prevent loss of eternal life because of failure to repent. Chastisements are not irredeemable — they are a final effort of Christ's mercy to save unrepentant sinners from hell. **Better to live through a chastisement, repent, and be redeemed than to die in your sins and suffer from the irredeemable chastisement of hell.**

The predominant sin that causes chastisements is pride. The Original Sin of Adam and Eve was due to their pride in wanting to be like God.

Jesus King of All Nations said, "Your pride blinds you to your God. Pride blinds! They think they see and know the truth, but what they perceive is smoke, it is all falsehood." (*Journal* 265). He said, "Pride hardens the soul and darkens the conscience thereby preventing the permeation of my grace which washes over it as water over a stone. **One must possess the precious virtue of humility in order to recognize and honor my sovereign Kingship.**

"There are many, even among my very ministers, who do not recognize this work of mine because they lack humility." (*Journal* 545-546). **"I shall once more receive the renewed honor and worship due to my sovereign Kingship. This re-acclamation of** my sovereign and divine rights is a great counterbalance for the great pride and sinfulness of these times." (*Journal* 689).

In His urgent warning of August 25, 2004, **Jesus King of All Nations said, "My children, I do not wish to strike you in my perfect justice. But if you remain obstinate of heart and blinded by your great pride, I must do so in order to save the greater number."** (*Journal* 313).

God's chastisements are not for destruction, but for *re-construction*—to bring us to repentance and conversion and back to Him and to His divine mercy through the forgiveness of our sins. Divine judgments are not to consume us, but to purify us. They are not to condemn us, but to redeem us. They are not an end, but a chance for a new beginning. We can bring about this new beginning through prayers, especially those contained in the Appendices, fasting, and the sacraments of Confession and Eucharist.

Through His chastisements, God warns and tests those who are near to His Heart. As the Book of Judith states, "Let us give thanks to the Lord our God for putting us to the test as He did our ancestors. Recall how He dealt with Abraham, and how He tested Isaac, and all that happened to Jacob in Syrian Mesopotamia while he was tending the flocks of Laban, his mother's brother. He has not tested us with fire, as He did them, to try their hearts, nor is He taking vengeance on us. But **the Lord chastises those who are close to Him in order to admonish them."** (Judith 8:25–27).

Sr. Lucia, one of the Fatima visionaries, wrote with respect to chastisements, "And let us not say that it is God who is punishing us in this way; on the contrary, it is people themselves who are preparing their own punishment. In His kindness, God warns us and calls us to the right path, while respecting the freedom He has given us; hence people are responsible."

St. Paul's Letter to the Hebrews says that chastisements are intended to make the righteous holy, just as an earthly father disciplines his children to help them to be good. It says,

> My child, do not regard lightly the discipline of the Lord, or lose heart when you are punished by Him; for **the Lord disciplines those whom He loves, and chastises every child whom He accepts.**

Endure trials for the sake of discipline. God is treating you as children; for what child is there whom a parent does not discipline? If you do not have that discipline in which all children share, then you are illegitimate and not His children.

Moreover, we had human parents to discipline us, and we respected them. Should we not be even more willing to be subject to the Father of spirits and live? For they disciplined us for a short time as seemed best to them, but He disciplines us for our good, in order that we may share in His holiness. Now, **discipline always seems painful rather than pleasant at the time, but later it yields the peaceful fruit of righteousness to those who have been trained by it.**

Therefore, lift your drooping hands and strengthen your week knees, and make straight paths for your feet, so that what is lame may not be put out of joint, but rather be healed. (Hebrews 12:5–13).

God does judge. Hell is eternal punishment for unrepented sin. It is a real consequence of wrongdoing and deservedly suffered. But to save us from hell, God chooses to impose chastisements. These are intended to discourage us from self-injury by wrongdoing and to encourage us to rectify our lives. Sin is separation from God and violation of His loving plan. Punishment shows sinners what they are doing to themselves. So, God permits humankind to experience the consequences of sin.

St. John Paul II said, "In the face of the evil that manifests itself in different ways in the world, man, afflicted and disconcerted, asks, 'Why?'" He continued,

God has responded to this anguished question that arises from the scandal of evil, not with an explanation of principle, as the wishing to justify Himself, but with the sacrifice of His own Son on the Cross. **In Jesus' death are found the apparent triumph of evil and the definitive victory of good; the darkest moment of history and the revelation of divine glory; the breaking point is the center of attraction and reconstruction of the universe.** "I," Jesus says, "when I am lifted up from the earth, will draw all men to myself." (John 12:32). The Cross of Christ is, for believers, [an] icon of hope because on it was accomplished the salvific plan of the love of God. (Pope John Paul II, *Angelus Address*, September 19, 2004).

People also ask, "What did we do to deserve a natural disaster?" In answer to this question, related to the Haitian earthquake on January 12, 2010, Thomas Wenski, later Archbishop of Miami, wrote,

> **When faced with our misfortunes or those of others, we can be tempted to ask ourselves: 'What did we do or what did these people do to deserve this?' Once in His ministry, Jesus spoke of the Galileans whom Pilate had executed. And He spoke of those killed when the Tower of Siloam collapsed. (See Luke 13:1–9)...**

> **Jesus says in the Gospel: don't think that those Galileans were the biggest sinners around. Don't think that those who died in the Tower were guiltier than anyone else.**

People also ask, "Why does God allow chastisements from evil people?" The lone gunman's Las Vegas Slaughter in 2017 resulted in 573 casualties, including 58 fatalities. It was the worst mass gun slaughter of civilians in American history. This was not merely a human criminal event; it was sin-inspired and directed by Satan — evil personified.

Evil is not created by God, it is the absence of the good that He has created, inspired by a real evil personality, Satan, with whom the human race has been in conflict since the Garden of Eden, when he tempted Adam and Eve into the Original Sin.

God allows evil caused by sin so that we can freely choose the good and reject evil with our own free will. He did not make us robots and cannot force us to love Him or to do good and avoid evil. However, He works all evil for good. (See Romans 8:28).

He allowed the most innocent, His only begotten Son, Jesus Christ, true God and true man, to be the victim of the sin and evil that Satan inspired, resulting in Jesus' own Crucifixion and death. However, God worked this evil for the good of the Resurrection of Jesus and the fulfillment of His promise of

eternal life for those who believe in Him. These are the mysteries of iniquity and redemptive suffering in the divine plan of love.

Jesus came to destroy the works of Satan (see 1 John 3:8), so we should not be fearful and fixated on the media reports of natural disasters and evils. They should inspire our hearts to open in prayer and fasting for the victims and their families and not lead us to craven fear for our own safety. Jesus told us, "Fear is useless; what is needed is trust." (Luke 8:50).

God creates everything good. Evil comes from creatures' abuses of their freedom, and punishment for sin is not arbitrarily imposed by God. Human punishment often has the character of a more or less vengeful reaction, but God's punishment has none of this character. It comes from love and the desire to save us. Without excluding created freedom, God "desires all men to be saved and to come to the knowledge of the truth." (1 Timothy 2:4). **Jesus comes to save, not to condemn.** (See John 3:17; 12:7).

God's justice ultimately consists of being faithful to His gifts of life and freedom. God simply cannot be unfaithful. (See 2 Timothy 2:12–13). God tries every means to win the love of sinners who initially reject Him, but still might repent. **In Our Lord Jesus, we see how far He goes in His love for the world. "God so loved the world that He gave His only Son." (John 3:16).**

God is merciful, but He is also just. His justice can be brought to nations through wars, violence, and natural disasters, resulting in the suffering of the guilty and, too often, the innocent. This suffering is mysteriously meritorious to those who accept it, abandon themselves, and offer it to God. Suffering also brings us to the repentance that brings God's merciful forgiveness, healing, and union with Him.

God's chastisements can be brought to us through God Himself directly, such as the Great Flood and the destruction of Sodom and Gomorrah; through His permissive Will at the hands of others, such as the two destructions of Jerusalem: first, by the Babylonians and, later, by the Romans; and through nature as when Isaiah wrote, "from the Lord of hosts you will be punished with thunder and earthquake and loud noise, with whirlwind and tempest and the flame of a consuming fire." (Isaiah 29:6).

God does not directly will moral evils such as war, violence, and terrorism, but allows them for a greater good—our conversion and sanctification. He may directly will physical evil from nature (such as the Great Flood and the destruction of Sodom and Gomorrah), however, He may avert (prevent) or mitigate (lessen) chastisements if people repent.

If there is no prevention and chastisements come, He may leave a remnant of righteous people, as He did with Noah and his family after the Great Flood and with Lot and his family after the destruction of Sodom and Gomorrah.

Our Lady told Fr. Gobbi, of the Marian Movement of Priests, "These are the times of the purification; these are the times when the justice of God will chastise this rebellious and perverted world, for its salvation. The purification has already begun within the Church: pervaded with error, darkened by Satan, covered with sin, betrayed and violated by some of its own pastors. Satan sifts you like wheat; how much chaff will soon be blown away by the wind of persecution!" (*To the Priests* 112).

Chastisements and God's Love

God really loves us, as is assured in Scripture, even if He allows us to suffer from chastisements.

"For God so loved the world that He gave His only Son, that whoever believes in Him should not perish but have eternal life. For God sent the Son into the world, not to condemn the world, but that the world might be saved through Him." (John 3:16–17).

The Lord passed before [Moses] and proclaimed,

> The Lord, the Lord,
> a God merciful and gracious,
> slow to anger,
> and abounding in steadfast love and faithfulness,
> keeping steadfast love for the thousandth generation,
> forgiving iniquity and transgression and sin,
> yet by no means clearing the guilty. (Exodus 34:6–7).

God allows chastisements for a greater good. He allows them to serve His divine plan of love—to help awaken the consciences of souls—thereby turning their hearts and minds to Him, their God and Savior. This brings God's merciful forgiveness, healing, and union with Him. Chastisements also allow souls to participate in God's redemptive act by sharing in the sufferings of Jesus. These sufferings are mysteriously meritorious to those who accept them, abandon themselves, and offer them to Him.

Hurricanes Katrina, Harvey, Irma, and Jose are among the long list of natural disasters of the 21st century that have inflicted widespread violence on man and nature. In 2011, a super outbreak of tornadoes claimed the lives of over 340 people in the southeastern United States. In Alabama, whole communities were wiped off the map. Only a few weeks earlier, a Japanese tsunami claimed 15,000 lives and, seven years before that, over 230,000 people were killed in an Indonesian tsunami.

No respecters of property or persons, these disasters decimated trailers, brick homes, shopping centers, and churches, killing people who were young, old, rich, poor, religious, and unreligious. To some people, it is evidence that we are alone in a chaotic, ungoverned, and disordered world. For others, it is evidence that we are in a world that was created but that is now fallen, a world in which we suffer as a result of the Fall of Adam and Eve and our own unrepented sinfulness.

The Book of Genesis says that, at each stage of Creation, God pronounced that what He had made was "good" and that the world was a hospitable place to live. It became less hospitable after the Fall. As the apostle Paul later put it, "Creation was subjected to frustration." (Romans 8:20).

The universal human desire to transcend the limitations of this fallen world is a sign that the present world is not what it once was or will one day be. **Paul suggests that, like a woman in labor, the whole of creation is in the throes of childbirth, waiting for redemption.**

So, tornadoes, hurricanes, tsunamis, volcanoes, and earthquakes are not the evolutionary products of a godless universe; they are the wails of a creation longing to be "liberated from its bondage to decay and brought into the freedom and glory of the children of God." (Romans 8:21).

Anyone who turns to God can be saved, for He is a merciful God. For those who do not turn to Him, He can only be slow to anger and push back the time of chastisement for a while, hoping that, in the interim, they bring forth the fruits of repentance. It is like the parable of the fig tree.

For three years, the owner of the fig tree looked for fruit from his tree and found none. He wanted to cut it down, but his gardener pleaded with him, "Let me fertilize it. Perhaps, this next year it will produce fruit." The tree was given one more year, but, if it were then without fruit, it would be cut down. (See Luke 13:6-9).

And so, the Blessed Virgin Mary, like the gardener, pleads with God for more time for sinners to repent. God gives them more time to bear the fruit of conversion, but, without conversion, they will be chastised and cut down like the barren fig tree.

Fear of chastisements is useless—what is needed is trust. "We should have confidence on the day of judgment..." (1 John 4:17). **"Be sincere of heart, be steadfast, and do not be alarmed when disaster comes. Trust Him and He will uphold you, follow a straight path and hope in Him."** (Sirach 2:2-6).

St. John wrote, "So we know and believe the love God has for us. God is love, and he who abides in love abides in God, and God abides in him. In this is love perfected with us, that we may have confidence for the day of judgment, because as He is, so are we in this world. There is no fear in love, but perfect love casts out fear. For fear has to do with punishment, and he who fears is not perfected in love." (1 John 9-10, 16-18).

Chastisements of the Innocent

God allows the chastisements of the innocent for His greater glory. Jesus Himself is the prime example. Jesus was the totally innocent one that suffered from chastisement. The prophet Isaiah prophesied, "But He was wounded for our transgressions; He was bruised for our iniquities; upon Him was the chastisement that made us whole; and with His stripes we were healed.....But the Lord laid upon Him the guilt of us all." (Isaiah 53:5-6).

Job was also an innocent who suffered from chastisements. Job's story is told in Scripture in the Book of Job. He was an innocent man who was "blameless and upright, who feared God and avoided evil." (Job 1:1). He had many children and animals, much property, and was "greater than any of the men of the East." (Job 1:3). God allowed that he suffer chastisements and lose it all.

The Book of Job shows that God allowed him to be chastised through Satan by means that still happen today: enemy raiders

(like today's terrorists); forces of nature, such as lightning and great wind (like today's hurricanes and tornados); a loathsome disease that caused boils and scabs (like today's AIDS and monkeypox); and the death and loss of property, animals, employees, and family.

Job is a model of a good attitude toward the chastisements of innocent people. He was humble and realized that God allows the chastisements of innocent people like himself. He recognized that God does not have to justify His actions to men, that He is almighty and omnipotent, and that one must humbly accept suffering, trusting in God that "all things work for good for those who love God." (Romans 8:28).

We should imitate Job and his acceptance of chastisements. Job said, "Naked I came forth from my mother's womb, and naked shall I go back again. The Lord gave and the Lord has taken away; blessed be the name of the Lord!" (Job 1:21). "We accept good things from God; and should we not accept trouble?" (Job 2:10).

Because of his acceptance, Job's life was restored with more than he had had before the chastisements. We should say with Job, "Happy is the man whom God reproves! The Almighty's chastening do not reject. For He wounds, but He binds up; He smites, but His hands give healing." (Job 5:17–18).

Finally, we should stop questioning God and trust in the ways of His divine providence. Job said, "I know that you can do all things and that no purpose of yours can be hindered. I have dealt with great things that I do not understand; things too wonderful for me, which I cannot know. I had heard of you by word of mouth, but now my eye has seen you. Therefore, I disown what I have said, and repent in dust and ashes." (Job 42:2–6).

Chastisements in the Bible

Our primeval history is revealed in Genesis, the first book of the Bible. In His goodness, God created Paradise, the Garden of Eden, our human parents, Adam and Eve, and the rest of His Creation. He warned Adam and Eve not to eat of the Tree of the Knowledge of Good and Evil, lest they die. However, evil soon entered creation. Satan, in the form of a snake, tempted Adam and Eve to doubt God's goodness. Satan lied to them and told them that they would surely not die, but would become like God if they ate of that tree. (See Genesis 3:4–5). So, they willfully chose to distrust God, disobeyed His warning, and lost sanctifying grace through Original Sin.

They, and all of their descendants, were chastised with death and the loss of grace, the earthly paradise, heaven, and eternal life. They, and all of humanity, were left to seek the truth with darkened intellects and to do good with weakened wills, concupiscence (the struggle between the spirit and the flesh,) the pains of work and childbirth, and with sin, suffering, and death. However, God gave them hope with the promise of redemption and power over sin. (See Genesis 3:17–19).

This was the beginning of God's pattern with humanity. He would warn humanity, then mercifully and justly chastise humanity for disobeying His warning, but would leave them with hope for the future.

The cause of sin is rooted in pride and disobedience. While humans can conquer temptations, they are free to choose to obey or disobey, but must suffer the consequences of disobedience from a God who still loves us and desires our happiness.

The *Catholic Catechism* explains that "man, tempted by the Devil, let his trust in his creator die in his heart and, abusing his freedom, disobeyed God's command. This is what man's first sin consisted of. All subsequent sin would be disobedience toward God and lack of trust in His goodness." (*CCC* 397).

After Adam and Eve's Original Sin, their son, Cain, killed his brother, Abel, in pride and anger against God and in envy of his brother. God punished him with banishment, but promised to protect him.

The sins of humanity continued. Genesis 6 tells us that next "the sons of God" married "the daughters of men." The "sons of God" refer to godly men and the "daughters of men" refer to ungodly women with whom they intermarried. This weakened the relationship of the human family with God and He chastised the world with the Great Flood. (See Genesis 6:1–7). However, He saved the remnant of Noah and his family.

After the Great Flood, the whole world spoke the same language, with the same vocabulary, but the sins of humanity continued.

Next, the people of Babel said, "Come, let us build ourselves a city, and a tower with its top in the heavens, and let us make a name for ourselves, lest we be scattered abroad upon the face of the whole earth." (Genesis 11:4). They wanted to build a city to glorify themselves in their own rebellious, secular society and not to glorify God. Because of this, God chastised them with the confusion of languages so that they could no longer understand each other's speech and He then dispersed them into many nations all around the world.

"This state of division into many nations is at once cosmic, social, and religious. It is intended to limit the pride of fallen humanity united only in its perverse ambition to forge its own unity as at Babel. But, because of sin, both polytheism and the idolatry of the nation and of its rulers constantly threaten this provisional economy with the perversion of paganism." (CCC 57).

However, **God's perfect Will is for the unity of all humanity. This unity will be restored only through Jesus King of All Nations. He said, "Unity and oneness in Spirit was my own prayer for all mankind and my Church as my own last testament before I gave my life as Savior of all mankind!** *'I lay down my life for my sheep.'* **(John 10:15). As I am One with my Father and the Holy Spirit, my Will is that all mankind be one in me, so that one faith, one fold, and one shepherd** *'And I will set up one shepherd over them...'* **(Ezekiel 34:23) will be gathered together under my sovereign Kingship as Lord. Yes, my beloved, by praying this chaplet I have had you labor for,** *'... but she out of her want has put in all that she had—all that she had to live on.'* **(Mark 12:44) and have taught you, you will replace my great sorrow with infinite joy!** *'They who sow in tears, shall reap in joy'* **(Psalms 125:5)."** (*Journal* 52).

"Your life imitates my Mother *'...be imitators of me...'* (Philippians 3:17) who labors in my grace by the power of the Holy Spirit *'...the labors wherein I had labored...'* (Ecclesiastes 2:11) to form, give birth, *'and she brought forth...'* (Luke 2:7) mature, help reconcile, *'...and that through Him He should reconcile to Himself all things...'* (Colossians 1:20) and mediate to me, your God, souls and nations of souls *'...a very great multitude.'* (Ezekiel 47:10) to obtain the extension of my Reign in the hearts of my people, *'thus mightily did the Word of the Lord spread and prevail.'* (Acts 19:20) and thus **I shall** unite all mankind, even unto the end of time, under my divine **Reign of Kingship. '... to the only God our Savior, through Jesus Christ Our Lord, belong glory and majesty, dominion, and authority, before all time, and now, and forever. Amen.' (Jude 1:25)." (Journal 53).**

After the dispersion of the people of Babel, the sins of humanity continued, including the worship of false gods, until about 2000 BC. Then God chose one man and one nation, the Patriarch Abraham and Israel (the Chosen People,) to learn obedience to God, first for themselves and then for all nations.

In order to gather together scattered humanity, God led Abram out from Ur to the land of Canaan. God later named him Abraham, meaning "the father of a multitude of nations." God made a covenant with him for all the nations and re-established the bonds of kinship between God and the human family. **God promised Abraham that he would be the father of many nations and that his descendants would be as countless as the number of the sands on the seashore. He promised him that, in his descendants, all the nations of earth would find blessing.** (See Genesis 17:6).

God also promised Abraham that He would bless his elderly wife, Sarah, with a son whom He would also bless; that he would give rise to nations; and that kings would issue from him. (See Genesis 17:16). He promised him and his descendants that He would be their God, they would be His people, and that He would give them the Promised Land of Canaan.

Abraham's descendants would be the trustees of these promises and were called to prepare for that day when God would gather all His children into the unity of the Church. They would be the root on to which the Gentiles would be grafted, once they, too, came to believe. (See CCC 60).

However, the Jews broke this covenant through their sins, especially with sodomy. The book of Genesis, chapter 19, tells us that the sins of Sodom and Gomorrah cried out to God. Because of this, God chastised them with annihilation. He sent two angels to Lot. They told him that God had sent them to destroy Sodom and Gomorrah because of the sins of the people. Then God rained fire and brimstone down from heaven and "He overthrew those cities, and all the valley, and all the inhabitants of the cities, and what grew on the ground." (Genesis 19:24). However, He first saved the righteous Lot and his family.

In 2018, a group of archaeologists and other scientists reported evidence for a theory that Sodom and Gomorrah were actually destroyed by a meteor strike. They theorize that it exploded at the low altitude of almost one mile, with the force of a ten-megaton atomic bomb, over the northeast corner of the Dead Sea.

They believe that the explosion rained down molten lava and killed approximately 50,000 people living in the approximately 400-square-mile region that was rendered uninhabitable for almost 700 years. According to them, the approximate date of the annihilation matches the time period corresponding to the event described in Genesis.

And the sins of the Jews continued. Around 1600 BC, God, in His justice, brought upon them the chastisement of their enslavement in Egypt. They had lived somewhat peacefully in Egypt from the time of Joseph's arrival there for about 100 years, but then, for about another hundred years, in slavery. When Abraham (then Abram) was in Canaan, God revealed to him the future enslavement of his descendants in Egypt and their eventual deliverance to the Promised Land.

"As the sun was about to set, a trance fell upon Abram, and a deep terrifying darkness enveloped him. Then the Lord said to Abram, 'Know for certain that your descendants shall be aliens in a land not their own [Egypt], where they shall be enslaved and oppressed. But I will bring judgment on the nation they must serve [Egypt], and in the end they will depart with great wealth....In the fourth time-span [the fourth generation] the others shall come back here [Canaan]....'" (Genesis 15:12–16).

The enslavement of the Jews in Egypt was a chastisement due to their sins. The prophet Ezekiel recounts, "They rebelled against me and refused to listen to me; none of them threw away the detestable things that had held their eyes, they did not abandon the idols of Egypt. Then I thought of pouring out my fury on them and spending my anger on them there in the land of Egypt; but I acted for my name's sake, that it should not be profaned in the sight of the nations among whom they were, in whose presence I had made myself known to them, revealing that

I would bring them out of the land of Egypt. Therefore, I led them out of the land of Egypt and brought them into the desert. Then I gave them my statutes and made known to them my ordinances, which everyone must keep, to have life through them." (Ezekiel 20:8–11).

God requested, through Moses, that the Egyptian Pharaoh let the Jews leave the country, but he continued to enslave them. So, God punished the Egyptians with the chastisement of ten plagues, including the last and the greatest of all, the death of their firstborn children.

Only then were the Jews finally released by Pharaoh. In His mercy, God liberated the Jews under the leadership of Moses, who led them in their Exodus out of Egypt, through the waters that God miraculously parted in the Red Sea, and into the desert.

However, the sins of the Jews continued with their disobedience against God in the desert by their worship of a molten golden calf. However, God still cared for them and fed them manna (a food from heaven) as He led them to the Promised Land.

The Book of Numbers tells us that, as the Jews approached the Promised Land, they sent men into it to scout out the land. The men returned and the majority reported that they did not have the strength to overcome the inhabitants. They said, "We are not able to go up against the people; for they are stronger than we." (Numbers 13:31). The Jews cried out against Moses, "Would that we had died in the land of Egypt!" (Numbers 14:2).

Because of their lack of trust in God's protection, He chastised them. He prevented any of that generation from entering the Promised Land and let them wander in the desert for 40 years, until they had all died. This continuing pattern of the sins of the Jews and God's chastisements demonstrates that God is always just, but also faithful, loving, and merciful toward humanity, giving hope for the future.

Just as the waters of the Red Sea miraculously parted, so did the waters of the River Jordan as Joshua led the Jews into the Promised Land around 1450 BC. God destroyed seven nations in the land of Canaan and gave the Jews the Promised Land as their inheritance, as He had promised Abraham. God reigned as the King of Israel for over 325 years.

However, the Jews eventually rejected the Kingship of God and demanded a human king, like the other nations. So, God gave them Kings—Saul, David, and Solomon—but they also sinned grievously against Him.

After the Jews had entered and conquered the Promised Land, they reached their greatest power in the Davidic Kingdom, with Jerusalem as its capital. **King David was succeeded by his son, Solomon, who reigned from 970 to 931 BC. He offended God by having a harem of 700 wives and 300 concubines, many of whom were pagans who did not worship the one true God but their own false ones. "His wives turned away his heart after their gods."** (1 Kings 11:4).

Because of the sins of Solomon, God said, "I will surely tear the Kingdom from you and will give it to your servant. Yet for the sake of David, your father, I will not do it in your days, but I will tear it out of the hand of your son." (1 Kings 11:11-12). This prophecy of the chastisement of division was carried out during the life of Solomon's son, Rehoboam. The 12 tribes of united Israel were divided into two kingdoms: the Southern Kingdom of Judah with the tribes of Judah and Benjamin and the Northern Kingdom of Israel with the remaining 10 tribes.

Sins continued, and so did the chastisements. The Northern Kingdom of Israel turned away from God, relied upon their own powers, and became a godless nation. As a consequence, God sent the pagan nation of Assyria to chastise them. Isaiah wrote," Ah, Assyria, the rod of my anger, the staff of my fury! Against a godless nation I send him, and against the people of my wrath I command him, to take spoil and seize plunder, and to tread them down like the mire of the streets." (Isaiah 10:5-6).

In 722 BC, the Assyrians invaded the Northern Kingdom and sent most of those people into exile, resettling the land with pagans that resulted in the eventual disappearance of the 10 tribes. In 586 BC, the Babylonians attacked Jerusalem in the Southern Kingdom. The prophet Jeremiah warned King Zedekiah, King of Judah, to surrender to King Nebuchadnezzar II, King of Babylon, but all of his warnings were ignored.

A long siege by the Babylonians caused famine and epidemics in Jerusalem, the destruction of the Temple, and the exile of the survivors into the Babylonian Captivity. King Zedekiah, the last king in the Davidic Line, was captured, his sons were slain before his very eyes, and then his own eyes were plucked out and he was led in chains to Babylon. **It was a great chastisement.** (See 2 Kings chapter 25).

The Jews were exiled in Babylon for 70 years. Later, in the late sixth century BC, after Babylon fell to Persia, some Jews returned to Jerusalem and began to rebuild the Temple.

God had warned Israel and Judah, "Give up your evil ways and keep my commandments and statutes, in accordance with the entire law which I enjoined on your fathers and which I sent you by my servants the prophets." However, they did not listen, but were as stiff-necked as their fathers, who had not believed in the Lord, their God. They rejected His statutes, the covenant which He had made with their fathers, and the warnings which He had given them." (2 Kings 17:13-15). That was the end of the Kingdoms of Israel and Judah.

From King David's descendants, God eventually brought to Israel a Savior, Jesus, according to His promise, as the King of All Nations. The angel Gabriel told Mary that her son, conceived by the Holy Spirit, was to be called "Jesus." He would be great, would be called "Son of the Most High," would inherit the throne of David, His father, would rule over the house of Jacob forever, and of His Kingdom there would be no end. (See Luke 1:32).

Because most of the Jewish people did not recognize Jesus as the Messiah, He prophesied the last great chastisement to them shortly before His death. When He drew near Jerusalem and saw the city, He wept over it, saying "For the days shall come upon you when your enemies will cast up a bank about you and surround you, and hem you in on every side, and dash you to the ground, you and your children within you, and they will not leave one stone upon another within you because you did not recognize the time of your visitation." (Luke 19:43–44).

He also prophesied the destruction of the Temple and the wrath of God upon the people. Jesus said to His disciples, "When you see Jerusalem surrounded by armies, know that its desolation is at hand. Then those in Judea must flee to the mountains. Let those within the city escape from it, and let those in the countryside not enter the city, for these days are the time of punishment when all the Scriptures are fulfilled. Woe to pregnant women and nursing mothers in those days, for a terrible calamity will come upon the earth and a wrathful judgment upon this people. They will fall by the edge of the sword and be taken as captives to all the Gentiles, and Jerusalem will be trampled underfoot by the Gentiles until the times of the Gentiles are fulfilled." (Luke 21:20–24).

Regarding the Temple, Jesus said, "The days will come when there shall not be left here one stone upon another that will not be thrown down." (Luke 21:6–7). His prophecy was fulfilled by the Roman General Titus in the year 70 AD. As Jesus had prophesied, not a stone upon a stone was left in the Temple, and it has never been rebuilt.

Jerusalem was sacked and burned and the Temple was destroyed. According to Josephus, the Jewish historian, over a million Jews lost their lives and the survivors were carried into slavery or they dispersed themselves throughout the nations.

However, God gave them hope for the future, prophesying their return. The prophets said, "I will bring them out from the peoples and gather them from the countries, and I will bring them into their own land." (Ezekiel 34:13). "I will restore the fortunes of my people Israel....I will plant them in their own land never again to be uprooted from the land I have given them." (Amos 9:14–15; Ezekiel 37:21–22).

"Who has ever heard of such a thing? Who has ever seen such things? Can a country be born in a day or a nation be brought forth in a moment? Yet no sooner is Zion in labor than she gives birth to her children." (Isaiah 66:8).

1878 years later, on May 14, 1948, the nation of Israel was born, literally in a single day.

20th Century Marian Prophecies of Chastisements – Fulfilled

God's chastisements are His secrets which He reveals to His prophets. They speak His words and reveal them to us so that by repentance and conversion we can mitigate or avoid them. "For the Lord God does nothing without revealing His secrets to His servants, the prophets." (Amos 3:7).

God revealed chastisements to His prophets so that those whom they warned could mitigate or avoid them. He revealed to Noah:

the Great Flood; to Abraham and Lot: the destruction of Sodom and Gomorrah; to Joseph: the seven-year famine in Egypt; to Moses: the plagues of Egypt; and to Jonah: the destruction of Nineveh. These were prophets sent by God in the times of the Old Testament. In modern times, He has sent His Mother as the prophetess of chastisements.

In her great love for us, Mary prophesied chastisements in the 20th century in order to bring us to conversion. She warned the world to repent and convert or to suffer from chastisements. The world did not listen or sufficiently respond to her requests and it has suffered.

In 1917, at Fatima, Portugal, during World War I, she appeared to three shepherd children. She prophesied destruction as a divine chastisement and punishment for sins. She said, "War is a punishment for sins" and that God was "about to punish the world for its crimes by means of war, famine, and persecutions of the Church and of the Holy Father." She also warned that if her messages were not obeyed, "nations will be annihilated."

Our Lady prophesied that if her requests for conversion and prayer were not fulfilled, the Holy Father would suffer grievously, as would St. John Paul II, much later, from his attempted assassination. She also prophesied that the errors of Russia would spread throughout the world, promoting wars and the persecution of the Church, as happened through Communism and today's neo-Marxism.

On July 13, 1917, **Our Lady revealed the vision of the Third Secret of Fatima.** Cardinal Joseph Ratzinger, later Pope Benedict XVI, interpreted this vision and said, "This represents the threat of judgment [chastisements] which looms over the world. Today the prospect that the world might be reduced to ashes by a sea of fire no longer seems pure fantasy: man himself, with his inventions, has forged the flaming sword. The vision then shows the power which stands opposed to the force of destruction – the splendor of the Mother of God and...the summons to penance....The vision speaks of dangers and how we might be saved from them."

In 1981, Mary began appearing in Church-approved apparitions at Kibeho, Rwanda. She emphasized the call to pray the Rosary and asked for penance and fasting, similar to her requests at Fatima.

Mary showed the visionaries images of savage murders, machetes, a "river of blood," people brutally killing each other, decapitated bodies, abandoned corpses with no one to bury them, and the putrefying remains of hundreds of thousands. These visions are now considered a prophecy of the ethnic genocide of almost 1 million people that later took place in that country.

On August 19, 1982, Mary appeared and, according to Fr. Gabriel Maindron, author of *Kibeho. Rwanda – A Prophecy Fulfilled. The Apparitions of Our Lady at Kibeho*, said, "The visionaries sometimes cried, their teeth chattered, they trembled. They collapsed several times with the full weight of their bodies during the apparitions, which lasted nearly eight hours without interruption. The crowd of about 20,000 present on that day was given an impression of fear — indeed, panic and sadness." Apparently, Mary herself was sad.

Immaculée Ilibagiza, Rwandan genocide survivor and author of *Our Lady of Kibeho*, wrote that Mary had the visionary, Alphonsine Mumureke, repeat three times into the microphone an apparent lament for the failure to respond to her requests, "You opened the door and they refused to come in. You opened the door and they refused to come in. You opened the door and they refused to come in."

Then Immaculée **reported, "Suddenly Alphonsine let out a gut-wrenching scream that cut through the startled crowd like a razor, 'I see a river of blood! What does that mean? No, please! Why did you show me so much blood? Show me a clear stream of water, not this river of blood!' the seer cried out, as the holy Mother revealed one horrifying vision after another. The young woman was subjected to so many images of destruction, torture, and savage human carnage that she pleaded, 'Stop, stop, please stop! Why are those people killing each other? Why do they chop each other?'"**

Alphonsine was next shown "a growing pile of severed human heads, which were still gushing blood. The grotesque sight worsened still as Our Lady expanded Alphonsine's vision until she beheld a panoramic view of a vast valley piled high with the remains of a million rotting, headless corpses, and not a single soul left to bury the dead."

Mary gave a clear warning. She said, "My children, it does not have to happen if people would listen and come back to God." She told them to warn government leaders, who belonged to the Hutu tribe, not to battle with the minority Tutsis.

Unfortunately, the warning was not heeded and, 12 years after the first apparitions, the two tribes entered a horrible civil war. One of the slaughters took place on the very spot where Mary had appeared. Twenty-five thousand people were killed in the place where pilgrims once knelt. The hands of a statue of Mary were shot off during the war and a bullet was embedded in her heart. Three of the visionaries were slaughtered in the mayhem.

Many of the deceased were chopped up and thrown in a river. As the visions prophesied, machete-wielding soldiers killed almost a million Rwandans in the span of a few short months. That was the highest killing rate in recorded history.

The Kibeho warnings were not just for Rwanda, but for the whole world. Mary said, "When I tell you this, I am not addressing myself strictly to you, child, but I am making this appeal to the world which is in revolt against God. I am concerned with and turning to the whole world to repent because otherwise the world is on the edge of catastrophe."

Mary told one of the visionaries at Rwanda, "Cleanse your hearts through prayer. The only way is God. If you don't take refuge in God, where will you go to hide when the fire has spread everywhere?"

The Rwandan people did not listen to Mary's motherly guidance and were unable to escape the tragic consequences of the genocide. When the terrifying scenes shown to the visionaries became reality, and the Church's approval came, it was simply too late.

Mary still appears throughout the world, pleading for prayer and fasting to bring conversions and peace. The alternative, she warns, is to suffer chastisements worse than those that have already occurred during the third millennium.

At Akita, Japan, on October 13, 1973, Mary appeared to Sr. Agnes Sasagawa and said, "If men do not repent and better themselves, the Father will inflict a terrible punishment on all humanity. It will be a punishment greater than the deluge [the Great Flood] such as one will never have seen before. Fire will fall from the sky and will wipe out a great part of humanity, the good as well as the bad, sparing neither priests nor faithful. The survivors will find themselves so desolate that they will envy the dead. The only arms which will remain for you will be the Rosary and the Sign left by my Son. Each day recite the prayers of the Rosary. With the Rosary, pray for the Pope, the bishops, and the priests." (Dan Lynch, *Medjugorje's Ten Secrets: How to Prepare*, John Paul Press, 2020, 78).

At Medjugorje, Bosnia-Herzegovina, on October 25, 1985, Mary appeared to Mirjana Soldo. Fr. René Laurentin, an authoritative theologian, reported that Mirjana said, "She showed me, as in a film, the realization of the First Secret. The earth was desolate. 'It is the upheaval of a region of the world.' She was precise. I cried." (Dan Lynch, *Medjugorje's Ten Secrets: How to Prepare*, John Paul Press, 2020, 95).

8. Chastisements of the Third Millennium

Many people today wonder about so many disasters, just as did the prophet Jeremiah. "You may ask yourself, 'Why is all this happening to me?' It is because of your many sins!" (Jeremiah 13:22).

Why is all this happening to us? The worst disasters in the history of the United States have all occurred in the last few decades. Why so many disasters? For the same reason — because of our many sins: legalized contraception, abortion, same-sex false marriages, false transgenderism, and so-called "physician-assisted suicide."

The 9/11 Attack on America

On September 11, 2001, the 9/11 Attack on America killed almost 3000 people and caused approximately $41 billion in property damage.

After the 9/11 Attack on America, Fr. James Bruse, the first spiritual director of the Secretary of the Jesus King of All Nations Devotion, said, "I see that as something getting ready to happen. I think it's a major wake-up call that's going on, and I think that all that I see — the weird temperatures, the polar caps, the earthquakes — there's a lot going on and I think we should all be prepared. I really do. I've had a lot more come back to Church and Confession. I think it's all different than a few years back. I think we're in a different era now. Christ is preparing us for the Kingdom of God, saying 'Be prepared,' but shouting it out now. It's as if Christ is saying 'Wake up! Let's get moving on our spirituality.' I believe it's building up to something big."

The Indian Ocean Tsunami

On December 26, 2004, the Indian Ocean Tsunami killed over 230,000 people in fourteen countries. It was one of the deadliest natural disasters in recorded history. Jesus King of All Nations warned of this chastisement and gave a confirming message after it occurred.

Jesus' Secretary received a message, on August 25, 2004, containing an urgent warning of a chastisement soon to come. Jesus said,

> Pray, pray, pray! Prayer offered to me through my holy Mother. Only she can avert the chastisement that now swiftly approaches. I cry out, my little one, to all mankind and, in particular, to my faithful ones! You must pray and offer sacrifices! A most fearful punishment is close at hand.
>
> Cities will be simultaneously affected. Great destruction, great loss of life. Great sorrow and pain. Smoke and fire. Wailing and lamentation.
>
> My children, I do not wish to strike you in my perfect justice. But if you remain obstinate of heart and blinded by your great pride, I must do so in order to save the greater number. My child, I tell you most solemnly that this event will take place on a holy day. I, the Lord, have spoken. (*Journal* 311–313).

The Indian Ocean Tsunami probably fulfilled Jesus' prophecy. As Jesus prophesied, the tsunami struck "on a holy day" (Sunday) and cities were "simultaneously affected" with "great destruction, great loss of life," and "smoke and fire" (crematory funeral pyres).

Jesus said that this disaster could have been averted, but not enough people prayed and offered sacrifices through His Mother's mediation as He had requested. **Two days after the tsunami struck, on December 28, the Feast of the Holy Innocents, Jesus gave another message. He said,**

> Daughter of my sacred Kingship! Cry out; cry out to my children! Repent! Repent and return to the Lord! Near is the Day of the Lord!! A day of swift and perfect justice. Purifying justice.
>
> My little one, I lament. I weep. My children do not hear. They do not see. They stop their ears that they may not hear. They cover their eyes that they may not see. They are willfully blind and willfully deaf.

I have shaken the earth to awaken the conscience of man.

Will they hear? Will they wake from their sleep in sin? If they do not, a yet more terrible catastrophe will befall mankind. Pray! Sacrifice! Invoke my most sacred, Eucharistic, and kingly Heart through my most holy Mother! (*Journal* 314–317).

The Indian Ocean Tsunami could have been averted, just like Jesus' prophesy of a Puerto Rican Tsunami in 1993, but there was an insufficient response of prayer and sacrifice. In the wake of this tsunami, **Alex Dias, the Catholic Bishop of Port Blair in the Andaman Islands, told the media, "I believe that the tsunami is a warning. A warning from God to reflect deeply on the way we lead our lives."**

Hurricane Katrina

On August 29, 2005, Hurricane Katrina killed almost 2000 people. This was the most destructive hurricane ever to strike the United States. The devastation in New Orleans and the surrounding Gulf Coast area caused billions of dollars in property damage and catastrophic loss to the region's rich cultural heritage.

New Orleans City Council President Oliver Thomas witnessed the horrors firsthand and, hearing talk of Sodom and Gomorrah, commented, "Maybe God's going to cleanse us."

It was generally acknowledged that New Orleans, the epicenter of the disaster, was a "sin city." The New Orleans *Southern Decadence* festival, which was scheduled to take place Labor Day weekend, was described by a French Quarter tourism site as "sort of like a gayer version of Mardi Gras" which is "most famous [or infamous] for the displays of naked flesh which characterize the event," with "public displays of sexuality...pretty much everywhere you look." The city was also renowned for occult practices, particularly voodoo.

The *American Spectator* reported that "New Orleans was ripe for collapse. Its dangerous geography, combined with a dangerous culture, made it susceptible to an unfolding catastrophe. Currents of chaos and lawlessness were running through the city long before [the hurricane struck] and they were bound to come to the surface under the pressure of natural disaster and explode in a scene of looting and mayhem."

Former New Orleans Archbishop Philip Hannan urged that the lesson of the storm not be lost — and insisted that it was a clear message from God. He said,

> I've been speaking at local parishes, and here's what I kept telling the people. I say, look, we are responsible not only for our individual actions to God, but in addition to that we are also citizens of a nation and, in the Old Testament as well as the New Testament, it says that a nation has a destiny and we are responsible whether we cause it or not for the course of morality in that nation. We are responsible as citizens for the sexual attitude, disregard of family rights, drug addiction, the killing of 45 million unborn babies, the scandalous behavior of some priests — so we have to understand that **certainly the Lord has a right to chastisement. If you ask me if the Lord knew of this, this was the greatest storm in the history of the nation. He is the Creator. He certainly permitted this. It would be as silly as asking if Henry Ford knew how a car worked.**

According to Archbishop Hannan, people who experienced it "are beginning to react according to that concept of morality." **He said that when he preached on the topic in the devastated area of Mandeville, where 1,000 attended Mass, "people loudly applauded. They want to be told the truth. We have reached a depth of immorality that we have never reached before. And the chastisement was Katrina."** He continued,

> I keep telling people, you have got to talk about this chastisement, you've got to let not only your children and grandchildren, but other people know about it — the others who have not gone through it, how much of a penance it was. To come back to your home and find it destroyed is an enormous shock, not only to the father and the mother, but to the children. **Because this is the worst storm in our history, it should become part of our heritage. We should tell our descendants just how terrible it was so they will understand that it was a chastisement and should improve our morality.**

I think it's up to us to preach very strongly and candidly and *directly* to say that this was a chastisement from God. God gave us our rights and therefore He gives us our duties too. We have got to pay attention to this chastisement. The Old Testament and the New. God has told us from the very beginning that we are responsible. To me it's inescapable if you read any Scripture at all.

Everyone I know, priests and bishops, believe that too. This storm was so disruptive, so destructive, that if you believe there is a Creator, He certainly knew or permitted it to happen. He certainly knew.

Katrina was an act of God upon a sin-loving and rebellious nation, a warning to all who foolishly and arrogantly believe there is no God, and that if He did exist, 'would not have done such a thing!' (Interview of Archbishop Hannan by the Catholic news website *Spirit Daily*, October 4, 2005).

The Haitian Earthquake

On January 12, 2010, the Haitian Earthquake killed almost 100,000 people, injured about 220,000 more, and left at least 1.5 million people homeless, with 250,000 residences and about 30,000 commercial buildings severely damaged.

Only five days later, on January 17, 2010, Jesus King of All Nations gave a consoling message after this devastating tragedy. He said, "Those who have lost their lives in this tragedy are victims of merciful love. Their sacrifice will not only help to secure their salvation but will also call down my great mercy upon their nation and the world....I allow such things in nature to serve my divine plan of love, to help awaken the consciences of souls, and thereby to turn their hearts and minds to me, their God and Savior, and also to allow them to participate in my redemptive act by sharing in my sufferings." (*Journal* 351–352).

The Japanese Earthquake/Tsunami

On March 11, 2011, the Japanese Earthquake struck. It was the most powerful earthquake ever to hit Japan and one of the five most powerful in the world since recordkeeping began in 1900. It

triggered a powerful tsunami with waves that towered 133 feet as they traveled inland. It destroyed entire towns, farms, factories, roads, railways, and electric lines. It left almost half a million people homeless. It moved the city of Honshu 8 feet east and shifted the earth on its axis 4 inches. It caused a number of nuclear accidents and a meltdown at three reactors, affecting hundreds of thousands of residents. It killed 16,000 people and caused $309 billion in property damage. It was one of the costliest natural disasters in history.

The Governor of Tokyo, Shintaro Ishihara, said that the Japanese Earthquake/Tsunami was "punishment from heaven" because the Japanese had become greedy. He also said, "Japanese politics is tainted with egoism and populism. We need to use the tsunami to wipe out egoism, which has attached itself like rust to the mentality of the Japanese people over a long period of time."

Militant Jihadist Muslims' Terrorist Attack in Paris, France

On November 13, 2015, a terrorist attack by militant jihadist Muslims in Paris, France, massacred 130 people. Five days later, on November 18, Jesus King of All Nations said in a message,

> **Chaos shall reign. More blood will be shed around the globe so long as the acknowledgment of my sovereign Kingship, my divine rights, is denied.**

> **This satanic group [militant jihadist Muslims] has been unleashed upon the world due to the great sinfulness of mankind. Wake up at last my people. Repent and be converted for I tell you if you do not the atrocities committed by this satanic and most evil group shall continue and grow. My mercy waits to be poured out through the practice of my Devotion of Jesus King of All Nations.**

> **Let it be known that the presence and veneration of this Image of mine shall shield souls from this danger. My sovereign power shall shield you from the viciousness of the enemy.** (*Journal* 653–654, 656, 658, 660).

A mass shooting is defined as three or more deaths in a single incident, occurring in a public place. Here are some of them:

Austin, Texas: A lone gunman killed 14 and wounded 31 at the University of Texas, on August 1, 1966;

San Ysidro, California: A lone gunman killed 21 people and wounded 19 at a restaurant, on July 18, 1984;

Killeen, Texas: A lone gunman killed 23 people and wounded 27 at a cafeteria, on October 16, 1991;

Blacksburg, Virginia: A lone gunman killed 32 people on Virginia Tech's campus, on April 16, 2007;

Newtown, Connecticut: A lone gunman killed 20 children and six adults at Sandy Hook Elementary School, on December 14, 2012;

San Bernardino, California: A husband and wife shot and killed 14 people and wounded 22 at a holiday party, on December 2, 2015;

Orlando, Florida: A lone gunman killed 49 people and wounded more than 50 at the Pulse Nightclub, on June 12, 2016;

Las Vegas, Nevada: A lone gunman killed 58 people and wounded more than 520 at the Harvest Festival concert on the Las Vegas Strip, on October 1, 2017;

Sutherland Springs, Texas: A lone gunman killed 26 people and wounded 20 at the First Baptist Church, on November 5, 2017; and

Parkland, Florida: On February 14, 2018, Ash Wednesday, a lone gunman killed 17 students and wounded 15 at a high school in Parkland, ironically named in 2017 as "the safest place in Florida."

In 2018, there were 307 mass shootings in the United States, so many that most people cannot remember them all. After a mass shooting at a Pittsburgh synagogue, on October 27, 2018, twelve more occurred in less than 3 weeks, with 79 shot and 23 of those killed. On November 7, at a bar in Thousand Oaks, California, 13 were killed.

Between July 28 and August 4, 2019, three mass shootings in the United States left 34 people dead and dozens more wounded in Dayton, Ohio; El Paso, Texas; and Gilroy, California.

On March 16, 2021, a gunman in Atlanta, Georgia, killed 8 during a series of shootings at three massage parlors.

On March 22, 2021, a gunman opened fire at a grocery store in Boulder, Colorado, killing 10 people.

Archbishop Samuel Aquila, for the Archdiocese of Denver, said that "incidents like this have become far too common in our country and our state.

"We must work to promote deeper conversion of hearts so that our lives are characterized by the virtue of charity, which allows us to love God and our neighbor, strengthening the fabric of society and preventing senseless acts of violence such as this one."

Many people ask, "Why did these mass killings happen?" These are not merely human criminal events, they were sins, inspired and directed by Satan, who is evil personified. Law enforcement authorities revealed that the Parkland, Florida, killer confessed that "demon voices" told him "what he needed to do to launch the deadly assault."

Evil is not created by God, it is the absence of the good that He has created, inspired by a truly evil personality, Satan, with whom the human race has been in conflict since the Garden of Eden when he tempted Adam and Eve into Original Sin.

"Without the knowledge Revelation gives of God, we cannot recognize sin clearly and are tempted to explain it as merely a developmental flaw, a psychological weakness, a mistake, or the necessary consequence of an inadequate social structure, etc. Only in the knowledge of God's plan for man can we grasp that sin is an abuse of the freedom that God gives to created persons so that they are capable of loving Him and loving one another." (CCC 387).

Wildfires

In the fall of 2017, wildfires lit up the American West as the three huge hurricanes of Harvey, Irma, and Maria hit in the East and caused cumulative damage of over $350 billion and deaths and psychological trauma to many.

In November of 2018, wildfires ravaged both ends of California. Over 30 people died in the fires. The Camp fire was the most destructive fire in state history. It virtually burned the town of Paradise to the ground, destroying thousands of homes and structures. The fires displaced hundreds of thousands of residents.

Governor Jerry Brown said, "This is not the new normal, this is the new abnormal. The chickens are coming home to roost, this is real here."

COVID–19

In its first six months, the COVID–19 pandemic left a death toll in America equivalent to 65 9/11 Attacks, millions out of work, everyday life upended, and roiling riots, lootings, and shootings.

On March 18, 2020, Jesus King of All Nations revealed a message to His Secretary, the mystic of the Jesus King of All Nations Devotion. He said that what we were seeing happening around us was the beginning of the chastisements that He has prophesied to correct the conscience of mankind. In my opinion, He was referring to the COVID–19 pandemic.

What is the remedy for what He described in His message below as "the ills of the world"?

He pleads with us to practice His Devotion in order that He may, as He said in His message, "pour out abundant blessings upon poor, aching mankind." He said, "This shall call down my mercy and my healing upon the world."

Jesus concludes with a Call to Action, "Take heed of my Words. Take action now."

Here is His complete message with my bracketed comments and His scriptural citations,

My children, pray my Devotion, enthrone my Image of Jesus King of All Nations.

What you see happening around you [the COVID-19 pandemic] is the beginning of the chastisements foretold by me to correct the conscience of mankind. *"Be watchful! I have told it all to you beforehand."* (Mark 13:23).

Once more I appeal to my holy Church to rapidly approve my Devotion of Jesus King of All Nations and allow the public practice of my Devotion and the enthronement of my Image. As I have said before, **this is the remedy for the ills of the world; the re-acclamation of my sovereign Kingship over all of mankind, over all nations.**

"Great and wonderful are your works, Lord God Almighty. Just and true are your ways, O King of the nations. Who will not fear you, Lord, or glorify your name? For you alone are holy. All the nations will come and worship before you, for your righteous acts have been revealed." (Revelation 15:3, 4).

This shall call down my mercy and my healing upon the world.

"But for you who fear my name, there will arise the sun of justice with its healing rays;" (Malachi 3:20).

Take heed of my words. Take action now.

"Turn to me and be safe, all you ends of the earth, for I am God, there is no other!" (Isaiah 45:22).

I wait to pour out abundant blessings upon poor, aching mankind.

"If you wish to return, O Israel, says the Lord, return to me." (Jeremiah 4:1).

Jesus previously revealed in the message below that the Jesus King of All Nations Devotion is the "crowning glory" of all of the devotions to Him.

He said,

> **This work is eternal for it is the proclamation of my
> sovereign and divine Kingship; the acknowledgment of
> my supreme authority over all creation; it is the song of
> praise sung by the Heavenly Court, by the angels who
> continually cry, "Holy, holy, holy!", as they claim my
> divine sovereignty.**

> **Contained within it is the totality of all of the devotions
> to my sacred and divine person for it is the crowning glory
> of all others; the absolute and supreme authority granted
> me by my Father. This authority which must be
> recognized by all and re-acclaimed by my holy Church.**
> (*Journal* 706, 708).

On March 21, 2020, Cardinal Raymond Leo Burke wrote, in
Message on the Combat against the Coronavirus,

> A person of faith cannot consider the present calamity in
> which we find ourselves without considering also how
> distant our popular culture is from God. It is not only
> indifferent to His presence in our midst but openly
> rebellious toward Him and the good order with which He
> has created us and sustains us in being....

> **In His justice, God recognizes our sins and the need of
> their reparation, while, in His mercy, He showers upon us
> the grace to repent and make reparation....**

> God never turns His back on us; He will never break His
> covenant of faithful and enduring love with us, even though
> we are so frequently indifferent, cold, and unfaithful. As the
> present suffering uncovers for us so much indifference,
> coldness, and infidelity on our part, we are called to turn to
> God and to beg for His mercy. We are confident that He will
> hear us and bless us with His gifts of mercy, forgiveness,
> and peace.

Cardinal António dos Santos Marto, Bishop of the Diocese of
Leiria-Fátima, Portugal, denied that the COVID–19 pandemic was
a chastisement from God. He said that those who believe it is do so
"out of ignorance, sectarian fanaticism, or insanity."

On the other hand, eminent Italian historian Professor Roberto de Mattei described the bishop of Fatima's words as "scandalous." He explained that "it contradicts not only the words of Our Lady of Fatima, who says that God is going to chastise the world by means of war, hunger, and persecutions of the Church and the Holy Father, but the teaching of Sacred Scripture, and the words of previous popes and saints."

The scriptural and historical record is clear that God punishes people and nations through war, plague, and famine. When Church prelates deny this, their denials are themselves a sign that we are really in a period of chastisement.

St. Thomas Aquinas explains, "When it is all the people who sin, vengeance must be made on all the people, just as the Egyptians who persecuted the children of Israel were submerged in the Red Sea, and as the inhabitants of Sodom were struck down *en masse*, or a significant number of people must be struck, such as happened in the chastisement inflicted for the adoration of the golden calf." (St. Thomas Aquinas, *Summa Theologica (Summary of Theology)*, II^a-IIae, Ques 108, Art 1, Reply to Objection 5).

On January 6, 1870, St. John Bosco had a vision in which it was revealed to him that "war, plague, and famine are the scourges with which the pride and malice of men will be struck down." The Lord said, "You, O priests, why do you not run to weep between the vestibule and the altar, begging for the end of the scourges? Why do you not take up the shield of faith and go over the roofs, in the houses, in the streets, in the piazzas, in every inaccessible place, to carry the seed of my Word. Do you not know that this is the terrible two-edged sword that strikes down my enemies and that breaks the wrath of God and men?" (Giovanni Battista Lemoyne, *Biographical memoirs of the venerable Don Giovanni Bosco*, 782).

Monsignor Nicola Bux, former theologian for the Vatican Congregations for the Doctrine of the Faith, for divine Worship, and for the Pontifical Celebrations Office, confirmed the March 18, 2020, message of Jesus King of All Nations that the COVID-19 pandemic plague was a chastisement.

In that message, Jesus King of All Nations had said, "What you see happening around you [the COVID-19 pandemic] is the beginning of the chastisements foretold by me to correct the

conscience of mankind." Jesus cited His Scripture, *"Be watchful! I have told it all to you beforehand."* (Mark 13:23).

Six days later, on March 24, Monsignor Bux gave a YouTube Address, *COVID-19 Caso o Castigo? (COVID-19 A Chance Event or a Chastisement?).* He said, "Today, the word 'chastisement' arouses scandal even among churchmen, because they have forgotten that, at the beginning of world history, after love, there is sin, anger, and judgment."

Monsignor Bux's implication is that the "sin" is idolatry and the "judgment" is the chastisement of the COVID-19 pandemic. He warned us about idolatry and referred to the worship of the Pachamama idols at the Amazon Synod in Rome, in October 2019.

Before the idols were placed in the Santa Maria church at the Amazon Synod, they were exhibited as part of a pagan ritual before the very eyes of Pope Francis. As he looked on, an Amazonian woman chanted to the idols. Several people carried the idols in procession to Pope Francis, who made the Sign of the Cross over them. After that, they were placed in the church.

Monsignor Bux said that idolatry is the "gravest sin....We gave in to idolatry...by kneeling before heaps of earth and worshiping idolatrous statues, even in St. Peter's Basilica."

In the third century, St. Cyprian of Carthage lived through a terrible plague in his diocese. He addressed his flock in a sermon (*De mortalitate*) and encouraged them to not be afraid of the plague or of death, but only of the loss of their souls, because "it is for him to fear death who is not willing to go to Christ. That pestilence and plague, which seems horrible and deadly, searches out the righteousness of each one and examines the minds of the human race..."

St. Cyprian's words speak to us today — not to fear bodily death, but to fear eternal death in hell and begin to practice the Jesus King of All Nations Devotion, personal holiness, and the spiritual and corporal works of mercy as the remedies to plagues, such as the COVID-19 pandemic.

At least 207 natural disasters were recorded globally in the first six months of 2020. In the United States, which led the world in COVID-19 fatalities, it was also a year that witnessed the greatest number of landfalls by tropical systems (storms and hurricanes) in recorded history; civil disruptions (as not seen in decades); massive tornadic systems across the land; floods; as well as wildfires that in California easily broke all-time marks, destroying acreage that collectively surpassed the single greatest wildfire in American history, the Peshtigo Fire of 1871, by tens of thousands of acres.

However, God in His mercy can still allow the aversion or mitigation of chastisements that we deserve.

9. Aversion and Mitigation of Chastisements

In His Will, God can rescue the devout from chastisements. St. Peter writes, "For if God did not spare the angels when they sinned, but condemned them to the chains of Tartarus and handed them over to be kept for judgment; and if He did not spare the ancient world, even though He preserved Noah, a herald of righteousness, together with seven others, when He brought a Flood upon the godless world; and if He condemned the cities of Sodom and Gomorrah to destruction, reducing them to ashes, making them an example for the godless people of what is coming; and if He rescued Lot, a righteous man oppressed by the licentious conduct of unprincipled people, then **the Lord knows how to rescue the devout from trial and to keep the unrighteous under punishment for the day of judgment…**" (2 Peter 2:4–9).

Chastisements can be averted (prevented or avoided) or mitigated (lessened in severity) if people respond to God's warnings. For example, the prophet Jonah warned Nineveh (ancient Iraq) that it would be destroyed in forty days. But the people repented, prayed, and fasted and the chastisement was averted. (See Jonah chapter 3).

History shows that heeding the call to repentance is critical. At the preaching of Jonah, Nineveh repented and was spared its chastisement. At the preaching of Jesus, Jerusalem did not repent and was chastised by its utter destruction by the Romans.

Sr. Lucia, one of the visionaries of Our Lady of Fatima, revealed that the world was spared from a chastisement of nuclear war that she said "would have occurred in 1985" but was averted because St. John Paul II made the collegial consecration of the world to the Immaculate Heart of Mary in 1984.

Our Lady told Fr. Gobbi, of the Marian Movement of Priests, "The purification can still be set back or shortened. Much suffering can still be spared you." (*To the Priests* 110). So, we should repent and pray in order to avoid or mitigate threatened chastisements.

Promises of Jesus King of All Nations and Mary for Aversion and Mitigation of Chastisements

To mitigate chastisements and to help us save souls, Jesus asked us to pray the *Novena in Honor of Jesus as True King* **and made us a promise.** He asked us to pray, "Forgive us, O sovereign King, our sins against you. Jesus, you are a King of mercy. We have deserved your just judgment. Have mercy on us, Lord, and forgive us. We trust in your great mercy! O most awe-inspiring King, we bow before you and pray; may your Reign, your Kingdom, be recognized on earth!" (*Journal* 29). **He promised us, "Each time you say these prayers, I will mitigate the severity of the chastisements upon your country."** (*Journal* 41).

Jesus also said, "A great catastrophe is about to descend on the world. Lessen this punishment with the spiritual weapons of frequent reception of the holy sacraments; loving, reverent attendance at the holy sacrifice of the Mass; and constant praying of the holy Rosary. When my Mother came to Fatima, she requested the praying of the Rosary daily. I now say constant! Let this prayer encompass your very hearts, minds, and souls offering it to me through my dear Mother for the salvation of souls." (*Journal* 341).

Our Lady of Akita, Japan, told Sr. Agnes in 1973, "I alone am able still to save you from the calamities that approach. Those who place their confidence in me will be saved."

Jesus King of All Nations said, "Only [my Mother] can avert the chastisement that now swiftly approaches. I cry out, my little one, to all mankind and, in particular, to my faithful ones! You must pray and offer sacrifices!" (*Journal* 311).

Mary said at Medjugorje,

I will pray to my Son not to punish the world, but I plead with you, be converted.

You cannot imagine what the Eternal Father will send to earth. That is why you must be converted. Renounce everything. Do penance. Express my thanks to all my children who have prayed and fasted. **I carry all this to my divine Son in order to obtain an alleviation of justice against the sins of mankind.** (June 24, 1983).

Regarding the lessening or mitigation of the punishment, Mary told the visionary Mirjana, on November 11, 1982, "I have prayed. The punishment has been softened. Repeated prayers and fasting reduce punishments from God, but it is not possible to avoid entirely the chastisement. Go on the streets of the city, count those who glorify God and those who offend Him. God can no longer endure that."

Mary said that chastisement is inevitable because we cannot expect the conversion of the entire world. However, chastisements can be mitigated by prayer and penance. According to Mirjana, we are close to chastisement and so she says to "convert yourselves as quickly as possible. Open your hearts to God."

Let us take hope in the words of Cardinal Joseph Ratzinger, later Pope Benedict XVI, who interpreted the vision of the Third Secret of Fatima. He wrote, on June 26, 2000, "The future is not in fact unchangeably set....The vision speaks of dangers and how we might be saved from them....There is no immutable destiny, that faith and prayer are forces which can influence history and that in the end prayer is more powerful than bullets and faith more powerful than armies....What remains...[is] the exhortation to prayer as the path of 'salvation of souls' and, likewise, the summons to penance and conversion."

Prophesied Seaquake in Puerto Rico – Averted

In April 1992, the Jesus King of All Nations Devotion's Secretary and her Spiritual Mother visited Bishop Enrico Rivera in Puerto Rico. With his permission, they prayed the Jesus King of All Nations devotional prayers before the exposed Blessed Sacrament, together with others in the church of Our Lady of Mount Carmel. This was the first time that the devotional prayers were prayed in public in a church with a bishop's permission.

Puerto Rico had suffered from heavy rains and flooding from January 5-6, 1992. The catastrophic event killed 23, injured 167, and caused property damage of approximately $155 million. As the rainy season began in May, the government became concerned about more flooding.

A government official called the Spiritual Mother and asked her to pray to Jesus King of All Nations for protection. While they were on the phone, the Spiritual Mother had a vision of a seaquake chastisement. A seaquake is an earthquake below sea level that can cause a devastating tsunami and destruction. Jesus told the Spiritual Mother to pray the *Chaplet of Unity* as the remedy and they prayed together over the phone.

Then, the government official spread the warning and the *Chaplet of Unity* remedy to other government officials and to a group of religious sisters. The Sisters prayed an all-night vigil and brought the message to the Bishop. All of them received the message with loving hearts open to the words of Jesus and they acted upon them in response to His request. They turned to Jesus and personally prayed the devotional prayers for mercy and to avert the threatened chastisement.

On May 22, 1992, in answer to their prayers of His Devotion, Jesus stopped and averted the seaquake chastisement that He had prophesied. Jesus heard their prayers and said,

> Some have already received me as their Lord and King in the Devotion that I have given you to give to the world, that of Jesus King of All Nations....I have heard the prayers of my people in repentance, and my most holy Mother has interceded on their behalf for these children. Recognize and honor my Mother!

> I have stopped the seaquake at this time, for it would have devastated the lands and the peoples; with the merciful scepter of my Kingship, I have done this! Yes indeed! My messengers were correct that I sent to tell my people of the devastation of the chastisement that was to occur today, the 22nd of May! In my justice, their horrible sins have justly deserved much more than this! But my faithful souls have prayed to me and recognized me as King of All Nations, and have spread my glory in this recognition!

> No, not all are praying, but enough have prayed to mitigate, as you know so well, my beloved, that it is my promise to those who honor me, and have embraced me and my Devotion as King of All Nations! **Yes, chastisements will come, but let them see, let them experience, let them bear witness to the mercy that I have given them that they were not harmed!**...

I have shown them that if they turn to me, their merciful King who desires to reign in their hearts, that I am a King of Mercy, a Father of Mercy, a Lord of Love who does not want their unnecessary deaths and condemnation of their souls because of their sins and stubbornness in pride.

Jesus continued in His message to warn us that if we don't wake up and see the lightning of His mercy, we will experience the thunder of His justice (chastisement). He said,

Have no doubt—the thunder of my justice was going to be heard! As thunder comes before the rain, so the thunder of my just judgment upon them was going to be heard first! Will my children wake up and see the lightning first? The lightning of the merciful rays of my mercy that I wish to strike their hearts with!

Will they notice me who AM? Will my people finally see with the light of my grace so that I can reign in their hearts?! Yes, I wish to be the light that comes before the Reign! The Reign of my merciful Kingship! Choose my people; choose how you wish to serve me!....

It is you, my special little ones, who have found the fulfillment of my promises not only for yourselves, but for your whole nation! **Remember what I have done for you, my people, of how I have spared you this time!**"

(Please see Appendix F, The Spiritual Mother's Message of Aversion of a Prophesied Seaquake Chastisement in Puerto Rico, on pg. 280, for the full message.)

Jesus spared them at that time, but not later from Hurricane Maria. On September 18, 2017, Puerto Rico was devastated by the 115 mile-per-hour hurricane. Tens of thousands were left homeless because of the winds and floods. Basic goods and services, such as food, water, and fuel, were in short supply. Electricity was out for virtually the entire island for a long time and was not fully restored for months. Nearly 85 percent of the island had no cellphone coverage. Much of the country's already-shaky economic base, including tourism and agriculture, was all but wiped out. **Over 1000 people were killed with over $50 billion in property damage. It was Puerto Rico's worst natural disaster.**

Nuclear War – Averted

In 1917, before the nuclear age, the Blessed Virgin Mary warned us, at Fatima, Portugal, that there could be an "annihilation of nations." Almost 60 years later, after the nuclear age, she warned us, at Akita, Japan, that if people did not repent and better themselves, "fire will fall from the sky and will wipe out a great part of humanity…"

Marthe Robin was a French mystic of the 20th century. She died in 1981. She revealed the danger of atomic bombs in utter simplicity, "This atom bomb—when one thinks that small nations will also have it and only two fools will be needed to ravage everything."

The danger of nuclear warfare was manifested by two such fools from small nations. They were the leaders of Pakistan and India, both of whom had nuclear weapons. They almost went to nuclear war in 1998.

On May 11 and 13, 1998, India conducted a total of five underground nuclear tests, breaking a 24-year self-imposed moratorium on nuclear testing. Pakistan followed, claiming five tests on May 28, 1998, and an additional test on May 30, for a total of six, to get one up on India.

The Indian tests, which completely surprised the U.S. intelligence and policy communities set off a worldwide storm of criticism. Many analysts judged that, by conducting nuclear tests, the Indian government hoped to consolidate its power by rallying strong national pro-nuclear sentiment.

On May 29, 1998, the Spiritual Mother of the Jesus King of All Nations Devotion phoned me and told me that she and others had been praying for peace between India and Pakistan. She said that Jesus King of All Nations gave her a message concerning their nuclear confrontation and the threat of nuclear war.

I asked her to please request Jesus to speak plainly, as He did to Moses face-to-face, so that everyone could understand it. In the message, Jesus asked, "Am I speaking plainly enough, my people?", as I had asked Him to do. And then He answered His own question, "I AM." This is a double play on words by Jesus who answers His own question as well as gives His name (I AM),

as He plainly told Moses face-to-face and as I had asked Him to speak to me.

Then Jesus gave the message to the Spiritual Mother contained in Appendix G, *The Spiritual Mother's Message of the Aversion and Mitigation of Nuclear War*, on pg. 287, that I recorded over the phone. In His message, Jesus thanked all those who had prayed for peace. He said, "Although they [India and Pakistan] persisted, the prayers were used to mitigate the 'wicked design' (Mark 7:21) of these pride-filled and arrogant nations."

Jesus King of All Nations mitigated a nuclear chastisement to a lesser chastisement of conventional warfare because of the prayers of the people. The conventional warfare continued between Pakistan and India from 1998 through 2002, with the loss of thousands of people, but not the millions that might have been killed through a nuclear confrontation.

In His message, Jesus said that the world needs arms of love and not the nuclear arms which bring only destruction. Jesus gave the Spiritual Mother a vision of an explosion inside an orange and the tremendous damage that it caused to its core and skin. He said that, likewise, nuclear explosions hurt the very core of the earth, its skin, and its course in space.

Jesus said that if nuclear war comes, the earth will be reduced to a potter's field, a field of blood. He was referring to His betrayal by Judas to the Sanhedrin for 30 pieces of silver, which Judas threw back to the Sanhedrin after Jesus was crucified. They viewed it as blood money and therefore illegal to put into their treasury. So, they used it instead to buy the potter's field as a burial ground for foreigners. It came to be known as "the Field of Blood." (See Matthew 27:7–8). Jesus implied that nuclear war would be a betrayal of Him and humanity and reduce the entire earth to a potter's field, a field of blood.

Jesus said, "It is time and past time to reconcile with your wife, reconcile with your husband, and 'heed carefully what you hear.' (Matthew 11:13). Reconcile with your children, reconcile with your neighbors, reconcile peoples and nations with one another."

Jesus concluded, "Am I speaking plainly enough, my people? I AM. My love for you is infinitely merciful, for I love you more than you can ever possibly know love."

The Great St. Louis Flood – Averted

On Sunday, August 1, 1993, I spoke at the St. Louis Eucharistic Congress during the height of the 1993 Great Flood of the Mississippi River. In my talk, I explained how Our Lady of Guadalupe interceded to save Mexico City from a horrible flood in 1634. The flood had already killed 30,000 people. The desperate citizens, imploring Our Lady's help, carried the Miraculous Image of Our Lady of Guadalupe through the knee-high floodwaters from the Basilica to the Cathedral in Mexico City. This was the first and only time that such a procession had taken place. The flood miraculously ended.

After my talk, some Congress participants asked me to imitate that procession and take the Missionary Image of Our Lady of Guadalupe to the flooding Mississippi River. This River was originally named the River of the Immaculate Conception. Our Lady of Guadalupe is a representation of the Immaculate Conception.

I made an announcement of a spontaneous procession with the Missionary Image to the River. About 200 people joined me and we processed from the Cathedral of St. Louis to the Great Arch of the Gateway to the West and down the flood-swept steps to the riverside.

Hundreds of onlookers joined us there and I sprinkled holy water into the river and prayed in the pouring rain for an abatement of the flood, the salvation of the dead, and the healing of the sufferers. We concluded by singing "America the Beautiful."

As we processed back, the rain suddenly stopped as we sang the very last note of the "Hail Holy Queen" hymn and the Cathedral bells unexpectedly rang out jubilantly at 5:20 PM! As we placed the Image into a van, a large flock of swallows suddenly swooped over us and circled continuously overhead. There were no other birds to be seen anywhere else.

The Mississippi River at St. Louis crested on that very day, August 1, 1993, at 49.6 feet, nearly 20 feet above flood stage. It had a peak flow rate of 1,080,000 cubic feet. At this rate, a bowl the size of Busch Memorial Stadium in St. Louis would be filled to the brim in 70 seconds!

The next day, the floodwaters began to recede! The Congress organizers credited this to Our Lady of Guadalupe.

A few years later, I received an email from Sara Connelly Zervos, who was in that procession. She reminded me of the grace of the receding of the Great Flood. She wrote,

> On August 1, 1993, you spoke at the St. Louis Eucharistic Congress with the Missionary Image of Our Lady of Guadalupe during the height of the Great Flood of 1993. The forecast for that weekend was for the flood stage to go to its highest level in history, and it did on that day at 49.6 feet, nearly 20 feet above flood stage, which was expected to inundate St. Louis.

> However, on that day, the small group at the Congress, led by you with the Missionary Image of Our Lady of Guadalupe, processed around the St. Louis Arch, praying for God's mercy through the Mother of God.

> The next day, the levees broke north of St. Louis and south of St. Louis, but St. Louis was saved. I was privileged by God to be there and witness this miracle.

10. Protection from Chastisements

In our Culture of Death, we see and read about militant jihadist Muslims on a barbaric rampage across the world, killing innocent people; acts of terror throughout the world; serial mass killings; and mothers murdering their own children, both before and after their birth.

These are great evils that the world has never experienced to this extent before. Other great evils include the dissolution of marriage and the family through no-fault divorce and same-sex false marriages; false transgenderism; anti-life evils such as contraception, abortion, embryonic experimentation, infanticide, so-called "physician-assisted suicide;" "euthanasia" killings; unjust wars; genocides; the sex trade; the drug trade; addictions; ecological destruction; and church, business, and political corruption. Never has God been more disbelieved, ignored, disobeyed, and blasphemed by so many.

Do you also notice the increasing chastisements that God is allowing from both nature and humanity because of these evils? These sins cry out to heaven for God's vengeance! Jesus King of All Nations said that He must chastise us "in order to save the greater number." Chastisements are not an end, but a chance for a new beginning. We can bring about this new beginning through His Devotion's prayers, His Image, His Medal, and through the sacraments of Confession and Eucharist.

St. John Paul II said, "God, in fact, is not indifferent before good and evil; He enters mysteriously the scene of human history with His judgment which, sooner or later, will unmask evil, defend the victims, and indicate the way of justice....The object of God's action is never ruin, pure and simple condemnation, or the annihilation of the sinner." (Pope John Paul II, *Address*, September 10, 2003). We must implore God for mercy to protect us from His justice.

Jesus told St. Faustina, "I am prolonging the time of mercy for the sake of [sinners]. But woe to them if they do not recognize this time of my visitation." (*Diary* 1160). "While there is still time, let them have recourse to the fount of my mercy;..." (*Diary* 848). "He who refuses to pass through the door of my mercy must pass through the door of my justice..." (*Diary* 1146).

Jesus told her, "I do not want to punish aching mankind, but I desire to heal it, pressing it to my merciful Heart. I use punishment when they themselves force me to do so; my hand is reluctant to take hold of the sword of justice. Before the Day of Justice, I am sending the Day of Mercy." (*Diary* 1588). "These rays [referring to the two rays in His Divine Mercy Image that are symbolic of the blood and water that flowed from His Sacred Heart while on the Cross] shield souls from the wrath of my Father. Happy is the one who will dwell in their shelter, for the just hand of God shall not lay hold of him." (*Diary* 299).

So, God can protect us from chastisements. He protected Noah and his family from the Great Flood; He protected the Jews from the chastisements against Egypt, particularly the death of their firstborn children; He protected Lot and his family from the chastisement of the destruction of Sodom and Gomorrah; and He protected the Ninevites from Jonah's prophesied destruction of their city because they repented. **In the modern age, He protected four Jesuit priests from the chastisement of the first atomic bomb.**

Protection from the Atomic Bomb

On August 6, 1945, the United States Air Force dropped the first atomic bomb on Hiroshima, Japan. It killed about 140,000 people.

The bomb exploded with a blinding flash, creating a giant fireball that vaporized practically everything and everyone within a radius of about a mile of the point of detonation. Over two thirds of the city's buildings were completely destroyed.

Four Jesuit priests and four other people were in their home, eight blocks from Ground Zero, the center of the attack, but they survived and the radiation from the bomb had no effect upon them. The radiation should have caused serious lesions and probably immediate death, but it did not. Over the course of the following years and examinations by dozens of doctors, no trace of radiation was found in any of them.

The priests believed that they were protected from this chastisement because, as Fr. Hubert Schiffer said, "We were

living the message of Fatima. We lived and prayed the Rosary daily in that home."

Jesus King of All Nations said, "My daughter, my little one, I offer again, to straying mankind, a treasure with which they may again turn aside my just judgment. It is my Devotion of Jesus King of All Nations. I tell you most solemnly, little one, that one of the fruits of this Devotion will be the buying of more time from my mercy in order that souls may be converted before it is too late." (*Journal* 303). "Pray, pray, pray! Prayer offered to me through my holy Mother. Only she can avert the chastisement that now swiftly approaches." (*Journal* 311).

Jesus respects our free will and leaves the choice to us to accept or reject both His admonition and the gift of His Devotion and His ensuing protection from chastisements.

Be Not Arrogant

In the face of chastisements, we are called to humble ourselves and not to arrogantly challenge them. God asked King Solomon for true humility in the face of chastisements. He said, "If I close heaven so that there is no rain, if I command the locust to devour the land, if I send pestilence among my people, **if then my people, upon whom my name has been pronounced, humble themselves and pray, and seek my face and turn from their evil ways, I will hear them from heaven and pardon their sins and heal their land.**" (2 Chronicles 7:13–14).

Rabbi Jonathan Cahn of Wayne, New Jersey, said that, after the 9/11 Attack on America, a passage in the Book of Isaiah was uncannily re-enacted in the United States, just the way it originally played out in Israel at the time of the great prophet Isaiah.

He quoted the book of Isaiah, what it meant to Israel, and how it was applied after 9/11 in America by some of our politicians. "The bricks are fallen down, but we will build with hewn stones: the sycamores are cut down, but we will change them into cedars." (Isaiah 9:10).

These words were first uttered by arrogant leaders in Israel in response to a limited strike by Assyria on the lands of Zebulun and Naphtali — an attack the prophet makes clear was actually part of a limited chastisement by God against apostasy. It wasn't meant to destroy the nation, but to awaken it.

However, instead, the response from the leaders in Israel was one of arrogance. The brick buildings were toppled, but they vowed to build bigger and better. The little sycamore trees may have been uprooted, but they vowed to plant bigger and better cedars in their place.

God, speaking through Isaiah, explained that as a result of their pride, arrogance, and failure to heed the harbinger, bigger and more potent attacks would follow. Because neither the Northern Kingdom of Israel nor the Southern Kingdom of Judah truly repented, the first was eventually swept away by Assyrian invaders and the people of the latter were carried off into the Babylonian Captivity for 70 years.

Rabbi Cahn said, "In the aftermath of the [9/11] Attack on America, the nation was stunned. Everyone was trying to make sense of what had happened—this unprecedented Attack on America. The very next day, September 12, Tom Daschle, the Senate Majority Leader presented America's response to the world."

Senator Daschle said, "America will emerge from this tragedy as we have emerged from all adversity—united and strong. Nothing...nothing can replace the losses of those who have suffered. I know there is only the smallest measure of inspiration that can be taken from this devastation. But there is a passage in the Bible from Isaiah that speaks to all of us at times like this." He then went on to read Isaiah 9:10, as discussed above.

Rabbi Cahn said that the senator had no idea what he was talking about. He thought that he was offering comforting words to a grief-stricken nation, but, in fact, he was actually embracing the spiritually defiant and arrogant words of the leaders of Israel, proclaiming their ancient and ominous vow to rebuild with their own strength without God. Senator Daschle didn't realize it, but he was actually inviting more chastisement on our nation as had the Jewish leaders upon theirs.

Be Not Afraid

Jesus King of All Nations said, "My children, dear children, do not despair. There is always hope. My holy and dear Mother has instructed you many times in many places how to bring down my mercy upon the world. This Woman of Hope still pleads for you all, her children." (*Journal* 319).

In an interview with me at Medjugorje, on October 3, 2009, visionary Mirjana Soldo told me, "Blessed Mary said, 'What I started in Fatima, I will finish in Medjugorje. My Heart will triumph.' If our Heavenly Mother's Heart will triumph, what is there to fear?"

In the same interview, Mirjana said, regarding the end of the world, "Well, the one who dies tomorrow, for that person the end of the world will happen tomorrow. That person will encounter God tomorrow. So, it is not important to talk about it at all. **It is important to talk about ourselves, to think of myself. What is my soul like? Is it ready to encounter God now, this very moment?"**

Mirjana told Medjugorje priest Padre Livio in an interview, "The Madonna always says not to talk about the secrets, but to pray. She says, 'Whoever relates to me like a mother, and to God like a father, has no fear.' The Madonna teaches us not to worry about the future and not to waste time speaking about the secrets, but to be ready to meet the Lord at any moment."

She concluded, "I do not understand why you should be afraid. I just want to say to all my brothers and sisters that you need not fear. The only ones that should be afraid are those who do not give the Lord first place in their hearts. If you have Our Lord and Our Lady in the first place of your heart, of what should you be afraid? That's why I do not want people to think that you should be afraid. There can be no fear if God and Our Lady are in first place in your heart". (Dan Lynch, *Medjugorje's Ten Secrets: How to Prepare*, John Paul Press, 2020, 105–106).

Jesus said, "Fear is useless, what is needed is trust." (Mark 5:36). Visionary Mirjana has no fear. She is a joyful woman with a devoted husband and two daughters. When asked why there would be secrets, Mirjana said, "I only know it is God's Will and all that is to happen. But I do want to say that there is no reason to fear, because the Blessed Mother does not want faith to come from fear.

That faith does not last. There is no reason to fear. She said that if we love God, we have peace of joy — no matter what transpires."

Because we are God's children, we should not fear anything. St. Paul reminds us that nothing can separate us from Christ's love. (See Romans 8:38-39). Therefore, we should look to the future with a trusting spirit.

Our response to the requests of the Blessed Virgin Mary and our openness to the Holy Spirit's guidance and protection will be our help. **All things work for good for those who love God** (see Romans 8:28), **so all prophesied secrets, warnings, and chastisements will ultimately lead us to an everlasting experience of love, peace, and joy.**

Mirjana told me, "A mother never scares her children and never gives them a reason to be afraid. She gives them hope and love. Blessed Mary is not coming to Medjugorje so that we are afraid of the future, but so that we have love and peace in the future with her. The most important thing is to respond to Mary's requests for conversion, faith, prayer, and fasting and not to be fearful of any secrets."

I asked Mirjana to comment on the statement made by her friend, Fr. Petar — **"Everything is closer and closer, God has to do something very quickly."**

She said, "We can comment in many ways, but maybe I'll be in front of God tomorrow. I won't have time to wait for secrets, **I must change myself today.** I always tell the pilgrims, 'Don't talk about secrets, don't think about secrets, think of yourself, **think of today, where are you today with God? Because you don't know what you will have tomorrow. '"**

Mirjana told Padre Livio, "Not only must we be ready in the future and face the future with great preparation, but we all have to be prepared at all times, because we do not know when God will call us. We must be ready at any moment and live every day in intimate union with God."

And, if God calls one of our innocent family members or friends through the evil acts of others, we must be forgiving.

The Protection Prayers and Promises of Jesus King of All Nations

God gives us means of protection through the Jesus King of All Nations Devotion. The Devotion contains prayers and promises for protection against chastisements. The promises to those who embrace the Devotion include protection from harm and mitigation of chastisements and all other forms of God's justice.

Jesus King of All Nations said, "Child, I have given a great remedy in my Devotion of Jesus King of All Nations. I ask my children to embrace this Devotion. To pray this Devotion. To invoke me as Jesus King of All Nations. My mercy and protection will cover those souls, families, and nations that invoke me thus. I will stretch forth to them my scepter of mercy that they may take firm hold and not let go of my Divine Will and law. I will cover them with my kingly mantle that my perfect justice may not reach them as it will reach those who have abandoned my law." (*Journal* 318).

To protect us from chastisements, Jesus King of All Nations revealed the *Novena in Honor of Jesus as True King,* to be prayed over each of nine consecutive days, consisting of an Our Father, a Hail Mary, and a Glory Be, followed by this prayer,

> O Lord our God, you alone are the most holy King and ruler of all nations. We pray to you, Lord, in the great expectation of receiving from you, O divine King, mercy, peace, justice, and all good things.
>
> Protect, O Lord our King, our families and the land of our birth. Guard us, we pray, most faithful one! Protect us from our enemies and from your just judgment.
>
> Forgive us, O sovereign King, our sins against you. Jesus, you are a King of mercy. We have deserved your just judgment. Have mercy on us, Lord, and forgive us. We trust in your great mercy.
>
> O most awe-inspiring King, we bow before you and pray; may your Reign, your Kingdom, be recognized on earth! Amen. (*Journal* 29).

Jesus said that whenever we pray these prayers, He promised that He would be less severe in His judgment of our nation, the

United States of America. He said, "My little one, this not only applies to your nation, but also all other nations. My child, each time you say these prayers, I will mitigate the severity of the chastisements upon your country. Whenever there is the threat of severe weather, recite these prayers, along with the prayers I will later teach you, and no harm will come to you or to those you pray for. This, my little one, applies not only to weather, but all forms of my justice." (*Journal* 41–42).

Jesus also revealed the *Chaplet of Unity* and promised to grant those who pray it "mercy, pardon, and protection in times of severe weather and plagues." (*Journal* 54). **He said "I extend this promise not only for yourselves, but also for individuals for whom you pray. No, my beloved, sin and the evils committed by mankind are too great, no longer will I spare my judgment to correct the conscience of mankind as a whole, but this Devotion and *Chaplet [of Unity]*, prayed with repentance, confidence, and love, will heal, save, and unite souls to my mercy who otherwise would be lost. Any harm or danger, spiritual or physical, whether it be to soul, mind, or body, will I protect these souls against."** (*Journal* 55–56).

Jesus also requested the reception of *Novenas of Holy Communions* in His honor and promised those who make these Novenas that they would receive an angel for each Communion of the Novena and also angelic protection. He promised that "the praying of this Novena for communities, nations, and the world, will also call down my angelic protection upon them. Because of the many evils in these end-times, it is my desire that you pray to me to send my angelic hosts to guide, guard, and protect you." (*Journal* 224).

For more information on the Prayers and Protections, please see Appendix B, The Prayers and Promises of the Devotion, on pg. 245.

Protection through the Medal of Jesus King of All Nations

Jesus also revealed His only Medal to the world and promised us protection if we wore it. He appeared in visions to His Secretary and requested that a Medal be struck in honor of Him as Jesus King of All Nations. He said, "My daughter, it is my most Holy Will and desire that a Medal be struck according to the likeness of me you have seen....This Image is a sign that I rule heaven and earth, and my Kingdom, my Reign, is near at hand....**I promise to offer the precious grace of final perseverance to every soul who will faithfully embrace this Devotion. My daughter, I am very anxious to have this done. I desire that this Medal be part of the overall Devotion to me as Jesus King of All Nations."** (*Journal* 75, 7, 76).

Jesus is on the front side of the Medal. He told His Secretary, "My child, you have been wondering whether or not the promise I once made to you for the praying of the prayers to me as Jesus King of All Nations (that of my protection from severe storms and all forms of my justice) is also to be granted to those who faithfully wear my Medal. My child, I tell you, that I do extend this promise of mine to the devotional wearing of my Medal....**I promise to the souls who will faithfully wear my Medal, the grace of protection from harm from all forms of my justice. This will especially be true of danger coming from natural disasters."** (*Journal* 188, 189).

St. Michael the Archangel is on the reverse side of the Medal. St. Michael the Archangel told her, "I again promise my protection to all who give glory and honor to God in this Devotion. Also, it is to serve as a reminder that the Most High has appointed me a particular guardian of His Church and of the Most Blessed Sacrament." (*Journal* 85).

Jesus also promised those who wear His Medal, "the grace of receiving in abundance the gifts of the Holy Spirit" (*Journal* 190); **"...a special degree of glory in heaven;...a special power over my Sacred Heart and the Immaculate Heart of my Mother;...the desire to please me in all things and thus come to perfection"** (*Journal* 191); **and "the grace to come to know the secrets of my love."** (*Journal* 193).

Jesus promised those priests who devotionally wear His Medal "the grace of greater devotion in ministering the sacraments." (*Journal* 181).

As with all sacramentals, there is no superstitious, magical benefit derived from wearing a medal. The efficacy of sacramentals depends upon the devotion, faith, and love of the person who uses them. Now is the time for everyone to wear the Medal to receive the promised protection of Jesus.

Protection through the Enthronement of the Image of Jesus King of All Nations

At a time when our Culture of Death is growing, with our government's seeking to limit our constitutional right to the free exercise of our religion, it is very appropriate to publicly come before the Image of Jesus King of All Nations to acknowledge Him as our True King and to pray for God's mercy for our families, parishes, dioceses, country, and all nations. He will surely graciously grant His mercy to those peoples and nations that acknowledge Him as True King! Jesus is our sure refuge in these most evil times. **Jesus said, "My daughter, great are the graces which will be granted through the proper veneration of this Image of mine."** (*Journal* 6).

Jesus said, **"This Image, my child, must become known. My daughter, those souls who venerate this Image of mine will be blessed with my peace."** (*Journal* 14–15).

Jesus invited us to pray before His Image and said, **"My children, come before my Image of Jesus King of All Nations and pray for your countries. Pray for your people. Pray for your families. Pray for my mercy which I will graciously grant to those peoples and nations that acknowledge me as True King! I AM your sure refuge in these most evil and truly dangerous times."** (*Journal* 24).

During the ceremony for the Enthronement of the Image of Jesus King of All Nations, a blessed Image of Jesus is displayed in a prominent place, formal prayers are prayed, and then each participant signs a Pledge and Certificate of the Enthronement to Jesus King of All Nations. **Jesus said, "Enthrone this my Image everywhere for I shall be powerfully present there and the power of my sovereign Kingship shall surely shield you from my just judgment."** (*Journal* 418).

Protection from Hurricanes Irma and Charley

The Jesus King of All Nations apostolate accepted Jesus' offer of the gift of His protection and was protected from Hurricanes Irma and Charley.

On the vigil of September 11, 2017, I was visiting my daughter in Kalispell, Montana, 50 miles from the raging, destructive, wildfires that darkened the setting sun with a haze of smoke. I was also concerned for our winter office in Venice, Florida, on its west coast, endangered by Hurricane Irma. The forecast was for the eye of the hurricane to proceed north and pass over Venice at 2 AM the next day, with a wind speed of 115 miles per hour and a projected storm water surge of 10 to 20 feet. If it did, it would have flooded and destroyed our manufactured-home office. During the previous year, I had consecrated the office to Jesus King of All Nations and enthroned His Image there, as He had requested of everyone.

At 9 PM, I finished my daily prayers to Jesus King of All Nations for protection against Irma and I was also wearing His Medal for which He had also promised protection. Just before I went to bed, I imaginatively stood on our property in Florida, lifted my right hand as a stop sign against Irma, and prayed, "In the name of Jesus King of All Nations, I command you winds to calm and you rain and storm surge to abate." Then I prayed the *Novena Prayer in Honor of Jesus as True King.*

The New York Times reported that as Irma approached Venice, its eye began to disintegrate. People told me that they saw the yellow breakups of the eye on their TV screens. The Los Angeles Times reported that at 9:23 PM, Irma's path unexpectedly changed in direction from due north to north-northeast. It eventually went around Venice and proceeded diagonally across the state to Jacksonville on the East coast.

Irma only grazed Venice with a wind speed of 70 miles per hour and a storm surge of only 1 foot, contrary to the predicted monster storm. Our home office did not suffer from a drop of water or even from any downed branches, twigs, or leaves, nor from a loss of electricity. Irma left it totally unscathed. I attribute this to the promised protection of Jesus King of All Nations, who is faithful and true.

The Psalm for the Mass the next day was Psalm 145, "I will extol you, O my God and King, and I will bless your name forever and ever. Let all your works give you thanks, O Lord, and let your faithful ones bless you. Let them discourse of the glory of your Kingdom and speak of your might."

So, following the instructions of Psalm 145, I wrote an article and extolled Jesus King of All Nations. I attributed His protection of our home office from Irma to His Medal, His prayers, His promises, and the enthronement of His Image. In my article, I blessed His name forever and discoursed of the glory of His Kingdom and His might.

Some might say that was arrogant of me, because many other people were also praying. I'm sure that they were and they might have their own protection stories to tell. However, this is my particular story of praying particular prayers for which Jesus gave particular promises for protection from natural disasters. Some prayers are definitely more efficacious than others, particularly when they are requested or revealed by Jesus and Mary, such as the Rosary, the Divine Mercy prayers, and the Protection Prayers of Jesus King of All Nations. **I give all the glory for this protection to Him and take none of it for myself and I encourage others to pray His prayers and ask for His promised protection.**

Two days later, I received an email that confirmed my article. Susan Kruger wrote,

> *Dan, while out of town we were able to monitor what was going on near our home by watching a West Palm Beach weather live stream (WPTV) on a laptop. I believe it was around 10 PM Sunday night, when **we observed exactly what you described. The chief meteorologist and a second meteorologist were discussing Irma's location, which was quite obvious on their truly amazing HD radar. Irma wasn't tracking as expected, but had jogged to the East.***
>
> *The storm's projected track from the officials in Miami had not changed, yet we could see the eye of the storm move East. The two meteorologists discussed it and were more than perplexed.*
>
> *Now that you've explained what was happening, **I'm delighted to say that I witnessed the miracle that our precious Jesus King of All Nations performed for you!***

I am confident that He protected our office from Hurricane Irma, because He had also protected it from Hurricane Charley!

On August 13, 2004, Hurricane Charley had headed for our Florida office while my staff and I were at our center in St. Albans, Vermont. It was 3 PM, the hour of mercy, and we had adjourned to our chapel and gotten on our knees, begging Jesus

King of All Nations for His protection and to spare the Florida office.

As we prayed for His mercy during the 3 o'clock hour, Hurricane Charley suddenly and unexpectedly took a sharp turn to the right, away from our office and headed directly for its landfall in Punta Gorda. This sharp turn, seemingly in response to our prayers, occurred at 3:48 PM, spared our office, and baffled scientists.

Charley had been traveling toward our office at just over 160 miles per hour when it suddenly changed direction only minutes before its predicted landfall near the office. Mark Saunders, a tropical storm expert, said, "There was a sudden intensification and a veering to the right of track, and we're all trying to work out why." I believe that Jesus King of All Nations fulfilled His promised protection in answer to our prayers.

Jesus King of All Nations promises us His protection and to mitigate the severity of the chastisements upon our country. He said, "Each time you say these prayers, I will mitigate the severity of the chastisements upon your country. Whenever there is the threat of severe weather, recite these prayers along with the prayers I will later teach you, and no harm will come to you or to those you pray for." (*Journal* 41–42). **He also promises "mercy, pardon, and protection in times of severe weather and plagues."** (*Journal* 54).

Jesus promises us His protection, but He also pleads with each one of us to change our hearts and embrace the gift of His Jesus King of All Nations Devotion. However, while Jesus gives us the grace to change our hearts, He respects our free will and leaves the choice to us to either accept or reject both His admonition and the gift of His Devotion. **We should all accept this gift from Jesus and embrace His Devotion to prevent His prophesied chastisements from nature, from man, and from heaven itself.**

11. The State of the World

"The spiritual crisis involves the *entire world*....People in the West are guilty of rejecting God....The spiritual collapse thus has a very Western character....Because [Western man] refuses to acknowledge himself as an heir [of spiritual and cultural patrimony], man is condemned to the hell of liberal globalization in which individual interests confront one another without any law to govern them besides profit at any price....Transhumanism is the ultimate avatar of this movement. Because it is a gift from God, human nature itself becomes unbearable for Western man. This revolt is spiritual at root." (Cardinal Robert Sarah, *Catholic Herald*, April 5, 2019).

Cardinal Sarah also addressed a conference in Paris, on May 25, 2019, regarding the state of the world,

> I am convinced that this civilization is living through its mortal hour. As once during the decline and fall of Rome, so today the elites care for nothing but increasing the luxury of their daily lives, and the people have been anaesthetized by even more vulgar entertainments.
>
> As a bishop, it is my duty to warn the West: behold the flames of barbarism threaten you! And who are these barbarians? The barbarians are those who hate human nature. The barbarians are those who trample the sacred under foot. The barbarians are those who despise and manipulate life and strive for "human enhancement"....
>
> The West is blinded by its lust for wealth! The lure of money that liberalism instills in hearts lulls the peoples to sleep! Meanwhile, the silent tragedy of abortion and euthanasia continues. Meanwhile, pornography and gender ideology mutilate and destroy children and adolescents. We have become so used to barbarity, it no longer even surprises us!...
>
> Underneath the surface of its fantastic scientific and technological accomplishments and the appearance of

prosperity, Western civilization is in a profound state of decadence and ruin! Like Notre-Dame Cathedral [that had recently burned], it is crumbling. It has lost its reason for being: to show forth and lead others to God.

In the third millennium, we are experiencing cataclysmic events. The state of the world is worse than it was at the time of the Great Flood. There are great evils that the world has never experienced to this extent before, such as the dissolution of the family through no-fault divorce, same-sex sexual acts, same-sex false marriage, contraception, abortion, embryonic experimentation, so-called "physician-assisted suicide," euthanasia, the sex trade, the drug trade, addictions, unjust wars, genocides, terrorism, ecological destruction, and business and political corruption.

Never has God been less believed, adored, or obeyed. Never has God been more ignored, blasphemed, and disobeyed. Many people live as if God does not exist. Many people are their own god, believing and doing whatever they want. Many people are self-absorbed materialists and many seek only money, glory, and power. Few people seek to know, love, and serve God and to be eternally happy with Him in heaven. The world is becoming more worldly and less godly.

In 1984, St. John Paul II wrote in *Reconciliation and Penance*, "The restoration of a proper sense of sin is the first way of facing the grave spiritual crisis looming over man today. But the sense of sin can only be restored through a clear reminder of the unchangeable principles of reason and faith which the moral teaching of the Church has always upheld."

On January 8, 2009, **Pope Benedict XVI** addressed representatives of the 177 countries which have diplomatic relations with the Vatican. This was his *"State of the World Address"*. He said, "Today, more than in the past, our future is at stake, as well as the fate of our planet and its inhabitants, especially the younger generation which is inheriting a severely compromised economic system and social fabric."

In a later interview with journalist Peter Seewald, the Pope said, "There are, of course, signs that frighten us, that worry us. But there are also other signs with which we can connect and which give us hope. We have indeed spoken at length already about the scenario of terror and danger...."

The Pope then referred to the drug trade and sex tourism and continued,

> You see, man strives for eternal joy; he would like pleasure in the extreme, would like what is eternal. But when there is no God, it is not granted to him and it cannot be. Then he himself must now create something that is fictitious, a false eternity.

> This is a sign of the times, that should be an urgent challenge to us, especially as Christians. We have to show and also live this accordingly that the eternity man needs can come only from God. That God is the first thing necessary in order to be able to withstand the afflictions of this time. That we must mobilize, so to speak, all the powers of the soul and of the good so that a genuine coin can stand up against the false coin — and in this way the cycle of evil can be broken and stopped.

> The important thing...is that a need for healing exists, that man can understand again somehow what redemption means. Man recognizes that if God is not there, existence becomes sick and man cannot survive like that. That he needs an answer that he himself cannot give. (Peter Seewald, *Light of the World: The Pope, The Church and the Signs Of The Times*, (Ignatius Press, Ft. Collins, CO 80522, 2010)).

In his traditional Christmas greeting to the Roman Curia, on December 20, 2010, **Pope Benedict XVI noted the parallels that exist between the state of our world and the decline of the Roman Empire. He said,**

"**There was no power in sight that could put a stop to this decline. All the more insistent, then, was the invocation of the power of God:** the plea that He might come and protect His people from all these threats. The disintegration of the key principles of law and of the fundamental moral attitudes underpinning them burst open the dams which until that time had protected peaceful coexistence among peoples."

We see in our world today what the Pope described in the decline of Rome. He said, "The sun was setting over an entire

world. Frequent natural disasters further increased this sense of insecurity."

Comparing our world to Rome, the Pope said, "For all its new hopes and possibilities, our world is at the same time troubled by the sense that moral consensus is collapsing, consensus without which juridical and political structures cannot function. Consequently, the forces mobilized for the defense of such structures seem doomed to failure.

"Alexis de Tocqueville, in his day," the Pope continued, "observed that democracy in America had become possible and had worked because there existed a fundamental moral consensus which, transcending individual denominations, united everyone. Only if there is a consensus on the essentials can constitutions and law function. This fundamental consensus derived from the Christian heritage is at risk wherever its place, the place of moral reasoning, is taken by purely instrumental rationality of which I spoke earlier.

"In reality, this makes reason blind to what is essential. To resist this eclipse of reason and to preserve its capacity for seeing the essential, for seeing God and man, for seeing what is good and what is true, is the common interest that must unite all people of good will. The very future of the world is at stake."

Without God, society and the world have no final goal and no reason to distinguish good from evil. In 2019, Pope Emeritus Benedict XVI wrote, "When God dies in a society, it becomes free, we were assured. In reality, the death of God in a society also means the end of freedom...because the compass disappears that points us in the right direction by teaching us to distinguish good from evil. Western society is a society in which God is absent in the public sphere and has nothing left to offer it. And that is why it is a society in which the measure of humanity is increasingly lost." (Pope Emeritus Benedict XVI, *Notes on the Abuse Scandal*, April 10, 2019).

Jesus King of All Nations said, "My words are being fulfilled as the world descends yet further into an abyss of sin and the suffering which results from it. Greater are the numbers of those who follow the enemy of mankind and in an unabashed manner.

"Never before has the corruption of sin been so great as it is in these days. Evil spreads unabated as a thick pestilence destroying those in its path. More and more you can clearly see the need for the veneration of my sacred Image and the practice of my Devotion." (*Journal* 539–540).

In 1976, when St. John Paul II was still **Cardinal Karol Wojtyla**, he gave a retreat to the Roman Curia. He **said that we may be** "**experiencing the highest level of tension between the Word and the anti-Word in the whole of human history....We may now be wondering if this is the last lap along that way of denial which started out from around the Tree of the Knowledge of Good and Evil.** To us, who know the whole Bible from Genesis to Revelation, no stretch of that route can come as a surprise. We accept with trepidation, but also with hope, the inspired words of the Apostle Paul, 'Let no man deceive you in any way, because first it is necessary for the rebellion to come, and for the man of sin, the son of perdition, to reveal himself.'" (2 Thessalonians 2–3).

The "way of denial" that began with the Fall of Adam and Eve by the eating of the forbidden fruit of the Tree of the Knowledge of Good and Evil may now have arrived, as Carinal Wojtyla said, at its "last lap."

The *Wall Street Journal* reported that **Cardinal Wojtyla also said, in 1976,**

> We are now standing in the face of the greatest historical confrontation humanity has gone through. I do not think that wide circles of the American society or wide circles of the Christian community realize this fully. We are now facing the final confrontation between the Church and the anti-Church, of the Gospel versus the anti-Gospel. This confrontation lies within the plans of divine Providence; it is a trial which the whole Church, and the Polish Church in particular, must take up.

> It is a trial of not only our nation and the Church, but, in a sense, a test of 2,000 years of culture and Christian civilization with all of its consequences for human dignity, individual rights, human rights, and the rights of nations.

Author George Weigel refers to this speech in his biography of St. John Paul II, *Witness to Hope*. He wrote, "These remarks are cited on the editorial page of the *Wall Street Journal*, November 9, 1978, and attributed to Wojtyla's 'last speech in the U.S. in September 1976, as quoted in the *New York City News* (an interim strike newspaper).'"

Jesus King of All Nations said, "The outrages offered by this most sinful generation to the all-holy majesty of the one true God are greater than ever before in the history of mankind; yes, far worse than even in the time of Noah and the Flood." (*Journal* 451).

Five months after the U.S. Supreme Court overturned the landmark 1973 *Roe v. Wade* ruling, which had granted women a right to an abortion, on Election Day 2022, voters across the country clearly signaled their choice.

Vermont, California, and Michigan voters approved ballot measures enshrining abortion rights into their state constitutions!

On November 15, 1990, Our Lady warned Fr. Gobbi, of the Marian Movement of Priests, while he was in the United States, **"Abortions — these killings of innocent children, that cry for vengeance before the face of God — have spread and are performed in every part of your homeland.** The moment of divine justice and of great mercy has now arrived! **You will know the hour of weakness and poverty, the hour of suffering and defeat, the purifying hour of the Great Chastisement."** (*To the Priests* 437).

Since the 1973 *Roe v. Wade* decision, more than 60 million unborn children have been killed by abortion in the United States. According to the World Health Organization, there are over 3,000 abortions per day in the United States and every year in the world there are an estimated 40-50 million abortions. This corresponds to approximately 125,000 abortions per day.

The Church is also in need of purification in light of its present state.

12. The State of the Church

"It seems certain to me that the Church is facing very hard times. The real crisis has scarcely begun. We will have to count on terrific upheavals. But I am equally certain about what will remain at the end: not the Church of the political cult...but the Church of faith. It may well no longer be the dominant social power to the extent that it was until recently; but it will enjoy a fresh blossoming and be seen as man's home where he will find life and hope beyond death." (Cardinal Joseph Ratzinger, *Faith and the Future*, Ignatius Press, 2009).

The Church is in a state of crisis arising from apostasy with the loss of faith and the loss of the sense of sin. This came from widespread sexual immorality in the laity with contraception, fornication, and adultery that led to abortion, infanticide, same-sex false marriage, and false transgenderism

Sexual immorality in the clergy led to widespread sexual abuse of minors, homosexual acts amongst the clergy, and the enabling of the abusers and the active homosexuals.

Those sins led to corruption in the administration of the Church and its finances and in heterodox (unorthodox teaching) statements of faith and morals within the hierarchy. They arose from a false sense of mercy at the expense of the salvation of souls and the pursuit of the Great Commission of Jesus to make disciples of all nations "teaching them to observe all that I have commanded you." (See Matthew chapter 28). And those sins have led to a decentralized Church, leaving national bishops' bureaucracies free to pursue heterodoxy in faith and morals.

On January 13, 2021, Peter Seewald, an author friend of Pope Emeritus Benedict XVI, formerly Fr. Joseph Ratzinger, corresponded with Carl E. Olson, editor of the magazine, *Catholic World Report*. Mr. Seewald referred to a critical essay that Fr.

Ratzinger had written in 1958, "The New Pagans and the Church." Concerning the Church, Mr. Seewald wrote,

> **Fr. Joseph Ratzinger had learned from the Nazi era that the institution alone is of no use if there are not also the people who support it. The task was not to connect with the world, but to revitalize the Faith from within. In his essay, the then 31-year-old noted, "The appearance of the Church of modern times is essentially determined by the fact that in a completely new way she has become and is still becoming more and more the Church of pagans…, of pagans who still call themselves Christians, but who in truth have become pagans."**

Mr. Seewald continued,

> If you read his essay today, it shows prophetic features. In it, Ratzinger stated that in the long run the Church would not be spared "having to break down piece by piece the appearance of her congruence with the world and to become again what she is: a community of believers."

> In his vision, **he spoke of a Church that would once again become small and mystical; that would have to find her way back to her language, her worldview, and the depth of her mysteries as a "community of conviction." Only then could she unfold her full sacramental power: "Only when she begins to present herself again as what she is, will she be able to reach again the ear of the new pagans with her message, who up to now have been under the illusion that they were not pagans at all."**…

> With that he followed the admonition of the Apostle Paul that the Christian communities must not adapt themselves too much to the world, otherwise they would no longer be the "salt of the earth" of which Jesus had spoken. (Catholic World Report, *The Life, Faith, And Struggle of Joseph Ratzinger: An Interview with Peter Seewald*, January 13, 2021).

In 1969, **Fr. Ratzinger gave a series of radio speeches,** later published in the book *Faith and the Future*. (Ignatius Press, 2009). He spoke about the then present state of the Church and its future. He said that he was convinced that the Church was going through an era similar to the Enlightenment and the French Revolution. He explained, "We are at a huge turning point in the evolution of mankind. This moment makes the move from medieval to modern times seem insignificant."

He compared the then present state of the Church to that at the time of Pope Pius VI, who was abducted by troops of the French Republic and died in prison in 1799. The Church was fighting against a force which intended to annihilate it definitively, confiscate its property, and dissolve religious orders. Today's Church could be faced with a similar situation if priests are merely reduced to social workers and the work of the Church becomes mostly political.

He said, "The process [of renewal] will be long and wearisome as was the road from the false progressivism on the eve of the French Revolution—when a bishop might be thought smart if he made fun of dogmas and even insinuated that the existence of God was by no means certain—to the renewal of the nineteenth century."

He prophesied that the future Church "will become small and will have to start pretty much all over again. It will no longer have use of the structures it built in its years of prosperity. The reduction in the number of faithful will lead to it losing an important part of its social privileges. It will be a more spiritual Church and will not claim a political mandate flirting with the Right one minute and the Left the next. It will be poor and will become the Church of the destitute."

He continued, "The big talk of those who prophesy a Church without God and without faith is all empty chatter. We have no need of a Church that celebrates the cult of action in political prayers. It is utterly superfluous. Therefore, it will destroy itself. What will remain is the Church of Jesus Christ, the Church that believes in the God who has become man and promises us life beyond death."

He prophesied that "when all the suffering is past, a great power will emerge from a more spiritual and simple Church" and that this renewed Church will be a sign of hope for those who have not yet come to know the love of God. Then, and only then, Cardinal Ratzinger concluded, will they see "that small flock of faithful as something completely new: they will see it as a source of hope for themselves, the answer they had always secretly been searching for."

Our Lady told Fr. Gobbi, *"The great trial has arrived for your Church.* Those errors which have brought people to the loss of the truth faith have continued to spread. Many pastors have been neither attentive nor vigilant and have allowed many rapacious wolves, clothed as lambs, to insinuate themselves into the flock in order to bring disorder and destruction." (*To the Priests* 437).

On March 25, 2005, **Cardinal Joseph Ratzinger**, later Pope Benedict XVI, **recited the following words** at the 9th Station of the Way of the Cross on Good Friday at the Colosseum, that was seen by the dying Pope John Paul II,

> Should we not also think of how much Christ suffers in His own Church? How often is the holy Sacrament of His presence abused, how often must He enter empty and evil hearts! How often do we celebrate only ourselves, without even realizing that He is there! How often is His Word twisted and misused!

> What little faith is present behind so many theories, so many empty words! How much filth there is in the Church, and even among those who, in the priesthood, ought to belong entirely to Him! How much pride, how much self-complacency! What little respect we pay to the Sacrament of Penance, where He waits for us, ready to raise us up whenever we fall!

> All this is present in His Passion. His betrayal by His disciples, their unworthy reception of His body and blood, is certainly the greatest suffering endured by the Redeemer; it pierces His Heart. We can only call to Him from the depths of our hearts, *Kyrie eleison* (Lord, have mercy.)

The state of the Church is heterodox, meaning it is moving away from orthodoxy in some respects. Jesus excoriated the scribes and Pharisees as frauds and hypocrites and for weighing people down with laws that they themselves did not follow. He told the people to do everything that they were told to do by their leaders, but not to follow their bad example.

Today's frauds and hypocrites in the Church are taking away some laws that they think are weighing the people down in an attempt to lighten a burden that Jesus said is already light with a yoke that is easy. Ironically, they call those who criticize them modern-day scribes and Pharisees.

Because of Pope Francis' ambiguous language and actions, many cardinals, bishops, and priests are now teaching that those men and women who are divorced and civilly remarried without an annulment and who are sexually active without repentance, a firm purpose of amendment, and Confession, may discern in their consciences that they may receive the Eucharist. They even go so far as to say that they might have a *duty* to receive the Eucharist for the sake of preserving their illicit marriages and for the sake of their children.

Some bishops are now blessing the false marriages of same-sex people who are sexually active with each other and are welcoming them to receive the Eucharist. These sacrilegious communions will only further weaken the Church, according to the teaching of St. Paul. (See 1 Corinthians 11:30).

A conference was held in Rome, on April 7, 2018, called *Catholic Church: Where Are You Going? Only a Blind Man Can Deny That There Is Great Confusion in the Church*. Cardinals, bishops, priests, and lay faithful issued a Declaration in which they testified to the Church's unchanging teaching on marriage, the sacraments, and absolute moral commandments. **A contingent from the audience shouted out, "People of God, stand up! We are the ones who have to act!"**

Cardinal Raymond Burke called the Vatican's response to the "scandalized reactions" from across the globe "highly inadequate," because it failed to reassert the Church's teaching on the immortality of the soul and the existence of hell. He said it also failed to state that Pope Francis repudiates the "erroneous and even heretical ideas attributed to him."

The *Catholic Church: Where Are You Going?* conference issued a Final Declaration that stated, "We are convinced that persons who are divorced and civilly remarried, and who are unwilling to live in continence, are living in a situation that is objectively contrary to the law of God and therefore cannot receive Eucharistic Communion."

At the conference, Cardinal Walter Brandmüller, former president of the Pontifical Committee for Historical Sciences, said that the faithful not only have the "right of free speech" in the Church, based on "the sense of faith and love," but also that they—according to their knowledge, responsibility, and prominent positions—"sometimes even have the duty to communicate [their opinion] to their spiritual shepherds when it is about the well-being of the Church." He therefore concluded, "It would be time for the Magisterium to pay appropriate attention to this witness of faith."

The People of God are encouraged by the Second Vatican Council (see Vatican II, *Lumen Gentium (Dogmatic Constitution on the Church)*, 33) **to be a living witness and instrument of the mission of the Church**, in virtue of the very gifts bestowed upon them and in accordance with the authentic Sacred Tradition of the Church. **They should testify and confess to the truths of the Church as summarized in the Final Declaration of the *Catholic Church: Where Are You Going?* Conference held in Rome, on April 7, 2018:**

1. A ratified and consummated marriage between two baptized persons can be dissolved only by death.

2. Therefore, Christians united by a valid marriage who join themselves to another person while their spouse is still alive commit the grave sin of adultery.

3. We are convinced that there exist absolute moral commandments which oblige always and without exception.

4. We are also convinced that no subjective judgment of conscience can make an intrinsically evil act good and licit.

5. We are convinced that judgment about the possibility of administering sacramental absolution is not based on the imputability of the sin committed, but on the penitent's intention to abandon a way of life that is contrary to the divine commandments.

6. We are convinced that persons who are divorced and civilly remarried, and who are unwilling to live in continence, are living in a situation that is objectively contrary to the law of God and therefore cannot receive Eucharistic Communion.

Many in the Church have failed to testify and confess, in accordance with the authentic Sacred Tradition of the Church, to the truths of the Church listed in this Final Declaration.

Almost five years before the Final Declaration, on June 6, 2013, Jesus King of All Nations had said that by the refusal of His ministers "to even listen to my Word, thus rejecting my Devotion of Jesus King of All Nations, you have helped to bring these things upon the world."

He explained, "Let it be known that my all-holy Word shall be accomplished. Let my Devotion be accepted by my holy Church and rebuff me no longer. Lift up your heads and see what is taking place around you! In society, in nature, and those placed over human authority! Violence, corruption, death, and destruction! The blood of the innocent and suffering of the marginalized cry out to heaven for justice!

"Know my ministers that by your refusal to even listen to my Word, thus rejecting my Devotion of Jesus King of All Nations, you have helped to bring these things upon the world as my Devotion was given as a healing remedy for the ills that afflict the world by acknowledging my sovereign rights over mankind and once more bringing the sacred truth to the hearts and minds of the faithful that they in turn might be the shining example, the sign of hope for the world which is sunk to a new level of corruption." (*Journal* 483, 484, 486).

Jesus concluded, "You see the great seriousness of these times. The very downfall of society and of the moral order; the corruption within my very Church are themselves great signs of the authenticity of my Devotion and my messages." (*Journal* 768).

Idols at the Amazon Synod

At the Amazon Synod in Rome in 2019, people placed statues of the Amazonian Pachamama (Mother Earth) in the Vatican Gardens. Some bowed down to the ground and prostrated themselves before them. Cardinal Gerhard Müller, formerly the head of the Congregation for the Doctrine of the Faith, called the statues "idols."

The idols showed a naked woman in late term pregnancy. Idolaters turn to her for fertility, good ecology, and good fortune instead of turning to the one true God and trusting in His goodness and providence. Pachamama is an object of veneration, a goddess to which some Bolivians sacrifice llamas, especially their fetuses. It is an earth deity worshiped by some Peruvians, rooted in pagan Incan beliefs and practices.

Bishop José Luis Azcona, of Marajó in the Amazon region, confirmed that Pachamama is a pagan goddess and denounced the rituals in the Vatican. In his homily, on October 16, 2019, in Brazil, he said, "In those rituals, there is the Devil, there is magic." The invocation of the statues in front of which even some religious have bowed in the Vatican (and I will not mention the religious order to which they belong) is the invocation of the mythical power of Mother Earth, to which they are asking blessings upon humanity or offering gestures of gratitude. **These are scandalous demonic sacrileges, especially for the little ones who can't discern."**

Moreover, some of the idols were brought into Santa Maria in Traspontina, a Catholic church, and displayed there. God's first commandment is, "I am the Lord your God, you shall have no false gods before me." (Exodus 20:3). "You shall not carve idols for yourselves in the shape of anything in the sky above or on the earth below or in the waters beneath the earth; you shall not bow down before them or worship them." (Exodus 20:4–5).

Idolatry is the greatest offense against Jesus King of All Nations. Idolatry denies His sovereign and divine Kingship and the acknowledgment of His supreme authority over all creation. It denies the absolute and supreme authority granted to Him by His Father. This authority must be recognized by all and re-acclaimed by His Church. (See *Journal* 706, 708).

The *Catholic Encyclopedia* teaches that, "Considered in itself, idolatry is the greatest of mortal sins. For it is, by definition, an inroad on God's sovereignty over the world, an attempt on His divine majesty, a rebellious setting up of a creature on the throne that belongs to Him alone."

When the prophet Ezekiel was brought in spirit by God into the Temple, he saw the idols of the house of Israel. Then he saw, "about twenty-five men, with their backs to the Temple of the Lord, and their faces toward the east, worshiping the sun toward the east."

Then God said to Ezekiel, "Have you seen this, O son of man? Is it too slight a thing for the house of Judah to commit the abominations which they commit here, that they should fill the land with violence, and provoke me further to anger? Lo, they put the branch to their nose. Therefore, I will deal in wrath; my eye will not spare, nor will I have pity; and though they cry in my ears with a loud voice, I will not hear them." (Ezekiel 8:16–18).

Likewise, at the church of Santa Maria during the Amazon Synod, some of the pews were turned around from the altar to face the Pachamama idol. About twenty-five people sat upon the pews with their backs to the altar and the Blessed Sacrament and with their faces toward the idol. They sat "with their backs to the Lord's Temple" as did the "about twenty-five men" that Ezekiel had seen. Will God now deal "in wrath" with us, as He had told the prophet Ezekiel?

St. Athanasius, writing in his *History of the Arians*, even takes the introduction of idols into churches in the fourth-century Egyptian persecution to be the worst possible wickedness, "When was ever such iniquity heard of? When was such an evil deed ever perpetrated, even in times of persecution? **They were heathens who persecuted formerly; but they did not bring their idols into the churches....This is a new piece of iniquity. It is not simply persecution, but more than persecution, it is a prelude and preparation for the coming of Antichrist."**

We should turn to the one true God, face Him in reparation, and implore Him to end these sacrileges. Let us join Bishop Athanasius Schneider, who encouraged all Catholics to offer prayers and reparation for "the abomination of the veneration of wooden idols perpetrated in Rome during the Amazon Synod."

In a November 2019 interview, regarding the idols at the Amazon Synod, **Archbishop Carlo Maria Viganò, former Apostolic Nuncio to the United States, said,**

> The abomination of idolatrous rites has entered the sanctuary of God and has given rise to a new form of apostasy, whose seeds — which have been active for a long time — are growing with renewed vigor and effectiveness. The process of the internal mutation of the faith, which has been taking place in the Catholic Church for several decades, has seen with this Synod a dramatic acceleration

toward the foundation of a new creed, summed up in a new kind of worship [*cultus*]. **In the name of inculturation, pagan elements are infesting divine worship in order to transform it into an idolatrous cult....**

Idolatry seals apostasy. It is the fruit of the denial of the true faith. It is born of mistrust in God and degenerates into protest and rebellion....

We cannot remain indifferent to the idolatrous acts that we have witnessed and left us dumbfounded. **These assaults against the holiness of our Mother Church demand from us a just and generous reparation. It is urgent that we rediscover the meaning of prayer, reparation, and penance, of fasting, of the "little sacrifices, of the little flowers," and, above all, of silent and prolonged adoration before the Blessed Sacrament....**

The Amazonian paradigm is therefore not the end of the transformation process at which the "pastoral-revolution" promoted by the current papal magisterium aims. It serves as a catwalk to ferry what remains of the Catholic edifice toward an indistinct Universal Religion....

Jesus prophesied, "When you see the desecrating sacrilege...there will be a great tribulation, such as has not been from the beginning of the world until now, no, and never will be." (Matthew 24:15, 21).

In 2019, Rome journalist Robert Moynihan asked **Archbishop Carlo Maria Vigano** in an interview, "But what is your message really, that God is about to chastise the Church, as Nineveh was threatened with destruction, or do you believe there is still a chance to renew the Church, through prayer and a renewal of priestly and lay spirituality?"

The Archbishop **replied,** "The two possibilities you offer are not mutually exclusive. **There may be both a chastisement, which will shake and diminish the Church, and also a reform and renewal of the Church, making her more resplendent in holiness. Both are possible."**

On May 11, 2010, on his way back to Rome from his visit in Fatima, **Pope Benedict XVI said** about the Fatima message that "there is also the fact that attacks on the Pope and the Church come not only from without, but the sufferings of the Church come precisely from within the Church, from the sin existing within the Church."

He continued, "This too is something that we have always known, but today we are seeing it in a really terrifying way: **that the greatest persecution of the Church comes not from her enemies without, but arises from sin within the Church, and that the Church thus has a deep need to relearn penance, to accept purification, to learn forgiveness on the one hand, but also the need for justice."**

Cardinal Gerhard Müller, former head of the Vatican's Congregation for the Doctrine of the Faith, appeared on EWTN's *The World Over* on October 6, 2022. He spoke about the supporters of the Synodal Way for the Church.

Cardinal Müller warned us that "the Catholic Church is facing a hostile takeover by people who think that doctrine is like the program of a political party that can be changed by votes."

He said, "Revelation is entrusted to the Church for faithful preservation, and not as the Synodal Way meant at the beginning, that this virtually randomly assembled body somehow has the right and authority to override the Church's sacramental constitution and reinterpret Revelation according to its meaning.

"What is being pursued here is nothing other than division," Cardinal Müller lamented. "It is a so-called reform with a crowbar.

"Nobody can make an absolute shift and substitute the revealed doctrine of the Church, but they have this strange idea of doctrine as only a theory of some theologians.

"The doctrine of the apostles is a reflection and manifestation of the Revelation of the Word of God. We have to listen to the Word of God in the authority of the Holy Bible, of Apostolic Tradition, and of the Magisterium. And, as the Council said before: that it is not possible to substitute Revelation, given once and forever in Jesus Christ, by another revelation."

The Cardinal reflected on Irme Stetter-Karp, President of the Central Committee of German Catholics, who had emphasized that it should be "ensured that the medical intervention of an abortion is made possible across the board."

Cardinal Müller said, "Whoever wants to guarantee these crimes, area-wide for the entire population, cannot pose as a reformer of the Church.

"After all, the Church is not the object of our reform. The Church is founded by Christ, cannot be reformed, is unsurpassable; only we can go the way and must go the way of repentance and renewal. We must reform and renew ourselves in Jesus Christ and thus give the answer to the challenges of today....Synods of Bishops have no authority and are in no way a Magisterial authority."

Jesus King of All Nations revealed in His intentions for the praying of His *Chaplet of Unity,* "Pray for my holy Church upon earth, the Church Militant, and, in particular, for my Vicar, the Pope, all cardinals, bishops, and priests, that together with the faithful they may be one in me as I AM One with the Father and the Holy Spirit. My Spouse, the Church, is wounded by the many sins of disunity arising from pride, selfish desires, and a great lack of charity. The enemy seeks anew to destroy my Spotless Bride. He shall not prevail!"

In 2015, Pope Emeritus Benedict XVI wrote a private letter to Vladimir Palko, a former Catholic statesman. In the letter he urged prayer against "the power of the Antichrist expanding."

In 2023, after the death of Pope Emeritus Benedict XVI, Mr. Palco released a portion of that letter which said,

> "We see how the power of the Antichrist is expanding, and we can only pray that the Lord will give us strong shepherds who will defend His Church in this hour of need from the power of evil." (Rod Dreher Blog, *American Conservative,* Benedict XVI: It is The Time of Antichrist, January 10, 2023).

Because of the terrible evils in the State and the Church, Jesus King of All Nations has prophesied a Great Chastisement for humanity.

13. The Coming Great Chastisement

Introduction

On August 3, 1973, Our Lady gave a message to Sr. Agnes in Akita, Japan. She prophesied that the Heavenly Father was preparing a Great Chastisement on all mankind. She said,

> My daughter, my novice, do you love the Lord? If you love the Lord, listen to what I have to say to you.
>
> It is very important...you will convey it to your superior.
>
> Many men in this world afflict the Lord. I desire souls to console Him to soften the anger of the Heavenly Father. I wish, with my Son, for souls who will repair by their suffering and their poverty for the sinners and ingrates.
>
> In order that the world might know His anger, **the Heavenly Father is preparing to inflict a Great Chastisement on all mankind. With my Son I have intervened so many times to appease the wrath of the Father. I have prevented the coming of calamities by offering Him the sufferings of the Son on the Cross, His Precious Blood, and beloved souls who console Him forming a cohort of victim souls. Prayer, penance, and courageous sacrifices can soften the Father's anger.** I desire this also from your community...that it love poverty, that it sanctify itself, and pray in reparation for the ingratitude and outrages of so many men.

The late Fr. Albert J. Hebert said, "This [Devotion to Jesus King of All Nations] is one of the last great efforts of Our Lord to pour out His mercy before His justice descends upon mankind in the Great Chastisement."

On June 25, 2009, **Jesus King of All Nations said,**

> A great catastrophe is about to descend on the world. Lessen this punishment with the spiritual weapons of frequent reception of the holy sacraments; loving,

reverent attendance at the holy Sacrifice of the Mass; and constant praying of the holy Rosary. When my Mother came to Fatima, she requested the praying of the Rosary daily. I now say constant! Let this prayer encompass your very hearts, minds, and souls, offering it to me through my dear Mother for the salvation of souls.

Yes, the times are so grave that I desire this great prayer of the holy Rosary to rise from the faithful as a sacrifice of propitiation. **Only through the Immaculate Heart of Mary will I have mercy on this sinful world. I have entrusted it to her. Therefore, you must come to me through her. Hurry my children. Run to Mary!** (*Journal* 341–342).

Three years later, on May 20, 2012, **Jesus King of All Nations said, "Let it be known that as I AM the all-merciful God, and that though my perfect, holy justice must be fulfilled, that I do not wish my people to be inordinately weighed down with consternation and fear at the coming chastisement."** (*Journal* 410).

Nevertheless, less than a month later, He said, "Let it be known and made clear, that soon, very soon, there shall come upon mankind the Great Chastisement which has been prophesied for many years yet held back by the most powerful intercession of my Immaculate Mother and the prayers and sacrifices of my faithful ones." (*Journal* 420).

Almost two years after that, on October 8, 2013, Jesus King of All Nations said,

Listen, O my people! Listen to the loving cry and lament of your God! How long I have appealed to you through my most holy Mother and my prophets to turn from your sinful ways and be fully converted to your God!

The situation in the world now reaches a critical point. Souls are steeped in the corruption of sin which cries to heaven for my cleansing action. My justice is coming, my people, to correct you and to save the greater number.

People are blinded in these present days to the reality of sin because they do not even recognize or acknowledge the existence of their God. Yet I love you still, my people, and I shall forever. Turn back to me. **The chastisement is at hand.** (*Journal* 495).

On July 7, 2016, in Dallas, Texas, Micah Xavier Johnson ambushed and fired upon a group of police officers, killing five officers and injuring nine others. Ten days later, Jesus said, "Hear me, at last, or the state of the world will continue to decline yet further until one day the Great Chastisement will fall upon you and you shall cry, 'Blessed is He who comes in the name of the Lord!'" (*Journal* 734).

On April 27, 2017, **Jesus King of All Nations revealed,**

> Let it be clearly known and without doubt, that the great events now beginning to unfold in the world have been foretold by me and by my most holy Mother.

> The great storm of cleansing that shall bring about the correction of the conscience of mankind has begun.

> Cling fast to the holy faith.

> Cling to my Mother's holy Rosary and seek refuge within her Immaculate Heart.

> These tremendous events were foretold by me as Jesus King of All Nations. Again, and again, I have pleaded for the acknowledgement of my Devotion by my holy Church.

> I warned of the consequences of not heeding my requests. Behold, they are almost upon you.

> There is still the opportunity to seek shelter under my sovereign Kingship. Take up my Devotion; enthrone my Image; and pray my prayers.

> I came in this Image and Devotion to extend to sinful mankind the scepter of my great mercy before it becomes necessary to wield it as the rod of my justice. I AM perfectly merciful and perfectly just.

> Seek my great mercy while there is yet time. Terror will fall upon this world while consciences sleep. Pray that the greater number shall be saved. (*Journal* 814, 816, 818, 820-821, 823–826).

In the apparitions to Edson Glauber at Itapiranga, Brazil, St. Joseph emphasized,

> [M]y Son Jesus is very indignant with the sins of humanity.

He desires to pour His divine justice upon all men that do not want to repent and continue obstinately in their sins. Look, my son, I hold His right hand, preventing Him from pouring out His justice upon all humanity. I ask Him, through the graces of my heart and for being worthy to live by His side, taking care of Him with the love of a father in this world, and for Him having loved me with the love of a son, **to not chastise the world for its crimes, but for all my little ones who honor and will honor this chaste heart of mine, should pour out His mercy upon the world.**

The world's many sins call humanity to repent and do penance, St. Joseph said, **"because God receives continued offenses from ungrateful men.** Today there are so many outrages, the sacrilege and indifference by all men. It is because of this that so many calamities like war, hunger, and disease occur and so many other sad things man has suffered because of man's rebellion against God."

St. Joseph made clear the consequences of rebellions. He said, "God lets men follow their own paths to show them all that, without Him, they will never be happy. He lets men go through so much suffering to also show them the consequences sin brings to their lives and so then the **divine justice punishes humanity because of their obstinance in not being obedient to God's Will."**

He pointed out that humanity is "increasingly obstinate in their crimes" because of concern for worldly pleasures "rather than the love of God and His Commandments. But **God's justice is close at hand in a way never seen before and will come about suddenly upon the whole world."**

Nevertheless, St. Joseph offers us hope. He said that all those who honor his chaste heart "will receive the grace of my protection from all evils and dangers. For those who surrender to me will not be slaughtered by misfortunes, by wars, by hunger, by diseases and other calamities, they will have my heart as a refuge for their protection. Here, in my heart, all will be protected against the divine justice in the days that will come. **All who consecrate themselves to my heart, honoring it, they will be looked upon by my Son Jesus with eyes of mercy.** Jesus will pour out His love and will take to the glory of His Kingdom all those I put in my heart."

Jesus King of All Nations appeared to **the Spiritual Mother of the Jesus King of All Nations Devotion** on the Feast of the Triumph of the Cross. She **wrote,**

> **For a space of time, He let me behold a heavenly chastisement, which is to come. Greater than any Hiroshima could ever be. It was a merciful calling from God; a chastisement of mercy because God's people's hearts were far from Him and they no longer revered Him as God.**
>
> I am speaking this because God asked me to say this to His people. **Repent! Come and be healed in the Sacrament of Confession.** Come and be healed by asking for forgiveness. Come and be healed with the merciful love that God offers us. (*Journal* 147–148).

On August 6, 1945, the first atomic bomb was dropped by the United States on Hiroshima, Japan, killing about 140,000 people. Three days later, on August 9, 1945, the second atomic bomb was dropped by the United States on Nagasaki, Japan, killing about 80,000 people. **Dr. Takashi Nagai was an innocent Christ-like figure who suffered from the chastisement of that bomb. He was a Japanese convert to Catholicism.**

At the time of the bombing, Takashi was working in the radiology department of Nagasaki Medical College Hospital, which was located only 1000 yards from Ground Zero. **He said, "There was a flash of blinding light. A giant hand seemed to grab me and hurl me three meters. The giant invisible fist had gone berserk and was smashing everything in the office and I listened to strange noises like mountains rumbling back and forth. Then came pitch darkness. Panic gripped my heart when I heard crackling flames and sniffed acrid smoke. I was conscious of my sins and directed my whole attention to the Lord, our judge, and asked His forgiveness."**

Takashi received a serious injury that severed his right temporal artery. Nevertheless, he joined the rest of the surviving medical staff and dedicated himself to treating the victims. On August 11, he found his house destroyed and the burnt bones of his wife, Midori, with her Rosary close to her among a heap of ashes.

On November 23, 1945, an outdoor Requiem Mass was celebrated in front of the ruins of the cathedral for the innocent victims of this chastisement that God had permitted. Takashi gave an exhortation filled with faith, comparing the innocent victims to a sacrificial offering to God in order to obtain peace. He said,

> **In an instant, eight thousand Christians were called into the hands of God, while in a few hours the fierce flames reduced to ashes this sacred territory of the East.** At midnight of that same night, the cathedral suddenly burst into flames and was burned to the ground. And exactly at that time in the Imperial Palace, his Majesty the Emperor made known his sacred decision to bring the war to an end....

> And now at last we have brought this great and evil war to an end. But in order to restore peace to the world it was not sufficient to repent. We had to obtain God's pardon through the offering of a great sacrifice.

> Before this moment there were many opportunities to end the war. Not a few cities were totally destroyed. But these were not suitable sacrifices; nor did God accept them. **Only when Nagasaki was destroyed did God accept the sacrifice. Hearing the cry of the human family, He inspired the Emperor to issue the sacred decree by which the war was brought to an end.**

> Our church of Nagasaki kept the faith during four hundred years of persecution when religion was proscribed and the blood of martyrs flowed freely. During the war, this same church never ceased to pray day and night for a lasting peace. Was it not, then, the one unblemished lamb that had to be offered on the altar of God? **Thanks to the sacrifice of this lamb, many millions who would otherwise have fallen victim to the ravages of war have been saved.**

> How noble, how splendid was that holocaust of August 9, when flames soared up from the cathedral, dispelling the darkness of war and bringing the light of peace! In the very depth of our grief, we reverently saw here something beautiful, something pure, something sublime. **Eight**

thousand people, together with their priests, burning with pure smoke, entered into eternal life. All without exception were good people whom we deeply mourn.

How happy are those people who left this world without knowing the defeat of their country! How happy are the pure lambs who rest in the bosom of God! Compared with them, how miserable is the fate of us who have survived!

Japan is conquered. Urakami is totally destroyed. A waste of ash and rubble lies before our eyes. We have no houses, no food, no clothes. Our fields are devastated. **Only a remnant has survived. In the midst of the ruins, we stand in groups of two or three looking blankly at the sky....**

And as we walk in hunger and thirst, ridiculed, penalized, scourged, pouring with sweat, and covered with blood, let us remember that Jesus Christ carried His Cross to the hill of Calvary. He will give us courage.

The Lord has given, the Lord has taken away. Blessed be the name of the Lord!

Let us give thanks that Nagasaki was chosen for the sacrifice. Let us give thanks that through this sacrifice peace was given to the world and freedom of religion to Japan.

May the souls of the faithful departed, through the mercy of God, rest in peace. Amen.

The lessons from Dr. Takashi Nagai are that the victims of chastisements include the innocents whose suffering is redemptive, as Jesus King of All Nations taught us after the devastating Haitian Earthquake. This is a sign of hope because God leaves a surviving remnant and the power of His Resurrection sustains them to be a people of peace with hope for the future.

The source for Dr. Takashi Nagai's story related above about the dropping of the atomic bomb on Nagasaki, Japan, is the 1988 book, *A Song for Nagasaki*, by Paul Glynn. He is an Australian Marist priest and writer who served as a missionary in Japan for twenty-five years.

Summary of the Rebellions of Humanity Against God That Led to Chastisements

The rebellions and sins of humanity against God led to horrific chastisements from Him as acts of mercy and justice in order to bring them back to Him.

Adam and Eve's rebellion in the Garden of Eden led to their fall from grace and brought sin, death, and the loss of eternal life to all humanity.

The rebellious pride of the builders of the Tower of Babel led to the confusion of languages and their dispersion around the earth.

The sins of the contemporaries of Noah led to the Great Flood.

The sins of the inhabitants of Sodom and Gomorrah led to the annihilation of the cities and their inhabitants.

The rebellions of the Jews on their way to the Promised Land led to their 40 years of wandering in the desert.

The rebellion of the ten northern Jewish tribes against King Rehoboam put an end to the United Monarchy and caused the division of the Kingdom of the Jews into North and South.

The sins of the Jews in the Northern Kingdom led to its conquest by the Assyrians and the disappearance of the Kingdom.

The sins of the Jews in the Southern Kingdom led to its conquest and their imprisonment in the Babylonian Captivity for 70 years.

The failure of the Jews to recognize Jesus King of All Nations as their Messiah King led to their conquest by the Romans, the killing of approximately one million people, the destruction of their Temple, and their dispersion to the nations for almost 2000 years.

The sins of the Protestant rebellions led to their disunity from the one, holy, catholic, and apostolic Church and the loss of many graces through most of its sacraments.

The neglect of the French kings to honor the request of Jesus King of All Nations to honor His Sacred Heart led to the beheading of the last French King, Louis XVI, and the French Revolution.

The sins of the French revolutionaries led to the Reign of Terror, successive unstable governments, almost constant wars, and Secularism.

The sins of the modern Secularists are now leading us to the Great Chastisement prophesied by Jesus King of All Nations and the subsequent fulfillment of His prophecy that "a Great Renewal of my Holy Church, of Mankind, and, indeed, of All Creation will follow the cleansing action of my justice."

Jesus King of All Nations said, "No, my beloved, sin and the evils committed by mankind are too great, no longer will I spare my judgment to correct the conscience of mankind as a whole, but this Devotion and *Chaplet [of Unity]* prayed with repentance, confidence, and love, will heal, save, and unite souls to my mercy who otherwise would be lost." (*Journal* 55).

The Great Chastisement

Our Lady told Fr. Gobbi, "The moment of divine justice and of great mercy has now arrived! You will know the hour of weakness and poverty, the hour of suffering and defeat, the purifying hour of the Great Chastisement." (*To the Priests* 437).

A Great Chastisement will come, as Jesus King of All Nations prophesied, because the nations have not followed the example of the inhabitants of Nineveh, who repented and were saved. Rather, the nations have followed the example of the inhabitants of Sodom and Gomorrah, who did not repent and were destroyed.

God chastises not only cities, like Sodom and Gomorrah, but nations, as well, when their inhabitants refuse to repent. There have been and there will be sins, which are followed by just and merciful preliminary chastisements, ultimately resulting in a Great Chastisement.

The author of the Second Book of Maccabees, in Scripture, tells us, "Now I beg those who read this book not to be disheartened by these misfortunes, but to consider that these chastisements were meant not for the ruin but for the correction of our nation. It is, in fact, a sign of great kindness to punish sinners promptly instead of letting them go for long. Thus, in dealing with other nations, the Lord patiently waits until they reach the full measure of their sins before He punishes them; but with us He has decided to do differently, in order that He may not have to punish us more severely later, when our sins have reached their fullness. He never withdraws His mercy from us. **Although He disciplines us with misfortunes, He does not abandon His own people. Let these words suffice for recalling this truth."** (2 Maccabees 6:12–17).

So, it seems that the preliminary chastisements that nations have suffered were intended by God for their correction. However, with the lack of correction and the continuance in horrific national sins, especially unrestricted abortion, **it seems that God is waiting until the sins of our Culture of Death reach their full measure before His Great Chastisement.**

On November 15, 1990, **Our Lady warned Fr. Gobbi,** of the Marian Movement of Priests, while he was in the United States, **"Abortions—these killings of innocent children that cry for vengeance before the face of God—have spread and are performed in every part of your homeland. The moment of divine justice and of great mercy has now arrived! You will know the hour of weakness and poverty, the hour of suffering and defeat, the purifying hour of the Great Chastisement."** (*To the Priests* 437).

In the 1940s, **Jesus told Polish Servant of God Rozalia Celak (Rosalie Celakówna),** "My child! Because of the sins and crimes committed by men around the world, God will send a terrible punishment. God's justice cannot stand these crimes. **The only countries that will remain will be those that recognize the Reign of Jesus Christ."**

On June 6, 2011, Jesus King of All Nations gave His message below to His Secretary by interior locution and guided her to the scriptural citations contained in the message that confirmed it. Jesus warns us of a Great Chastisement about to fall upon this sinful world in order to "correct the conscience of mankind as a whole." This chastisement will be an act of His perfect justice tempered by His infinite mercy.

Jesus asks us to embrace His gift of the Jesus King of All Nations Devotion. Through the practice of His Devotion, we will receive graces of conversion, healing, and protection. He said,

> **Urgency! Urgency my people!** *"Thus says the Lord God: See, I will lift up my hand to the nations, and raise my signal to the peoples;"* (Isaiah 49:22). **Great is the**

chastisement that is ready to descend upon this sinful world to correct the consciences of individuals and the conscience of mankind as a whole! My Sacred, kingly, and Eucharistic Heart, which burns as a conflagration of divine love for mankind, urges me on to mercy, yet the weightiness of mankind's sins compels my perfect justice to be poured out. *"Because you are haughty of heart, and say, 'A god am I! I occupy a godly throne in the heart of the sea!' And yet you are a man, and not a god, however you may think yourself like a god."* (Ezekiel 28:2).

My perfect justice, however, is always tempered by my infinite mercy. It is, indeed, itself an act of mercy whenever my justice is accomplished for I AM mercy itself and there is no action either within or without the divine Godhead that is not imbued with mercy as it is part of my very nature as God. It is in fact the crowning glory of all of my divine attributes.

"But you are a God of pardons, gracious and compassionate, slow to anger and rich in mercy; you did not forsake them. Though they made themselves a molten calf and proclaimed, 'Here is your god who brought you up out of Egypt,' and were guilty of great effronteries, yet in your great mercy you did not forsake them in the desert." (Nehemiah 9:17, 18, 19).

Those who are filled with my spirit of love understand well this divine science, but those filled with the spirit of this world, the spirit of self-indulgence and of prideful arrogance, cannot grasp how the very justice of God is, in fact, merciful.

I correct my children out of love for them. *"Those whom I love, I reprove and chastise. Be earnest, therefore, and repent."* (Revelation 3:19). **I delight not in the suffering of my children. I desire to awaken their darkened consciences that they may recognize their sinfulness and be converted and that there may be a renewal of hearts and minds thereby causing the world itself to be renewed.** *"The one who sat on the throne said, 'Behold, I make all things new.' Then He said, 'Write these words down, for they are trustworthy and true.'"* (Revelation 21:5).

"I will sprinkle clean water upon you to cleanse you from all your impurities, and from all your idols I will cleanse you. I will give you a new heart and place a new spirit within you, taking from your bodies your stony hearts and giving you natural hearts." (Ezekiel 36:25–26).

Until the heart of man changes, the world will not and cannot change. Greater and greater will be the catastrophes in nature which itself rebels against the sinfulness of the children of men. The earth itself writhes in horror at the weight of corruption and uncleanness it supports. It cries out for justice against its inhabitants.

"Lo, the Lord empties the land and lays it waste; He turns it upside down, scattering its inhabitants:....The earth is utterly laid waste, utterly stripped, for the Lord has decreed this thing. The earth mourns and fades, the world languishes and fades; both heaven and earth languish. The earth is polluted because of its inhabitants, who have transgressed laws, violated statutes, broken the ancient covenant. Therefore, a curse devours the earth, and its inhabitants pay for their guilt; Therefore, they who dwell on earth turn pale, and few men are left." (Isaiah 24:1, 3–6).

"The earth will burst asunder, the earth will be shaken apart, the earth will be convulsed. The earth will reel like a drunkard, and it will sway like a hut; its rebellion will weigh it down,..." (Isaiah 24:19, 20).

Violence, wars, and hatred will grow yet greater until finally mankind will bring upon himself a great punishment, then will follow the chastisement that will fall directly from heaven. *"the time of trial that is going to come to the whole world to test the inhabitants of the earth. I am coming quickly. Hold fast to what you have, so that no one may take your crown."* (Revelation 3:10, 11). **Heed my warnings, oh my people. Turn from your sinful ways, at last, before it is truly too late.** *"Return to the Lord and give up sin, pray to Him and make your offenses few. Turn again to the Most High and away from sin, hate intensely what He loathes;....How great the mercy of the Lord, His forgiveness of those who return to Him!"* (Sirach 17:20–21, 24). (*Journal* 366–375).

Hear me at last or the state of the world will continue to decline yet further until one day the Great Chastisement

will fall upon you and you shall cry, "Blessed is He who comes in the name of the Lord!" (*Journal* 734).

Embrace my Devotion of Jesus King of All Nations for it is a great mercy given by your God for these most perilous times. Contained within it are gems of all manner of grace given through the mediation of my Immaculate Mother. Graces of forgiveness, healing, and renewal of minds and hearts. *"for a tree is known by its fruit."* (Matthew 12:33). Why are my people not taking advantage of this gift of mine?

Let this be done. Let my gift be accepted with faith and great confidence in my kingly mercy and divine generosity. *"when you open your hand, they are filled with good things."* (Psalms 104:28).

Where is your faith, oh my people? You bind my hands through your lack of faith. *"Go to this people and say: 'You shall indeed hear but not understand. You shall indeed look but never see. Gross is the heart of this people; they will not hear with their ears; they have closed their eyes, so they may not see with their eyes and hear with their ears and understand with their heart and be converted, and I heal them.'"* (Acts 28:26–27).

Yours is the choice. I leave you free to accept or reject both my admonition and my gift. *"but the Lord's mercy reaches all flesh, reproving, admonishing, teaching, as a shepherd guides his flock; merciful to those who accept His guidance, who are diligent in His precepts."* (Sirach 18:11, 12–13). (*Journal* 376–379).

Our Lady told Fr. Gobbi that, because humanity has not accepted her repeated call to conversion, there is about to fall upon it the greatest chastisement which the history of mankind has ever known. She said,

You live unconscious of the fate which is awaiting you. You are spending your days in a state of unawareness, of indifference, and of complete incredulity. How is this possible when I, in so many ways and with extraordinary signs, have warned you of the danger into which you are running and have foretold you of the bloody ordeal which is just about to take place?

Because this humanity has not accepted my repeated call to conversion, to repentance, and to a return to God, there is about to fall upon it the greatest chastisement which the history of mankind has even known. **It is a chastisement much greater than that of the [Great] Flood. Fire will fall from heaven and a great part of humanity will be destroyed.**

The Church of Jesus is wounded with the pernicious plague of infidelity and apostasy. In appearance, everything remains calm and it seems that all is going well. In reality, she is being pervaded with an ever-widening lack of faith which is spreading the great apostasy everywhere. Many bishops, priests, religious, and faithful no longer believe and have already lost the true faith in Jesus and in the Gospel. For this reason, the Church must be purified, with persecution and with blood.

There has also entered into the Church disunity, division, strife, and antagonism. The forces of atheism and Masonry, having infiltrated within it, are on the point of breaking up its interior unity and of darkening the splendor of its sanctity. These are the times, foretold by me, when cardinals will be set against cardinals, bishops against bishops, and priests against priests, and the flock of Christ will be torn to pieces by rapacious wolves, who have found their way in under the clothing of defenseless and meek lambs. Among them, there are even some who occupy posts of great responsibility and, by means of them, **Satan has succeeded in entering and in operating at the very summit of the Church. Bishops and priests of the holy Church of God, how great today is your responsibility! The Lord is about to demand of you an account of how you have administered His vineyard. Repent, seek pardon, make amends, and, above all, be once again faithful to the task which has been entrusted to you.**

Sin is being committed more and more, it is no longer acknowledged as an evil, it is sought out, it is consciously willed, and it is no longer confessed. Impurity and lewdness cover the homes built by your rebellion....

My Heart is bleeding because I see your roads even now smeared with blood, while you live in an obstinate unconsciousness of that which awaits you. (*To the Priests* 332).

The Coming Great Chastisement might be the fire falling from the sky that might wipe out a great part of humanity, as prophesied by the Blessed Virgin Mary in Akita, Japan. That would be much worse than the destruction caused by the atomic bombs over Hiroshima and Nagasaki, Japan in 1945.

In Nagasaki, Our Lady told Fr. Gobbi, "In this city, there also exploded the atomic bomb, causing tens of thousands of deaths in a few brief instants, a chastisement and terrible sign of what man can do when, distancing himself from God, he becomes incapable of love, of compassion, and of mercy. This is what the whole world could become if it does not welcome my invitation to conversion and return to the Lord. From this place, I renew my anguished appeal to all the nations of the earth." (*To the Priests* 582).

Two world wars and two atomic bombs have taught us nothing. Those who do not learn from history are doomed to repeat it. **We must learn the need to repent and return to God to enter the Era of Peace, an age of faith with God to replace the doomed age of reason without God.**

So, we must endure chastisements, but with hope that mankind again will call upon God and live with faith and reason according to the law of God. We must maintain our hope and help to usher in a Culture of Life and a Civilization of Love in the Era of Peace that will come.

Jesus' chastisements are not vengeful punishments, but really acts of mercy to bring people to repentance, as Jesus said in the Scriptures, "Fear is useless, what is needed is trust." (Luke 8:50). **The best answer to fear is what Jesus King of All Nations Himself said, on December 28, 2004, two days after the Asian Tsunami struck. "I have shaken the earth to awaken the conscience of man."** However, He also cited Proverbs 1:33, *"But he who obeys me dwells in security, in peace, without fear of harm."* (*Journal* 316, 393).

Jesus King of All Nations said for those who embrace His Devotion, "I will cover them with my kingly mantle that my perfect justice may not reach them as it will reach those who abandon my law. My children, dear children, do not despair. There is always hope.... All is coming to fulfillment. Be at peace. Trust in my mercy and love. Pray to my holy Mother. Entrust your life to her. Receive the sacraments worthily and frequently. Obey my holy Spouse, the Church. Remain faithful. I love you. I bless you." (*Journal* 318–319, 321).

Our Lady told Blessed Elena Aiello, "The only valid means for placating divine justice is to pray and do penance, returning to God with sincere sorrow for the faults committed, and then the chastisement of divine justice will be mitigated by mercy. Humanity will never find peace if it does not return to my Immaculate Heart as Mother of Mercy and Mediatrix of Men; and to the Heart of my Son, Jesus!" (December 8, 1956).

Likewise, Jesus King of All Nations said, "Mankind must recognize my divine Kingship, my divine rights over them! It is only in me, my child, that mankind will find peace." (*Journal* 160).

Our Lady summarized the reasons for the Coming Great Chastisement. She told Fr. Gobbi,

> Humanity has not accepted my motherly request to return to the Lord along the road of conversion of heart and of life, of prayer, and of penance. Thus, it has known the terrible years of the Second World War, which brought about tens of millions of deaths and vast destruction of populaces and of nations.

> Russia has not been consecrated to me by the Pope together with all the bishops and thus she has not received the grace of conversion and has spread her errors throughout all parts of the world, provoking wars, violence, bloody revolutions, and persecutions of the Church and of the Holy Father.

> Satan has been the uncontested dominator of the events of this century of yours, bringing all humanity to the rejection of God and of His law of love, spreading far and wide division and hatred, immorality and wickedness, and legitimating everywhere divorce, abortion, obscenity,

homosexuality, and recourse to any and all means of obstructing life....

The Church will know the hour of its greatest apostasy. The man of iniquity will penetrate into its interior and will sit in the very Temple of God, while the little remnant which will remain faithful will be subjected to the greatest trials and persecutions. Humanity will live through the moment of its Great Chastisement and thus will be made ready to receive the Lord Jesus who will return to you in glory. (*To the Priests* 425).

Although the Great Chastisement may seem slow in coming, St. Peter tells us it is because the Lord is merciful and wants to bring us to repentance. "Therefore, you rebuke offenders little by little, warn them, and remind them of the sins they are committing, that they may abandon their wickedness and believe in you, O Lord!" (Wisdom 12:2).

St. Peter wrote, "But do not ignore this one fact, beloved, that with the Lord one day is as a thousand years, and a thousand years as one day. The Lord is not slow about His promise as some count slowness, but is forbearing toward you, not wishing that any should perish, but that all should reach repentance." (2 Peter 3:8-9).

The Remnant

Jesus King of All Nations promised us that, after the Great Chastisement, there will be a remnant left of "good and holy people." He said, "So greatly does this world require divine cleansing that only by means of the purifying power of fire shall it be renewed and its soil, the soil of the heart of man, emerge rich and fertile, ready to receive the seed of the divine Word and thus produce a harvest of holiness and virtue. A good and holy people shall the remnant be." (*Journal* 455).

The Coming Great Chastisement may be like the fire prophesied by the prophet Malachi that will separate the just from the wicked, setting the wicked on fire, but protecting the

just remnant who fear God's name and who will receive the healing rays of the sun of justice in an Era of Peace. Malachi said,

> Those who fear the Lord and trust in His name shall be mine, says the Lord of hosts, my own special possession, on the day I take action.
>
> And I will have compassion on them, as a man has compassion on his son who serves him.
>
> Then you will again see the distinction between the just and the wicked; Between the one who serves God, and the one who does not serve Him.
>
> For lo, the day is coming, blazing like an oven, when all the proud and all evildoers will be stubble, And the day that is coming will set them on fire, leaving them neither root nor branch, says the Lord of hosts.
>
> But for you who fear my name, there will arise the sun of justice with its healing rays. (Malachi 3:16–20).

The Coming Great Chastisement may also be like the darkness and the trembling of heaven and earth prophesied by the prophet Joel when God will sit in judgment and chastise all the nations around, on the Day of Yahweh in the Valley of the Verdict, but will be a shelter for His people in an Era of Peace. Joel said,

> Sun and moon grow dark, the stars lose their brilliance. Yahweh roars from Zion, He thunders from Jerusalem; heaven and earth tremble.
>
> But Yahweh will be a shelter for His people, a stronghold for the Israelites.
>
> 'I shall avenge their blood and let none go unpunished,' and Yahweh will dwell in Zion. (Joel 4:15–16, 21).

God warns us of a Great Chastisement, but the righteous and devout may be preserved as a remnant of righteousness. As St. Peter wrote, "the Lord knows how to rescue the devout from trial."

He also wrote, "For God did not spare the angels when they sinned, but condemned them to the chains of Tartarus and handed them over to be kept for judgment; and if He did not spare the ancient world, even though He preserved Noah, a herald of righteousness, together with seven others, when He brought a Flood upon the godless world; and if He condemned the cities of Sodom and Gomorrah to destruction, reducing them to ashes, making them an example for the godless people of what is coming; and if He rescued Lot, a righteous man oppressed by the licentious conduct of unprincipled people...then the Lord knows how to rescue the devout from trial and to keep the unrighteous under punishment for the Day of Judgment..." (2 Peter 2:4-9).

After the chastisement of the Great Flood, God left the remnant of Noah and his family, and after the chastisement of the destruction of Sodom and Gomorrah, He left the remnant of the family of Lot.

Ezekiel prophesied that the Babylonian Captivity of the Jews was a chastisement for their sins. They were dispersed to the nations. However, there was the promise of the return of a remnant, that God would be their God, and they would be His people. (See Ezekiel chapter 36). **God will also leave a remnant after the Coming Great Chastisement.**

Edson Glauber, the visionary from Itapiranga, Brazil, said,

> **The Chastisement will come to the world. Our Lady said that before the Chastisement comes, there will be a huge rumble in the sky, a thunder that will shake the four corners of the earth. The Chastisement will be terrible! Humanity will know, in this way, what the price is of sin and disobedience.**

> It will seem as it is fire! It will seem that the sky is full of reddish and orange flames for a long time. This will make the earth very hot and all the vegetation will die slowly. After, everything will be dry and the water will not quench the thirst of people.

> When this happens, it will seem that there are two suns in the sky. And, this will be very impressive at night, causing emotions and amazement in many people. There will be no use in running away, because where could you go?

> The Chastisement is inevitable. When all will be at its highest point, there will appear in the sky the three Sacred Hearts of Jesus, Mary, and Joseph, giving a sign of

protection, comfort, and hope to all those who were faithful to God, to His Commandments, and to His Church.

At that time, **Our Lady will cover with her mantle the families that had responded to her appeals. She will defend and protect them from the Chastisement that will fall on the world.** (*Terra da Fe' (Land of Faith) Volume II,* Galileu Borsa Limo Manaus, 2004).

The Remedy

So, what is the remedy? What is the solution?

In the 17th century, Jesus foresaw the outbreaks of the French revolutions in the 18th and 19th centuries. As a remedy against them, He revealed to St. Margaret Mary the devotion to His Sacred Heart. Through her, He revealed His request of King Louis XIV to consecrate himself to the Sacred Heart of Jesus and to give Him public homage. His requests were not fulfilled and the French Revolution came as a chastisement.

Similarly, **Jesus King of All Nations has prophesied an imminent Great Chastisement and, as a remedy against it, He revealed His Devotion and His request for the enthronement of His Image everywhere. Jesus King of All Nations said, "In these times, only one thing will be given as a remedy. I myself AM that remedy!"** (*Journal* 159).

On March 18, 2020, **Jesus King of All Nations said** that what we were seeing happening around us was the beginning of the chastisements that He has prophesied to correct the conscience of mankind. In my opinion, He was referring to the COVID–19 pandemic. He also gave us what He described as, "the remedy for the ills of the world."

He said, **"Once more I appeal to my holy Church to rapidly approve my Devotion of Jesus King of All Nations and allow the public practice of my Devotion and the enthronement of my Image. This is the remedy for the ills of the world; the re-acclamation of my sovereign Kingship over all mankind, over all nations."**

God is seemingly calling out to us, "You need me!" There is no other leader, or political, legal, or monetary solution. We are beyond human redemption and only God can save us.

On the very same day as the terrorist mass killings at the San Bernardino holiday party, December 2, 2015, Jesus King of All Nations revealed a message for us to "Awake! A great catastrophe is about to befall you!"

This is His message, together with the scriptural citations to which He led His Secretary to confirm the message,

Awake! Lift up your heads my people! Do you not see the signs all around you?! A great catastrophe is about to befall you!

"And He said to them, 'Oh, how foolish you are! How slow of heart to believe all that the prophets spoke!'" (Luke 24:25).

Let my bishops take up my Devotion of Jesus King of All Nations, for it has been given as a remedy and a protection in these most dangerous times!

"Shall I not open for you the floodgates of heaven, to pour down blessing upon you without measure?" (Malachi 3:10).

Is it not clear what is taking place? Violence and godlessness increase daily. Hatred and a complete disrespect for life grow wantonly. There is no sense of sin or of the divine throughout the earth! What is about to descend upon mankind is due to his great sinfulness.

I have warned you time and time again but you still refuse to listen and my holy Church does not recognize the urgent need of the approval of my Devotion!

"Why do these people rebel with obstinate resistance? Why do they cling to deceptive idols, refuse to turn back? I listen closely: they speak what is not true; No one repents of his wickedness, saying, 'What have I done!' Everyone keeps running his course, like a steed dashing into battle." (Jeremiah 8:5–6).

I have told you of the remedy. That of the public practice of my Devotion and veneration of my Image. Let as much as can still be done to bring this about be done. Let those who are able enthrone my Image in their homes, parishes, and dioceses.

"Behold, I will treat and assuage the city's wounds; I will heal them, and reveal to them an abundance of lasting peace....They shall be in fear and trembling over all the peaceful benefits I will give her." (Jeremiah 33:6, 9).

You see I AM infinitely merciful and accept a smaller amount than my justice requires. This is the pre-eminence of my divine mercy. It is my greatest divine attribute.

"Though our living Lord treats us harshly for a little while to correct us with chastisements, He will again be reconciled with His servants." (2 Maccabees 7:33).

Heed my words, my bishops, my prelates, and afford your flocks the offered graces of mercy and protection!

"Woe to my foolish shepherd who forsakes the flock!" (Zechariah 11:17).

Do all that you possibly can!

Do not be afraid of the opinion of man, fear rather displeasing your God!

"Do not despise prophetic utterances. Test everything; retain what is good." (1 Thessalonians 5:20–21). *(Journal 664–679).*

In light of the ongoing violence, mass murders, wars, militant jihadist Muslim terrorism, and the abuse and corruption in the Church and the State, we should remember that Jesus has told us, "Let not your heart be troubled." (John 14:1). "In this world you will have trouble. But take heart! I have overcome the world." (John 16:33).

Everyone wants to know what's going to happen, and when. However, we should not focus on the what and the when, but on *how* to be ready for the chastisements prophesied by Jesus and Mary. We should focus on what we should do and how we should be.

When Pope Benedict XVI visited Fatima, on May 11, 2010, He said, "The Lord told us that the Church would constantly be suffering, in different ways, until the end of the world....We need to relearn precisely these essentials: conversion, prayer, penance, and the theological virtues. This is our response: we are realists in expecting that evil always attacks, attacks from within and without, yet that the forces of good are also ever present and that,

in the end, the Lord is more powerful than evil and Our Lady is for us the visible, motherly guarantee of God's goodness, which is always the last word in history."

During the Mass at Fatima, on May 13, 2013, in the presence of half a million people, the Pope reaffirmed that "the demanding but consoling message the Virgin left us at Fatima is full of hope. It is a message that focuses on prayer, penance, and conversion, a message projected beyond the threats, dangers, and horrors of history, inviting humankind to have faith in the action of God, to cultivate great hope, and to experience the grace of the Lord in order to love Him, the source of love and peace. In Fatima, **the Blessed Virgin Mary invites us to walk with hope, letting ourselves be guided by the 'wisdom from on high' which was manifested in Jesus, the wisdom of love, to bring the light and joy of Christ into the world."**

Too many people ask too many questions about converting. They ask, "What will others think? Am I able to return to God? What will it be like? What must I give up?" We should not be asking these questions. They are of no help. They will not help us to be ready.

Jesus said to His disciples, **"Stay awake! For you do not know on which day your Lord will come."** (Matthew 24:42). **Jesus King of All Nations revealed in His Litany that He is "the only remedy for a world so ill."** (*Journal* 282).

We must accept the remedy of Jesus King of All Nations and respond *NOW*. People did not respond to Mary's requests at Quito, Paris, Champion, Fatima, and Kibeho and they suffered from the prophesied chastisements.

Are You Prepared?

Have you turned to God in reconciliation and trust and accepted His Will for your life? That was the question that passenger Fred Beretta had to answer as US Airways flight 1549 approached The Miracle on the Hudson, on January 15, 2009.

Seconds before the plane hit the Hudson River in New York City, God asked Fred, *"Where will you turn to now? Will you reconcile and trust? You must choose."* **As the plane hurtled toward the water and his expected death, the flight attendants kept repeating, "Brace for impact, brace for impact!" A surge of adrenaline coursed** through Fred's body and the world seemed to suddenly halt. The silent voice came again, *"Will you accept my Will for your life?"*

Fred knew that he needed to reconcile to the fact that, as he later wrote, he "was not in control, and either in pride and anger he could turn away from God or in humility turn fully to Him and accept His Will, however inscrutable it was and regardless of the consequences. **The river was coming for me and I had to decide."**

Fred decided "Yes" and he and all of the other passengers survived the airplane's crash landing on the Hudson River. (Frederick Beretta, *Flight of Faith*, (Charlotte, North Carolina: St. Benedict Press, 2009), 36–37).

The river of death and judgment is also coming for each of us and each of us is called to answer "Yes" to the question that God put to Fred, *"You must choose. Will you accept my Will for your life?"*

Let us be prepared to accept God's Will, as was Fred. We should prepare for and protect ourselves against the prophesied coming chastisements. Let it not be for us as it was in the days of Noah. Jesus said, "For as it was in the days of Noah, so it will be at the coming of the Son of Man. In those days before the Flood, they were eating and drinking, marrying and giving in marriage, up to the day that Noah entered the ark. They did not know until the Flood came and carried them all away." (Matthew 24:37–39).

We should not fear the works of Satan or any chastisements that God may allow, but pray for their aversion or mitigation and the grace to endure them. **"There is hope for your future, says the Lord."** (Jeremiah 31:17).

14. The Triumph of the Immaculate Heart of Mary, the New Pentecost, and the Era of Peace

The Triumph of the Immaculate Heart of Mary

Pope Benedict XVI said that praying for the Triumph of the Immaculate Heart...is equivalent in meaning to our praying for the coming of God's Kingdom. (Peter Seewald, *Light of the World: The Pope, The Church and the Signs Of The Times*, (Ignatius Press, Ft. Collins, CO 80522, 2010), 166).

Our Lady told Fr. Gobbi, of the Marian Movement of Priests, "The Triumph of the Immaculate Heart will coincide with the triumph of Jesus in His glorious Reign." (*To the Priests* 339).

Jesus King of All Nations told His Secretary, "My Kingdom, my Reign, is near at hand....My most holy Mother is preparing the great triumph. The Triumph of her Immaculate Heart ushers in the Reign of my love and mercy." (*Journal* 7, 14). **The Kingdom of God, for which Christians have prayed for over 2000 years, will come soon with the Reign of Jesus King of All Nations through the Triumph of the Immaculate Heart of Mary.**

On February 2, 1634, Our Lady of Good Success alluded to her triumph. She said, "In order to dissipate this black cloud that prevents the Church from enjoying the clear day of liberty, there will be a formidable and frightful war....This night will be most horrible, for, humanly speaking, evil will seem to triumph. This, then, will mark the arrival of my hour, when **I, in a marvelous way, will dethrone the proud and cursed Satan, trampling him under my feet and fettering him in the infernal abyss. Thus, the Church and Country will be finally free of his cruel tyranny.**"

The Triumph of the Immaculate Heart of Mary and the Era of Peace were first prophesied by Our Lady of Fatima on July 13, 1917, when she told the three visionary shepherd children, "In the end, my Immaculate Heart will triumph. The Holy Father will

consecrate Russia to me and she will be converted, and an Era of Peace will be granted to the world."

As Jesus is the head of the Mystical Body of Christ, the Church, so Mary is its heart and we are its humble feet, walking our pilgrimage in faith, directed by the head through the heart. This heart is like a prism diffusing all graces from the pure light of the Holy Trinity in all its varied colors to us. It is the gate of heaven through which passes the love of God to renew the whole world.

The word "heart" as used in Scripture often means the higher part of the soul, the interior perfections. With reference to Mary, it refers to her Immaculate Conception, fullness of grace, and blessedness. (See Luke 1:28, 42).

Mary's Immaculate Heart exists in her glorified body, which still loves and suffers for all humanity. Mary's Heart is immaculate because it is without sin as a consequence of her Immaculate Conception. It is the center of her ever-virgin being, which perfectly loves God and us. As she is united with the Sacred Heart of Jesus, so, too, is she united with our hearts and our lives, joys, and sorrows.

Her Immaculate Heart also symbolizes her interior life where she reflected on her joys and sorrows, her virtues and hidden perfections, her virginal love for God, and her maternal love for Jesus and all humanity. (See Luke 2:19, 51).

Her Heart is also the heart of a mother, a real living motherly heart which watches over us, hears our cries, and helps us by her tender care for us.

She knows, at every moment, everything that concerns us — our fears, anxieties, faults, temptations, and sins. As our Spiritual Mother, her Immaculate Heart mediates our prayers to God and dispenses God's graces to us.

As a mirror, her Heart reflects the most pure light of the Trinity, where the Father finds His design intact and perfectly realized, and from which He receives His greatest glory from a creature.

The centrality of her being is symbolized by her physical heart as the seat of her love and her spiritual heart as the seat of her interior perfections and her entire interior affective and moral life.

Mary revealed at Fatima that Jesus wants to establish devotion to her Immaculate Heart in the world. If we truly love Our Lady, we should heed her request to consecrate ourselves to her Immaculate Heart. Jacinta, one of the Fatima visionaries, said that God has entrusted peace to the Immaculate Heart of Mary. Mary, in turn, told Sr. Lucia, another Fatima visionary, that she would be her refuge and the way that would lead her to God.

At Fatima, Mary said, "Finally, my Immaculate Heart will triumph." Medjugorje visionary Mirjana told me that Mary had told her, "I want to say one thing that is very important. Blessed Mary said, 'What I started at Fatima, I will finish in Medjugorje, my Heart will triumph.' If the Heart of our Mother will triumph, we don't need to be scared of anything. It's only important to put our life in her hands and not to think about secrets. We should think about the messages and what she asked for us, so that we can help her Immaculate Heart to triumph."

Padre Livio told Mirjana that Mary, Queen of Peace, was coming to build us a new world of peace, the end of which is to bring us to the light of a closer relationship with God. Mirjana responded to him, "Yes, yes. I'm sure that eventually we will see this light. We shall see the triumph of the Heart of Our Lady and Jesus."

In 2009, Pope Benedict XVI offered a prayer on the anniversary of the first apparition of Our Lady of Fatima regarding the Triumph of her Immaculate Heart. He prayed,

> [Mary,] you promised the three children of Fatima that "in the end, my Immaculate Heart will triumph." May it be so! May love triumph over hatred, solidarity over division, and peace over every form of violence! May the love you bore your Son teach us to love God with all our heart, strength, and soul. May the Almighty show us His mercy, strengthen us with His power, and fill us with every good thing. (See Luke 1:46–56). (Pope Benedict XVI at Caritas Baby Hospital in Bethlehem, May 13, 2009).

One year later, the next anniversary of the first apparition of Our Lady of Fatima, Pope Benedict XVI said in his homily at Fatima, "We would be mistaken to think that Fatima's prophetic message is complete." He went on to look forward to the 2017 centenary of Fatima, expressing his hope that "the seven years which separate us from the centenary of the apparitions [may] hasten the fulfillment of the prophecy of the Triumph of the Immaculate Heart, to the glory of the Blessed Trinity."

Our Lady told Fr. Gobbi that the Triumph of her Immaculate Heart "will be a cause of amazement, even to the angels of God, a joy to the saints in heaven, a consolation and great comfort for all the just on earth, mercy and salvation for a great number of my straying children, a severe and definitive condemnation of Satan and his many followers. In fact, at the very moment when Satan will be enthroned as lord of the world and will think himself now the sure victor, I myself will snatch the prey from his hands. He will find himself empty-handed and, in the end, the victory will be exclusively my Son's and mine. This will be *the Triumph of my Immaculate Heart in the world.*" (*To the Priests* 29).

Our Lady explained, "This victory will take place with the fall of practical atheism throughout all the world, with the defeat of the Masonic and Satanic forces, with the destruction of the great power of evil, and with the full triumph of God in a world then completely purified by the great merciful chastisement." (*To the Priests* 579).

Our Lady also told Fr. Gobbi, **"The Triumph of my Immaculate Heart will be realized through a new birth of Jesus in the hearts and the souls of my poor wandering children. Only have confidence, and do not let anxiety or discouragement take hold of you. The future that awaits you will be a new dawn of light for the whole world, now at last made clean."** (*To the Priests* 89).

The Triumph of the Immaculate Heart of Mary means the triumph of goodness over the evil state of the world. It is the triumph of grace over sin, of faith over atheism, of love over hate, of virtue over vice, of life over death. It is the triumph of a loving motherly heart who wants to save her spiritual children on earth from evil and, by her intercession, obtain the grace from her Son, Jesus, for Him to reconcile them to Himself and to obtain an Era of Peace.

Jesus King of All Nations said, "Evil has already been defeated. Along with its fruit, which is death, it has been nailed to the Cross. It and its father [Satan] have been completely vanquished." (*Journal* 748, 750).

The New Pentecost

On the first Pentecost, ten days after Jesus had ascended into heaven, Mary and the apostles were gathered in prayer in the cenacle, the upper room of the Last Supper. Suddenly a sound came from heaven like the rush of a mighty wind that filled the house, and tongues as of fire appeared and rested on each of one of them. They were all filled with the Holy Spirit and began to speak in other languages, as the Spirit gave them utterance.

At the sound of the wind, a multitude of Jews from many nations, who spoke many languages, gathered outside. The timid apostles were transformed, boldly came out, and courageously preached to the Jews as the Spirit led them. All of the Jews miraculously understood them in their own native language.

When they heard Peter's preaching, they were cut to the heart and asked, "Brethren, what shall we do?" Peter said to them, "Repent and be baptized, every one of you, in the name of Jesus Christ for the forgiveness of your sins; and you shall receive the gift of the Holy Spirit." About 3000 received His word and were baptized that very day. (See Acts chapters 1–2).

We should hope and pray that the New Pentecost will be even more powerful and miraculous than the first Pentecost. May the Holy Spirit pour Himself out to bring millions of sinners to repentance and salvation.

On December 25, 1961, at the convocation of the Second Vatican Council, **Pope John XXIII prayed to the Holy Spirit, "Divine Spirit, renew your wonders in this our age as in a new Pentecost, and grant that your Church, praying perseveringly and insistently with one heart and mind together with Mary, the Mother of Jesus, and guided by blessed Peter, may increase the Reign of the divine Savior, the reign of truth and justice, the reign of love and peace. Amen."**

On May 9, 1975, Pope Paul VI wrote in *Gaudete in Domino (On Christian Joy)*, "So great are the needs and the perils of the present age, so vast the horizon of mankind drawn toward world coexistence and powerless to achieve it, that there is no salvation for it except in a new outpouring of the gift of God. Let Him then come, the Creating Spirit, to renew the face of the earth!"

In 1992, in Latin America, **St. John Paul II said, "Be open to
Christ, welcome the Spirit, so that a new Pentecost may take place
in every community! A new humanity, a joyful one, will arise
from your midst; you will experience again the saving power of
the Lord."**

On April 19, 2008, in a homily in New York City, **Pope Benedict
XVI said, "Let us implore from God the grace of a new
Pentecost....May tongues of fire, combining burning love of God
and neighbor with zeal for the spread of Christ's Kingdom,
descend on all present!"**

Later, on July 20, 2008, in his homily at World Youth Day in
Sydney Australia, **Pope Benedict XVI said that the power of the
Holy Spirit can create a new world and a new age.**

> The power of the Holy Spirit does not only enlighten and
> console us. It also points us to the future, *to the coming of
> God's Kingdom*....This power can create a new world: it can
> "renew the face of the earth!" (See Psalms 104:30).
> Empowered by the Spirit, and drawing upon faith's rich
> vision, a new generation of Christians is being called to help
> build a world in which God's gift of life is welcomed,
> respected, and cherished—not rejected, feared as a threat,
> and destroyed. A new age in which love is not greedy or
> self-seeking, but pure, faithful, and genuinely free, open to
> others, respectful of their dignity, seeking their good,
> radiating joy and beauty. A new age in which hope liberates
> us from the shallowness, apathy, and self-absorption which
> deaden our souls and poison our relationships.
>
> **Dear young friends, the Lord is asking you to be
> prophets of this new age, messengers of His love, drawing
> people to the Father and building a future of hope for all
> humanity.**

On October 8, 2013, **Jesus King of All Nations said,**

> **My Spirit shall once more descend in a new Pentecost: a
> new Pentecost replete with the cleansing fire of His love.
> A fire ablaze with the love and justice of God. "*I will pour
> out my spirit.*" (Isaiah 44:3).**
>
> Then shall the earth emerge cleansed from the defilement
> of sin and souls shall rejoice as they bathe anew in the

copious mercy of God. Light shall spread throughout the world which is at present in a great darkness. Even consciences are in complete darkness.

"For those deserved to be deprived of light and imprisoned by darkness, who had kept your sons confined through whom the imperishable light of the Law was to be given to the world." (Wisdom 18:4).

O how I wish that they were upright and filled with divine Light! Hold fast my faithful ones. Remain strong in the holy faith. (*Journal* 496–500).

Our Lady told Fr. Gobbi,

The Holy Spirit will come, as a heavenly dew of grace and of fire, which will renew all the world. Under His irresistible action of love, the Church will open itself to live the new era of its greatest holiness and will shine resplendently with so strong a light that it will attract to itself all the nations of the earth.

The Holy Spirit will come, that the Will of the Heavenly Father be accomplished and the created universe once again reflect His great glory.

The Holy Spirit will come, to establish the glorious Reign of Christ, and it will be a Reign of grace, of holiness, of love, of justice, and of peace. With His divine love, He will open the doors of hearts and illuminate all consciences. Every person will see himself in the burning fire of divine truth. It will be like a judgment in miniature. And then Jesus Christ will bring His glorious Reign in the world.

The Holy Spirit will come by means of the Triumph of my Immaculate Heart. For this, I am calling upon you all today to enter into the cenacle of my Heart. Then you will be prepared to receive the gift of the Holy Spirit which will transform you and make you the instruments with which Jesus will establish His Reign. (*To the Priests* 383).

Jesus told Elizabeth Kindelmann,

The Spirit of Pentecost will flood the earth with His power and a great miracle will gain the attention of all

humanity. This will be the effect of grace of the Flame of
Love [which is Jesus Christ Himself].

Due to a lack of faith, earth is entering into darkness, but
earth will experience a great jolt of faith. People will believe
and will create a new world. By the Flame of Love,
confidence and faith will take root. **The face of the earth
will be renewed because "something like this has not
happened since the Word became flesh." Earth, although
flooded with sufferings, will be renewed by Our Lady's
intercession.** (Elizabeth Kindelmann, *The Flame of Love: The
Spiritual Diary of Elizabeth Kindelmann*, 61).

Our Lady also told Fr. Gobbi,

**The great mercy will come to you as a burning fire of
love and will be brought by the Holy Spirit, who is given
to you by the Father and the Son, so that the Father may
see Himself glorified and the Lord Jesus may feel Himself
loved by all His brothers.**

The Holy Spirit will come down as fire, but in a manner
different from His first coming: it will be a fire which will
burn and transform everything, which will sanctify and
renew the earth from its foundations. It will open hearts to
a new reality of life and lead all souls to a fullness of
holiness and of grace. **You will know a love that is so great
and a sanctity that is so perfect that it will be such as you
had never known before. It is in this that the Spirit will
be glorified: in bringing everyone to the greatest love for
the Father and for the Son.** (*To the Priests* 357).

The Era of Peace

**Although the prophecy of a Great Chastisement may fill some
people with dread, fear, and horror, still there is a horizon of hope
beyond it—the Era of Peace that will emerge from the Culture of
Death.**

Regarding the daily intentions for His *Chaplet of Unity*, **Jesus King
of All Nations said to His Secretary, with His scriptural citations
included, "Offer my *Chaplet of Unity* on Saturdays for the
proclamation of the dogma of Mary, Mediatrix of All Graces, and
Co-Redemptrix. My holy Mother will receive this honor from my**

Church. It is my Will. So it shall be. *'these things are recorded in the chronicle of his pontificate,'* (1 Maccabees 16:24). **This dogma is to be a great light for the nations and usher in the Era of Peace.** The enemy is furious at the prospect of this dogma and is ferociously fighting to prevent it. Legions of demons have been assigned the task of destroying this work, so much do they fear Mary, the Woman of Revelation. The gates of hell shall not prevail against my Holy Will. Amen, amen, so I say, so it shall be. For I AM, the Eternal One, the Only One, the Lord of all. *'They will fight with the Lamb, but the Lamb will conquer them, for He is Lord of lords and King of kings, and those with Him are called, chosen, and faithful.'* (Revelation 17:14). My blessing to you." (*Journal* 337).

On July 13, 1917, **Mary told the three children at Fatima, "a period [or an era] of peace will be granted to the world."** Sr. Lucia, one of the Fatima visionaries, referred to it both as a "period of peace" and an "era of peace." I will use the term "Era of Peace" because it was the term used by St. John Paul II and by Our Lady in her messages to Fr. Gobbi.

On June 25, 1995, **at Medjugorje, Mary said, "Pray for peace so that as soon as possible a time of peace, which my Heart waits for impatiently, may reign."**

Cardinal Mario Luigi Ciappi, papal theologian for Popes Pius XII, John XXIII, Paul VI, John Paul I, and John Paul II, **said, "Yes, a miracle was promised at Fatima, the greatest miracle in the history of the world, second only to the Resurrection. And that miracle will be an Era of Peace, which has never really been granted before to the world."** (Lawrence G Lovasik, *The Apostolate's Family Catechism*, 35).

Pope Pius XI wrote, "It is God's task to bring about this happy hour and to make it known to all;....When it does arrive, it will turn out to be a solemn hour, one big with consequences, not only for the restoration of the Kingdom of Christ, but for the pacification of...the world. We pray most fervently, and ask others likewise to pray for this much-desired pacification of society." (Pope Pius XI, *Ubi Arcani Dei Consilio (On the Peace of Christ in His Kingdom)*, 14).

Sr. Lucia said, "The period of peace does not refer to civil peace." This peace is not merely the absence of external conflict. **It is a positive interior quality, a gift from Jesus.** (See John 14:27).

It is God's own peace, which is beyond all understanding. (See Philippians 4:7).

Luz de Maria is an Argentinian mystic and mother. Bishop Juan Abelardo Mata, of Nicaragua, granted an *Imprimatur* **for the messages that she received from Our Lady** from 2009 to September 2017.

These messages include the following prophecies, with some lack of clarity in the translation.

The Era of Peace is coming for mankind. [An] era in which everything will be reborn; man, purified and fused with God's Will; creation, which will then feel in harmony with mankind. Total and complete happiness. Peace and harmony are coming. In order for mankind to overcome that great transition, it must first come to be purified and eradicate such a high degree of offenses with which my Son's Most Sacred Heart is hurt. Evil has entered the Church. The Devil has infiltrated the Church causing some of my beloved to collapse in respect to faith and the dogmas. God is the same today, tomorrow, and always; the modernism that has transgressed tradition cannot change that. (January 30, 2011).

The new dawn will come for my children. Evil will not find a place among men and all will be peace. My children will see in all of creation the seed of my love. Your Mother will camp with her children; the lost gifts will be deserved by man again and I will see myself pleased in each human being. All of the Cosmos will vibrate with the beating of my Heart to a single unique rhythm, and man will breathe my peace in total concordance." (February 26, 2011).

The Era of Peace will be a gift from God and not earned by human effort. This peace is not obtainable without responding to Mary's pleas for repentance, conversion, and faith, prayer, and fasting.

It is the peace that St. John Paul II prayed for at the Basilica of Our Lady of Guadalupe: "with the peace of God in our conscience, with our hearts free from evil and hatred, we will be able to bring to all true joy and true peace, which comes to us

from your Son, Our Lord Jesus Christ, who with God the Father and the Holy Spirit lives and reigns forever and ever. Amen."

The Era of Peace may seem to be slow in coming, but it is not being delayed. God only wants to give time for people to repent, convert, and return to Him. Many will convert, even from among those who now deny the existence of God.

St. John Paul II said, "I once more express my conviction, born of faith, that God is even now preparing a great springtime for the Gospel." (Pope John Paul II, *Address to U.S. Bishops of Boston and Hartford*, September 2, 2004).

After the Great Chastisement and the cleansing action of God's justice, Satan will be vanquished and humanity will live holy lives, almost without sin, almost a regaining of Paradise, which had been lost by the Original Sin of Adam and Eve. Unceasing love, happiness, and divine joy will signify this future clean world.

St. John Paul II said, "God wants to restore in creation the original harmony that He established *'in the beginning'*....A creation in which God and man, man and woman, humanity and nature are in harmony, in dialogue, in communion. This plan, upset by sin, was taken up in a more wondrous way by Christ, who is carrying it out mysteriously but effectively in the present reality, in the expectation of bringing it to fulfillment." (Pope John Paul II, *General Audience*, February 14, 2001).

On May 13, 1995, the anniversary of her first apparition at Fatima, Our Lady prophesied to Fr. Gobbi that St. John Paul II would announce the era [of peace] that would spring up after the purification of the earth.

She said, "It is precisely through the sacrifice of this, the first of my beloved sons [St. John Paul II], that divine justice will be espoused to a great mercy. After the time of the trial, which will be one of purification for all the earth, there will spring up upon the world the New Era foretold and announced by him [St. John Paul II]; and thus, in these final times, he invites you all to cross the bright thresholds of hope." (*To the Priests* 545).

Using almost the same exact language, several years later, St. John Paul II wrote in *The Church in America*, "Now is the time of the New Evangelization to lead the People of God in America to cross the threshold of the third millennium with renewed hope."

Later, he announced the New Era that Our Lady had prophesied
would be announced by him. He wrote,

**At the dawn of the new millennium, we wish to propose
once more the message of hope which comes from the
stable of Bethlehem: God loves all men and women on
earth and gives them the hope of a new era, an Era of
Peace.**

His love, fully revealed in the Incarnate Son, is the
foundation of universal peace. When welcomed in the
depths of the human heart, this love reconciles people with
God and with themselves, renews human relationships,
and stirs that desire for brotherhood capable of banishing
the temptation of violence and war. (Pope John Paul II,
*Message of Pope John Paul II for the Celebration of the World Day
of Peace*, January 1, 2000).

St. John Paul II talked about this New Era again at an *Address*,
on September 10, 2003,

God, in fact, is not indifferent before good and evil; He
enters mysteriously the scene of human history with His
judgment which, sooner or later, will unmask evil, defend
the victims, and indicate the way of justice....

However, the object of God's action is never ruin, pure
and simple condemnation, the annihilation of the sinner. It
is the prophet Ezekiel himself who refers to these divine
words, "Do I indeed derive any pleasure from the death of
the wicked?...Do I not rather rejoice when he turns from his
evil way that he may live?...For I have no pleasure in the
death of anyone who dies, says the Lord God. Return and
live!" (Ezekiel 18:23, 32).

In this light, one can understand the meaning of our
canticle, brimming with hope and salvation. **After the
purification through trial and suffering, the dawn of a
New Era is about to begin,** which the prophet Jeremiah
already announced when speaking of a "new covenant"
between the Lord and Israel. (See Jeremiah 31:31–34).

**Our Lady described the New Era to Fr. Gobbi, on the Solemnity
of the Assumption, August 15, 1991, as the defeat of Satan and his
universal reign where "Christ reigns in the splendor of His**

glorified body, and the Immaculate Heart of your Heavenly Mother triumphs in the light of her body, assumed into the glory of Paradise." She said,

The New Era, which awaits you, corresponds to a particular encounter of love, of light, and of life between Paradise, where I am in perfect blessedness with the angels and the saints, and earth, where you, my children, live in the midst of many dangers and innumerable tribulations. This is the heavenly Jerusalem, which comes down from heaven upon earth, to transform it completely, and to thus shape the new heavens and the new earth.

The New Era, toward which you are journeying, is bringing all creation to the perfect glorification of the Most Holy Trinity. The Father receives His greatest glory from every creature which reflects His light, His love, and His divine splendor. The Son restores His Reign of grace and of holiness, setting free every creature from the slavery of evil and of sin. The Holy Spirit pours out in fullness His holy gifts, leads to the understanding of the whole truth, and renews the face of the earth.

The New Era, which I announce to you, coincides with the complete fulfillment of the Divine Will, so that at last there is coming about that which Jesus taught you to ask for, from the Heavenly Father: "your Will be done, on earth as it is in heaven." [Matthew 6:10]. This is the time when the Divine Will of the Father, the Son, and of the Holy Spirit is being accomplished by the creatures. From the perfect fulfillment of the Divine Will, the whole world is becoming renewed, because God finds there, as it were, His new Garden of Eden, where He can dwell in loving companionship with His creatures.

The New Era, which is just now beginning, brings to you a full communion of life with those who have preceded you and who, here in Paradise, enjoy perfect happiness. You see the splendor of the heavenly hierarchy; you communicate with the saints of Paradise; you relieve the purifying sufferings of the souls who are still in purgatory. You experience, in a strong and visible way, the consoling truth of the communion of saints.

The Triumph of the Immaculate Heart of Mary, the New Pentecost, and the Era of Peace

The New Era, which I am preparing for you, coincides with the defeat of Satan and of his universal reign. All his power is destroyed. He is bound, with all the wicked spirits, and shut up in hell, from which he will not be able to get out to do harm in the world. Herein, Christ reigns in the splendor of His glorified body, and the Immaculate Heart of your Heavenly Mother triumphs in the light of her body, assumed into the glory of Paradise.

In the midst of the innumerable sufferings of the times through which you are living, you look upon me as a sign of sure hope and of consolation, because I am the luminous door which opens up the New Era that has been prepared for you by the most Holy Trinity. (*To the Priests* 453).

The remnant survivors of the Great Chastisement, the beneficiaries of the Triumph of the Immaculate Heart of Mary and the New Pentecost, will live in the New Era that includes not only peace, but the Great Renewal of the Holy Church, of Mankind, and of All Creation. The Kingdom of God will be restored with the Reign of Jesus King of All Nations and the ultimate defeat of the power of Satan. There will be one flock, with one shepherd, in a Kingdom of love, peace, and joy in the Civilization of Love for which St. John Paul II always prayed.

15. The Great Renewal of the Holy Church, of Mankind, and of All Creation

T.S. Eliot, a British author considered one of the 20th century's major poets, wrote, "The World is trying the experiment of attempting to form a civilized but non-Christian mentality. The experiment will fail; but we must be very patient in awaiting its collapse; meanwhile redeeming the time: so that the Faith may be preserved alive through the dark ages before us; to renew and rebuild civilization, and save the World from suicide." (T. S. Eliot, *Thoughts after Lambeth*, 1931).

Jesus King of All Nations said, "I promised by holy covenant never to flood the earth in totality again; no, this time my all-holy justice shall come through fire.

"So greatly does this world require divine cleansing that only by means of the purifying power of fire shall it be renewed and its soil, the soil of the heart of man, emerge rich and fertile, ready to receive the seed of the divine Word and thus produce a harvest of holiness and virtue. **A good and holy people shall the remnant be. Repent, for time is even shorter than before."** (*Journal* 453, 455, 462).

St. John the Evangelist wrote, "Then I saw a new heaven and a new earth. The former heaven and the former earth had passed away, and the sea was no more....[for] the old order has passed away. The one who sat on the throne said, **'Behold, I make all things new.'"** (Revelation 21:1–5).

The hope of the Great Renewal of the holy Church began in the 17th century when Our Lady prophesied to Mother Mariana de Jesus Torres, at Quito, Ecuador, that during the twentieth century the Church would "find herself attacked by terrible hordes of the Masonic sect....The vices of impurity, blasphemy, and sacrilege will dominate in this time of depraved desolation."

However, she promised a complete restoration. In February 1634, she said, "There will be occasions in which everything will

seem to be lost and paralyzed. **This will be, then, the happy beginning of the complete restoration.**"

In the late 20th century, Our Lady told Gladys Quiroga de Motta, at San Nicolas, Argentina, "A new time has begun. A new hope has born; attach yourselves to this hope. **The very intense light of Christ is going to be reborn, for just as on Calvary, after Crucifixion and death, the Resurrection took place, the Church too will be born again through the strength of love.**"

St. Louis de Montfort wrote, "We are given reason to believe that, toward the end of time and perhaps sooner than we expect, God will raise up people filled with the Holy Spirit and imbued with the spirit of Mary. Through them, **Mary, Queen most powerful, will work great wonders in the world, destroying sin and setting up the Kingdom of Jesus, her Son, upon the ruins of the corrupt kingdom which is this great earthly Babylon.** (Revelation 18:20)." (St. Louis de Montfort, *Treatise on True Devotion to the Blessed Virgin*, 58–59). "Is it not true that your Will must be done on earth as it is in heaven. Is it not true that your Kingdom must come? **Did you not give to some souls, dear to you, a vision of the future renewal of the Church?**" (St. Louis de Montfort, *Prayer for Missionaries*, 5).

Pope Leo XIII said,

> We have attempted and persistently carried out during a long pontificate toward two chief ends: in the first place, toward the restoration, both in rulers and peoples, of the principles of the Christian life in civil and domestic society, since there is no true life for men except from Christ; and, secondly, to promote the reunion of those who have fallen away from the Catholic Church either by heresy or by schism, since it is most undoubtedly the Will of Christ that all should be united in one flock under one Shepherd. (Pope Leo XIII, *Divinum Illud Munus (On the Holy Spirit)*, 10).

Pope Paul VI followed up on this and said, "The unity of the world will be. The dignity of the human person shall be recognized not only formally but effectively...Neither selfishness, nor arrogance, nor poverty...[shall] prevent the establishment of a true human order, a common good, a new civilization." (Pope Paul VI, *Urbi et Orbi (To the City and to the World)*, April 4, 1971).

St. John Paul II also expressed this hope and said, "This is our great hope and our invocation, 'Your Kingdom come!' —a Kingdom of peace, justice, and serenity, which will re-establish the original harmony of Creation." (Pope John Paul II, *General Audience*, November 6, 2002).

Our Lady told Fr. Gobbi, of the Marian Movement of Priests,

Through [priests who are faithful, those who listen to me, those who love me,] I will again shine more resplendently in the Church, after the great purification....The Mother has, from Jesus, the power to bring back home the children who have gone astray.

But I have need of humble and courageous priests, ready to let themselves be laughed at, ready to let themselves be trampled on for me.

It will be through these priests, humble, laughed at, and trampled on, that I will form the cohort that will make it possible for me to bring to Jesus an innumerable number of children, now purified by the great tribulation.

And it will be a new Church where my Son Jesus will reign at last! (*To the Priests* 10).

Mystic Edson Glauber, of Itapiranga, Brazil, received several messages from Mary and Jesus concerning the Great Renewal. These messages include that the Lord is returning to fulfil all His promises and also the following messages,

His Kingdom on earth will be as it is in heaven. (July 8, 2000). Strive for the Kingdom of Heaven; not long remains before your and the world's definitive liberation from all evil. God is sending me, your most holy Mother, in order to prepare you for the great final battle against all evil....You are already in the times of the great transformations of the world and the Lord God is already marking His chosen ones, those who are obedient to heaven's voice. (September 29, 2003). I desire [to have] saints for my Kingdom of Love. **The earth will yet be a great paradise. First will come the sorrows, but then will come the great transformation, when all will be renewed and all things will be made new. Humanity will be revived in love and peace. Thus, my Kingdom on earth will be as in heaven.** (March 23, 2004).

There will be no more suffering. There will be no more weeping. God will wipe away the tears of all those who hope with patience and do not lose faith. Little children, take heart. Courage. A while more and everything will be transformed. (August 7, 2005).

Our Lady told Fr. Gobbi, "After the time of the great suffering, there will be the time of the great rebirth and all will return. Humanity a new garden of life and of beauty. The Church a family. Oh yes! Enlightened by truth, nourished by grace, consoled by the presence of the Spirit! Jesus will restore His glorious Reign. He will dwell with you. You will know the new times, the New Era. You will see a new earth and new heavens." (*To the Priests* 357).

The renewed Church, cleansed by sufferings, will again be clothed in humility and simplicity and will be poor as at her beginning. After the chastisements, there may be no means of constructing great buildings and wearing ornate clothing. There will be no striving for money, power, fame, and glory. There will be only one flock and one shepherd as Jesus prophesied. The Blessed Virgin Mary will be the Mediatrix of All Graces and the Queen of the New Era.

Throughout history, God periodically renewed the earth and humanity through certain people who found favor with Him. During the period of the rampant corruption of the world before the Great Flood, Noah found favor with God and God protected him and his family from the Flood and chose Noah to be the head of a renewed humanity.

During the period of idol worship in Ur, Abraham found favor with God and God chose him to leave Ur and to be the Patriarch of a renewed humanity in the Promised Land.

During the period of the Jews' enslavement in Egypt, Moses found favor with God and God chose him to lead the Jews out of Egypt to the Promised Land, in a covenant relationship with Him.

During the period of the Roman occupation of the Promised Land, Jesus Christ found favor with God the Father who chose Him to lead all of humanity to eternal life in a new covenant relationship with Him through the forgiveness of sins.

Now, in the period of the apparent triumph of Secularism, Jesus King of All Nations promises us that, after the Great Chastisement, there will come the Great Renewal of the Holy Church, of Mankind, and of All Creation.

On May 20, 2012, Jesus King of All Nations said,

> Therefore, let it also be known that a Great Renewal of my Holy Church, of Mankind, and, indeed, of All Creation will follow the cleansing action of my justice. How greatly I love my people! It is for your good, O mankind, that I allow my justice to be poured out in order to awaken your conscience and correct your sinful behavior. Yet you see how dearly I love you in that I continually warn you and even seek to comfort you in the pain of the cleansing which is almost upon you.

> Return to me, my people. I love you infinitely and eternally for such is my very nature as God; the one true God, the sovereign King of all that is.

> Pray and trust in me, my faithful ones. I will not abandon you in the dark and cloudy day which rapidly approaches. Stay close to my Immaculate Mother; cling to her holy Rosary; invoke her Immaculate Heart.

> Take up my Devotion of Jesus King of All Nations for in its practice you shall find for yourselves a haven of grace, mercy, and protection. Enthrone this my Image everywhere, for I shall be powerfully present there and the power of my sovereign Kingship shall surely shield you from my just judgment.

> Be strong and do not lose hope. I AM with you to save you. (*Journal* 414–419).

Jesus echoed this message of hope, on December 13, 2016,

> Do not lose hope my children. Though it seems all is lost, it is not so. I AM the Lord and Master of History and the times ever unfold under the power of my almighty hand.

> Trust in me and stay strong in the holy faith. I love you. I will never leave you or fail you for I AM faithful and true. (*Journal* 798, 800).

Jesus King of All Nations also said, "I correct my children out of love for them. I delight not in the suffering of my children. **I desire to awaken their darkened consciences that they may** recognize their sinfulness and **be converted that there may be a renewal of hearts and minds thereby causing the world itself to be renewed."** (*Journal* 370).

"**The earth shall be renewed. The blight of sin eradicated. This will result from the Triumph of the Immaculate Heart of Mary. Stand firm in the holy faith.**" (*Journal* 349–350).

So, let us respond to Jesus' requests: be hopeful, stay strong in the faith, trust Him, implore His mercy, and pray to survive the prophesied Great Chastisement and to be a part of the remnant, the Triumph of the Immaculate Heart of Mary, the New Pentecost, and the Great Renewal of hearts and minds, of the Holy Church, of Mankind, and of All Creation that Jesus has promised. It will not be the end of the world that is coming, but the end of the era of the Culture of Death and the beginning of an Era of Peace and the Great Renewal of the Church.

The Great Chastisement, the Great Renewal, and the Era of Peace may be similar to what the prophet Haggai prophesied. He said, "This is what the Lord Almighty says, 'In a little while I will once more shake the heavens and the earth, the sea and the dry land. I will shake all nations, and what is desired by all nations will come, and I will fill this house with glory,' says the Lord Almighty. '…The glory of this present house will be greater than the glory of the former house,' says the Lord Almighty. 'And in this place, I will grant peace,' declares the Lord Almighty." (Haggai 2:6–9).

The Great Renewal of the Church will come with the renewal of the priesthood. It will begin when priests live in the friendship of Jesus from a great return to the adoration of His real presence in the Eucharist.

In 2007, Jesus began to give a series of revelations in the form of heart-to-heart locutions to a priest who adored Him in the Blessed Sacrament. The priest compiled the locutions into a journal with the title *In Sinu Iesu (In the Bosom of Jesus).* **These words come from the Latin and refer to how St. John reclined on Jesus' Heart during the Last Supper.** (See John 13:23).

Jesus told the priest, "All of heaven weeps over the sins of my priests which are a grievous affront to my own priesthood. Every time a priest sins, he sins directly against me and against the most Holy Eucharist toward which his whole being is ordered. When a priest approaches my altar laden with sins that have not been confessed or for which he has not repented, my angels look on with horror, my Mother grieves, and I am again wounded in my hands and my feet and in my Heart."

Jesus told the priest that there would be a renewal of the priesthood. He said, "I am about to renew the priesthood of my Church in holiness. I am very close to cleansing my priests of the impurities that defile them. Soon, very soon, I will pour out graces of spiritual healing upon all my priests. I will separate those who will accept the gift of my divine friendship from those who will harden their hearts against me. Those who do not live in my friendship betray me and impede my work. They detract from the beauty of holiness that I would see shine in my Church."

Jesus explained to the priest,

If priests lived in my friendship, how different my Church would be...Many of the sufferings and hardships experienced with my Church at the hands of her ministers, my priests, would not exist.

Even after two thousand years of Eucharistic presence in my Church, I remain unknown, forgotten, forsaken, and treated like a thing to be kept here or there. Priests keep themselves apart from me. Their lives are compartmentalized. They treat with me only when duty obliges them to do so. Because of their loneliness, they look for love in other places and in creatures unworthy of the undivided love of their consecrated hearts to fill the emptiness within with vain pursuits, with lust, with possessions, with food and drink.

The sins of my priests call for reparation. The renewal of my priesthood in the Church will proceed from a great return to the adoration of my real presence in this the Sacrament of my love [the Eucharist]. This is the remedy for the evil that has so disfigured my holy priesthood in the Church. I want priest adorers and reparators, priests who will adore for priests who do not adore, priests who will make reparation for priests who do not make reparation for themselves or for others. Priests will be renewed in holiness and purity when they begin to seek me out in the Sacrament of my love.

The great renewal of the priesthood in my Church will begin when priests understand that I want them to live in the company of my Immaculate Mother. I will pour out the Holy Spirit upon all priests in the form of a purifying fire. Those who welcome that fire will emerge from it like gold from the furnace, shining with holiness and with a wonderful purity for all to see. Those who refuse my fire will be consumed by it.

The renewal of the priesthood and of all creation may bring it back to its primal splendor in such a way that the Heavenly Father may again be pleased to be reflected in it and to receive His greatest glory from all creation. The Immaculate Heart of Mary will prepare a little remnant who remain faithful to Christ, to the Gospel, and to the Church and with whom Jesus will bring about His glorious Reign in the world.

The Great Renewal of the Holy Church, of Mankind, and of All Creation was described by Our Lady to Fr. Gobbi. She said, "The time has come when the desert of this world will be renewed by the merciful love of the Father who, in the Holy Spirit, desires to draw all to the divine Heart of the Son so that His Reign of truth and grace, of love, of justice and peace may at last shine in the world. The Church and the world will thus be able to attain a splendor which they have never before known." (*To the Priests* 164).

On the Feast of Christ the King, Our Lady told Fr. Gobbi, "Jesus Christ is King, because it pertains to His divine mission to bring the created universe back to the perfect glorification of the Father, purifying it with the burning fire of the Holy Spirit, in such a way that it may become completely freed of every spirit of evil, of every shadow of sin, and thus be able to open itself to the enchantment of a new earthly paradise. Then will the Father be glorified and His name be held holy by all creation. In this creation, renewed by a perfect communion of life with the Father, Jesus Christ will restore His Reign of glory, so that the work of His divine redemption may attain its perfect fulfillment.

"The Holy Spirit will open hearts and minds in such a way that all will be able to carry out the Will of the Father and the Son, so that, as in heaven so also on earth, the Divine Will may be perfectly accomplished." (*To the Priests* 482).

Our Lady reaffirmed these prophecies of the Great Renewal of the Holy Church, of Mankind, and of All Creation when she told Fr. Gobbi,

> My victory is being accomplished in the Church, which I enlighten with my faith, assist with my presence, and comfort with my motherly tenderness. I myself am leading her by the hand, in this time of the purification, toward her greatest splendor which will reclothe her, making of her the greatest light for all the nations of the earth....
>
> My complete victory will come about with the Triumph of my Immaculate Heart in the world. Then the miracle of divine mercy, in the power of the Holy Spirit, will renew the face of the earth and it will again become a fragrant and precious garden in which the most Holy Trinity will be pleased to be reflected and will receive from the whole created universe its greatest glory. (*To the Priests* 554).

Jesus King of All Nations said that He would send "the cleansing fire of His love. A fire ablaze with the love and justice of God. Then shall the earth emerge cleansed from the defilement of sin and souls shall rejoice as they bathe anew in the copious mercy of God." (*Journal* 496, 498).

Elizabeth Kindelmann of Hungary received messages from Jesus and Mary for all the world. These messages received the *Imprimatur* of Cardinal Peter Erdő on June 6, 2009.

Our Lady revealed to Elizabeth that, as Mediatrix of All Graces, she will share that "Grace of Union with God," with which her Immaculate Heart is filled, with mankind in order to incapacitate Satan's power, which is leading more and more souls to damnation.

This "great effusion of grace which she wants to extend to the whole world" will be "the greatest outpouring of grace since the Word became flesh" and will be "comparable to the first Pentecost." She will "place the healing power of her maternal goodness at the root of evil" and heal the sense of separation from God that we feel in our fallen state.

She said that this will be an era of grace never known before on earth. However, because of our free will, in order for her to give us this grace, we must ask for it. She requested that, in order to bring this day closer, we should pray to her, "Blessed Mother, save us by means of the Flame of Love of thy Immaculate Heart!" and include this petition in the "Hail Mary" by praying, "...pray for us sinners, and spread the effect of grace of thy Immaculate Heart's Flame of Love over all of humanity, now and at the hour of our death. Amen." Our Blessed Mother asked that "as many as know my name, I want that they know that this I will do!"

Jesus told Elizabeth that the grace from the Flame of Love of the Immaculate Heart of Mary will be "the greatest grace given to mankind since the Incarnation" and "will be to your generation what Noah's Ark was to Noah." Jesus said that this great miracle will be a torrential flood of grace similar to the first Pentecost and also a renewal of the earth, as Jesus King of All Nations had also prophesied.

Our Lady said,

> The Flame of Love full of blessings springing from my Immaculate Heart...must go from heart to heart. It will be the great miracle of light blinding Satan. It is the fire of love and peace among men; and we will suppress fire with fire: the fire of heat with the fire of love, so that many souls can be saved from eternal damnation. I am asserting that there has never been before such a similar outpouring. It is the greatest miracle I am doing. I obtained this grace on your behalf from the Eternal Father by virtue of the five blessed wounds of my divine Son.

Jesus said,

> **I could compare this torrential flood of grace to the first Pentecost. It will submerge the earth by the power of the Holy Spirit. All mankind will take heed at the time of this great miracle. The torrential flow of the Flame of Love of my most holy Mother is coming. The world which is darkened already by a lack of faith will undergo formidable tremors and then people will believe!....This renewing of the earth tested by suffering will take place through the power and imploring force of the Blessed Virgin!**

Our Lady told Fr. Gobbi,

The glorious Reign of Christ is…to establish His Reign in your midst and to bring all humanity, redeemed by His most precious blood, back to the state of His new terrestrial paradise. (*To the Priests* 435).

And Jesus will reign! Jesus, for whom all has been created. Jesus, who became incarnate, who became your brother, who lived with you, who suffered and died on the Cross to bring humanity to a new creation through the gift of the redemption and so that His Reign might slowly spread itself from the depths—from hearts—to souls, to individuals, to families, to society.

Jesus, who taught you the prayer, the daily prayer, in order to invoke the coming of His Reign upon earth, will at last see fulfilled this prayer of His. He will reign. He will restore His Reign and this creation will return, as a garden where Christ will be glorified, where His Kingship will be welcoming and exalted. This will be a universal Reign of grace, of beauty, of harmony, of communion, of sanctity and justice, and of peace. (*To the Priests* 357).

Your Heavenly Mother wants to enfold each one of you in the secure refuge of her Immaculate Heart, to protect you in the time of the great trial, and to prepare you to receive Jesus, who is about to return to establish His glorious Reign among you.…

The glorious Reign of Christ will be established after the complete defeat of Satan and all the spirits of evil and the destruction of Satan's diabolical power. Thus, he will be bound and cast into hell, and the gates of the abyss will be shut so that he can no longer get out to harm the world. And Christ will reign in the world.

The glorious Reign of Christ will coincide with the triumph of the Eucharistic Reign of Jesus, because in a purified and sanctified world, completely renewed by love, Jesus will be made manifest above all in the mystery of His Eucharistic presence.

The Eucharist will be the source from which will burst forth all His divine power, and it will become the new sun, which will shed its bright rays in hearts and souls, and then in the life of individuals, families, and nations, making of all one single flock, docile and meek, whose sole shepherd will be Jesus. Your Heavenly Mother is leading you on toward these new heavens and this new earth, a Mother who is gathering you today from every part of the world, to prepare you to receive the Lord who is coming. (*To the Priests* 505).

That which is being prepared is so great that its equal has never existed since the creation of the world. Prepare yourselves with humility, with faith, with intense prayer. Prepare yourself by gathering together, each and all, in the spiritual cenacle of my Immaculate Heart. Prepare yourselves in silence and in expectation. (*To the Priests* 435).

Let us meditate on Psalm 96,

I

Sing to the Lord a new song;
    sing to the Lord, all the earth.
Sing to the Lord, bless His name;
    proclaim His salvation day after day.
Tell His glory among the nations;
    among all peoples, His marvelous deeds.

II

For great is the Lord and highly to be praised,
    to be feared above all gods.
For the gods of the nations are idols,
    but the Lord made the heavens.
Splendor and power go before Him;
    power and grandeur are in His holy place.

III

Give to the Lord, you families of nations,
  give to the Lord glory and might;
  give to the Lord the glory due His name!
Bring gifts and enter His courts;
  bow down to the Lord, splendid in holiness.
Tremble before Him, all the earth;
  declare among the nations: The Lord is King.
The world will surely stand fast, never to be shaken.
  He rules the peoples with fairness.

IV

Let the heavens be glad and the earth rejoice;
  let the sea and what fills it resound;
  let the plains be joyful and all that is in them.
Then let all the trees of the forest rejoice
  before the Lord who comes,
  who comes to govern the earth,
To govern the world with justice
  and the peoples with faithfulness.

In silence, and in expectation, let us confidently await in hope the Triumph of the Immaculate Heart of Mary, the New Pentecost, the Era of Peace, the Great Renewal of the Holy Church, of Mankind, and of All Creation, and the glorious Reign of Jesus King of All Nations.

16. Hope for the World

"But this I call to mind, and therefore I have hope: The steadfast love of the Lord never ceases, His mercies are new every morning...For the Lord will not cast off forever, but, though He cause grief, He will have compassion according to the abundance of His steadfast love for He does not willingly afflict or grieve the sons of men." (Lamentations 3:21–22, 31–32).

Even though the Great Chastisement is imminent, we are called to be hopeful and to take heart and realize that our efforts are not in vain. Jesus King of All Nations said, "Do you know, my little one, that if it were not for the love of the faithful few, my Father would have long ago destroyed the earth which is full of the guilt of sin? My child, make known this truth to my faithful children, so that they may take heart and realize that your lives of love and prayer are not in vain. Indeed, they are helping to save the world and to restore it to the beauty with which its Creator endowed it." (*Journal* 301).

On September 12, 2001, the day after the 9/11 Attack on America, St. John Paul II addressed the pilgrims gathered in St. Peter's Square, Rome,

> Yesterday was a dark day in the history of humanity, a terrible affront to human dignity. After receiving the news, I followed with intense concern the developing situation, with heartfelt prayers to the Lord. How is it possible to commit acts of such savage cruelty? The human heart has depths from which schemes of unheard-of ferocity sometimes emerge, capable of destroying in a moment the normal daily life of a people.

> But faith comes to our aid at these times when words seem to fail. Christ's Word is the only one that can give a response to the questions which trouble our spirit. **Even if the forces of darkness appear to prevail, those who believe in God know that evil and death do not have the final say.**

Christian hope is based on this truth; at this time our prayerful trust draws strength from it.

Through the prophet Jeremiah, God announced, "I know well the plans I have in mind for you, says the Lord, for your welfare, not for woe! Plans to give you a future full of hope." (Jeremiah 29:11). While the Jews suffered from the chastisement of the Babylonian Captivity, they received hope from Jeremiah that they would one day return to their homeland in Israel. (See Jeremiah chapter 30).

Jeremiah said, "Thus says the Lord, Cease your cries of mourning, wipe the tears from your eyes. The sorrow you have sown shall have its reward, says the Lord, they shall return from the enemy's land. There is hope for your future, says the Lord; your sons shall return to their own borders." (Jeremiah 31:16–17).

St. Paul wrote, "Hope will not leave us disappointed, because the love of God has been poured out in our hearts through the Holy Spirit who has been given to us." (Romans 5:5). "Hope is the confident expectation of divine blessing." (CCC 2090).

When I interviewed Mirjana, the Medjugorje visionary, I asked her if she had this same confidence that we will receive God's blessing. She said, "Yes, yes, because God is my Father and He loves us and He sends His Mother for so many years here to Medjugorje to help us to find Jesus, to find a good way, where we will meet Jesus and have real peace. Look at me. I am always joking, smiling, living my life with God and Blessed Mary with hope, because my faith is hope. I hope in God's love. I hope that He will judge me with love, I don't think about secrets."

Cardinal Ratzinger, later Pope Benedict XVI, wrote, "The vision of the third part of the 'secret' [of Fatima], so distressing at first, concludes with an image of hope: no suffering is in vain, and it is a suffering Church, a Church of martyrs, which becomes a signpost for man in his search for God." (Cardinal Joseph Ratzinger, *Theological Commentary*, May 13, 2000).

St. John Paul II recognized signs of hope for the world. He said, "With full confidence, let us place under the vigilant intercession of Holy Mary...the prospect of the third millennium. The third millennium remains for us a horizon of very stimulating reflections, because it makes us look forward in hope. The Blessed Mary is the guide in the new exodus toward the future."

In his Apostolic Letter, *On the Coming of the Third Millennium*, Pope John Paul II wrote, "Only God knows what the future holds. But we are certain that He is the Lord of history and directs it to His own end with our cooperation in hope. It will be the fulfillment of a divine plan of love for all humanity and for each one of us. That is why, as we look into the future, we are full of hope and are not overcome with fear. The journey...is a great journey of hope."

"Hope is the theological virtue by which we desire the Kingdom of Heaven and eternal life as our happiness, placing our trust in Christ's promises and relying not on our own strength, but on the help of the grace of the Holy Spirit." (CCC 1817).

Pope Benedict XVI said, "Jesus, with His death on the Cross and His Resurrection, has revealed to us His countenance, the countenance of a God so great in love as to communicate to us an indestructible hope, a hope that not even death can crack, because the life of those who entrust themselves to this Father always opens up to the perspective of eternal beatitude." (Pope Benedict XVI, *Angelus Address*, December 2, 2007). Pope Benedict called Mary the "Star of Hope" because she leads the way to Jesus Christ, the true light.

While our hope is placed in the eternal city, yet we must labor in the earthly city and transmit hope for its peace. This was what St. Augustine did during the fall of the Roman Empire. Pope Benedict wrote about what St. Augustine did. "Amid the serious difficulties facing the Roman Empire—and also posing a serious threat to Roman Africa, which was actually destroyed at the end of Augustine's life—this was what he set out to do: to transmit hope, the hope which came to him from faith and which, in complete contrast with his introverted temperament, enabled him to take part decisively and with all his strength in the task of building up the city." (St. Augustine, *Spe Salvi (Saved by Hope)*, 23).

This task of "building up the city" is hope-in-action through which we strive to realize our lesser and greater hopes and to work toward a better city and world. In "building up the city," we need the greater and lesser hopes that keep us going day by day. "But these are not enough," Pope Benedict concluded, "without the great hope, which must surpass everything else. This great hope can only be God, who encompasses the whole of reality and who can bestow upon us what we, by ourselves, cannot attain." (St. Augustine, *Spe Salvi (Saved by Hope)*, 31).

Jesus King of All Nations gave a message to the Secretary's Spiritual Mother entitled *The Source and Culmination of Hope.* He said, "O mankind, see the covenant of hope, my blood poured out over all souls for your salvation. Am I not the source of hope? The Alpha and the Omega, the beginning and the end of every rainbow?"

Mary is the Mother of Hope. She is the Mother of Jesus Christ who is our hope as the conqueror of sin and death. As a people of hope, we are not afraid, but look forward to the victory of good over evil, peace over war, truth over lies, love over hate, and life over death. We look forward to the Triumph of the Immaculate Heart of Mary, the New Pentecost, the Era of Peace, and the Great Renewal of the Holy Church, of Mankind, and of All Creation, the glorious Reign of Christ, and the return to the state of His new terrestrial paradise, eternal salvation, and an existence full of happiness in God.

St. John Paul II wrote, "God is preparing a great springtime for Christianity, and we can already see its first signs....Christian hope sustains us in committing ourselves fully to the new evangelization and to the worldwide mission, and leads us to pray as Jesus taught us, 'Thy Will be done, on earth as it is in heaven.' (Matthew 6:10)." (Pope John Paul II, *Redemptor Missio (Mission of the Redeemer)*, 86).

He also said, "This is our great hope and our invocation, 'Your Kingdom come!' — a Kingdom of peace, justice, and serenity, which will re-establish the original harmony of Creation." (Pope John Paul II, *General Audience*, November 6, 2002).

This hope reminds us of Our Lady of Guadalupe's assurance to St. Juan Diego, "Do not fear any illness or vexation, anxiety or pain. Am I not here who am your Mother?" Our Lady of Guadalupe is the Star of the New Evangelization and, as our Mother of Hope, she leads us in hope as we entrust ourselves with all of our hearts to God's great and generous promises.

In his Apostolic Letter, *On the Coming of the Third Millennium*, **St. John Paul II closed his remarks and wrote, "Christians are called to prepare...by renewing their hope in the definitive coming of the Kingdom of God, preparing for it daily in their hearts in the Christian community to which they belong, in their particular social context, and in the world of history itself."**

Jesus King of All Nations reminded us of this hope and said, "Do not lose hope but trust ever more strongly in my mercy, power, and love. I AM in absolute control. I AM the Almighty, the King of All Nations." (*Journal* 764). **"Nothing is wasted my children. It is all gathered up into the treasury of my Most Sacred Heart and applied to the redemption of souls and of the world."** (*Journal* 763).

Jesus concluded, "Take up my Devotion of Jesus King of All Nations, for in its practice you shall find for yourselves a haven of grace, mercy, and protection. Enthrone my Image everywhere, for I shall be powerfully present there and the power of my sovereign Kingship shall surely shield you from my just judgment. Be strong and do not lose hope. I AM with you to save you." (*Journal* 418–419).

So, we confidently await in hope what St. John Paul II called "the definitive coming of the Kingdom of God" and heed the words of Jesus King of All Nations, "Pray, pray, pray! Do not lose hope my people! Do not surrender your holy faith! Stay close to me in the Holy Eucharist! Stay close to me through my Immaculate Mother! I AM here for you! I AM here with you! Trust in me utterly for I love you!" (*Journal* 468).

17. What We Should Do

Secularist states representing the Kingdom of Satan have been at war against the Kingdom of God since Jesus Christ was a baby and King Herod tried to kill Him. The prophet Simeon prophesied at the Presentation of the infant Jesus in the Temple that He would be a sign of contradiction.

That was because Jesus would later say, "I am the way, the truth, and the life" and "I am a King, but my Kingdom is not of this world." Jesus stood in direct contradiction to the Secularist State of Rome as the King of the Kingdom of God and contradicted Caesar, the head of the Kingdom of Satan, including those who said to Pontius Pilate, "We have no king but Caesar."

The enemies of Jesus came for Him and arrested Him in the Garden of Gethsemane, tortured Him, and crucified Him. They came for Jesus' subjects during King Herod's persecution of 42 AD and arrested and killed many of them. They came for His subjects during the persecutions of the Roman emperors and killed many of them.

After the fall of the Roman emperors, Christendom reigned for over the 1300 years without any persecutions against the Kingdom of God until the French Revolution of 1789, when they killed King Louis XVI and the French Catholics in the Reign of Terror and in the genocide of the Vendée region. Then came Jesus, in 1840, who identified His enemies to Sr. Mary of St. Peter as the Freemasons, Socialists, and Communists.

In 1917, the Blessed Virgin Mary came from heaven and appeared to three young children at Fatima, Portugal. She prophesied that Russia, then on the verge of defeat in World War I, would spread her errors throughout the world. Then came the Russian Revolution with the murder of Czar Nicholas and his entire family and the persecution and killings of Christians and their clergy. This was followed by the racist Nazi National Socialists who did the same and, in addition, killed millions of innocent Jews.

As prophesied by Our Lady of Fatima, Russia spread throughout the world its errors of Socialism, Secularism, and atheistic materialism with the persecution and killings of Christians and their clergy that continues today in China, North Korea, Cuba, Vietnam, and Venezuela.

The modern Secularists in Europe and North America have begun to follow the practices of their Secularist predecessors. Christians suffer persecution from the intolerance of the Secularists and through their economic punishments of dissident Christians who refuse to recognize or follow their dictates to recognize evil as good, such as with contraception, abortion, homosexuality, same–sex false marriage, and false transgenderism. Like Jesus Christ and our Christian predecessors, we must stand in contradiction to them even if Christ's enemies come for us, as they did for Blessed Jerzy Popieluszko.

Fr. Jerzy was a martyred Polish priest. On October 19, 1984, he was tortured and assassinated by three Polish security services agents. Fr. Jerzy was an outspoken voice of the Church in Poland against the totalitarian Communist regime. He once said, "The priest is called to bear witness to the truth, to suffer for the truth, and if need be to give up his life for it."

During the early 1980s, Fr. Jerzy celebrated special Masses for the Polish patriots who were imprisoned under martial law for defending the dignity of the workers. These Masses were called Masses for the Country. He proposed a vision of freedom through non-violent psychological resistance at a time when fear and repression were the norm. Below are some of his quotes from some of those Masses, with the dates in parentheses.

A Christian fulfills his duties only when he is stalwart, when he professes his principles courageously, and he is neither ashamed of them nor renounces them because of fear or material needs. Woe betide a society whose citizens do not live by fortitude! They cease to be citizens and become more like slaves. It is fortitude which creates citizens, for only a courageous man is conscious of all his rights and duties. If a citizen lacks fortitude, he becomes a slave and causes immeasurable harm not only to himself but to his family, his country, and the Church. Woe betide State authorities who want to govern citizens by threats and fear! Fortitude is an essential part of one's life as a citizen. That is why fortitude is, for a Christian, the most important duty after love. (Fr. Jerzy Popieluszko, April 1983).

The essential thing in the process of liberating man in the nation is to overcome fear. Fear stems from threats. We fear suffering, we fear losing material goods, we fear losing freedom or our work. And then we act contrary to our consciences, thus muzzling the truth. **We can overcome fear only if we accept suffering in the name of a greater value. If the truth becomes for us a value worthy of suffering and risk, then we shall overcome fear—the direct reason for our enslavement. Christ told His followers, "Be not afraid of those who kill the body, and after that have no more that they can do."** (Luke 12:4). (Fr. Jerzy Popieluszko, October 1982).

As the children of God, we cannot be frightened slaves for Christ's Kingdom. We must believe that we will live through all the hard times and will reach a brighter future, but on condition that we are guided by greatness of spirit, courage of thought and action, that we are guided by law and conscience, truth and justice, by the consciousness that God loved the world so much that He gave His Son as an example. (Fr. Jerzy Popieluszko, June 1984).

St. Peter tells us,

Beloved, do not be surprised at the fiery ordeal which comes upon you to prove you, as though something strange were happening to you. But rejoice in so far as you share Christ's sufferings, that you may also rejoice and be glad when His glory is revealed.

If you are reproached for the name of Christ, you are blessed, because the spirit of glory and of God rests upon you. But let none of you suffer as a murderer, or a thief, or a wrongdoer, or a mischief-maker; yet if one suffers as a Christian, let him not be ashamed, but under that name let him glorify God. For the time has come for judgment to begin with the household of God; and if it begins with us, what will be the end of those who do not obey the Gospel of God?...Therefore, let those who suffer according to God's

Will do right and entrust their souls to a faithful Creator."
(1 Peter 4:12–19).

"According to the Lord, the present time is the time of the Spirit and of witness, but also a time still marked by 'distress' and the trial of evil which does not spare the Church and ushers in the struggles of the last days. It is a time of waiting and watching." (CCC 672).

Let us recognize the current crises in the Church and in the world as a purification from God. We have seen how God has shone His spotlight on the dark evil in the Church through the sexual abuse crises. We have seen how God has also shone His spotlight on the dark evil in the world through its sexual abuse crises in media, entertainment, and sports and in its governmental corruption.

In reality, we are not fighting only human beings, but demons as well. St. Paul tells us, "For our struggle is not against flesh and blood, but against the rulers, against the powers, against the world forces of this darkness, against the spiritual forces of wickedness in the heavenly places." (Ephesians 6:12).

Let us recognize, as St. Paul tells us, "God's household, which is the Church of the living God, the pillar and foundation of the truth." (1 Timothy 3:15). But, if the foundation weakens, the pillar and the Church will fall. However, **we have the promise of Christ that the gates of hell shall never prevail against His Church and we hope and believe that He will replace the broken pieces of its crumbling foundation with new and stronger ones in support of the pillar and the Church.**

God is in control! The crises in the Church and the world and all of His chastisements are part of His providential plan and His permissive Will, which He allows for the greater good of the Great Renewal of His Holy Church, of Mankind, and of All Creation.

Let us respond to the first words of St. John Paul II upon his acceptance of his papacy, on October 16, 1978, when he stepped onto the balcony at St. Peter's and said, "Be not afraid. Open our hearts to Christ."

Let us not be afraid of the world's mocking, rejection, or persecution of us. Let us say, as Jesus did, "Father forgive them, for they don't know what they're doing." (Luke 23:34). Let us not be angry or join the growing throng of apostates who are leaving the Church. As Peter said to Jesus, "Lord, to whom shall we go? You have the words of eternal life." (John 6:68).

"So then, brothers and sisters," as St. Paul writes, "stand firm and hold fast to the teachings we passed on to you, whether by word of mouth or by letter." (2 Thessalonians 2:15).

Since the Ascension of Jesus, God's plan has entered into its fulfillment. We are already at "the last hour." "Already the final age of the world is with us, and the renewal of the world is irrevocably under way; it is even now anticipated in a certain real way, for the Church on earth is endowed already with a sanctity that is real but imperfect." (CCC 670).

We can help perfect the sanctity of the Church by responding to St. John Paul II's *Plan for the Third Millennium* and his call for personal holiness.

As members of the lay faithful, we are called by our Baptism to be apostles to bring the Gospel message into the temporal realities of the world, such as our family, neighborhood, work, parish, culture, media, politics, sports, etc.

We are part of the priesthood of the laity who offer, by means of the hands of the priest in the Eucharist, Christ's body and blood, soul and divinity with our entire existence as praise and thanksgiving to God, as intercessors for the needs of the world, and in reparation and atonement for our sins and the sins of the whole world.

The Eucharist must be the source and summit of our Christian life. This leads to what St. Josemaría Escrivá called a "priestly soul and a lay mentality." From this Eucharistic source, we can propose the Gospel message as the best way to solve the personal and social problems of our times; as the best way to seek peace and justice in the family and among peoples; and as the best way to build what St. John Paul II called "a Culture of Life and a Civilization of Love."

As Lay Apostles, we are special in God's plan for the New Evangelization. Our mission is to allow the Sacred Heart of Jesus to flow through us as one of His arteries to bring His grace, mercy, and love to His body, the Church. We can each be a Lay Apostle!

We don't need any special education or training. We just need to be ourselves and practice our faith, hope, and love. But we should do more than we are doing now.

Here are the steps that we should take to be ready for the Great Chastisement,

1. Embrace the Jesus King of All Nations Devotion as He requested. He calls us to conversion and sanctification by turning away from sin to Him with our whole heart, mind, and soul. Repent, believe, convert, and ask with faith for His forgiveness and help.

   You may doubt that it's possible to convert. That is not true. Just remove your doubt and have faith that God can and will bring you to conversion and forgive you for your sins in the Sacrament of Confession with your true contrition and firm purpose of amendment. If you fall again, do not get discouraged, but rise up and return to the confessional and eventually God will free you from your sins.

2. Recognize the Reign of Jesus King of All Nations in your hearts, your minds, your souls, and on earth. Pray, offer sacrifices, and receive the sacraments, especially Confession and Eucharist, and adore Jesus in the Blessed Sacrament.

3. Pray the daily Rosary, the Chaplet of Divine Mercy, and the prayers revealed by Jesus King of All Nations. Wear His Medal, enthrone, display, and venerate His Image for your protection and practice devotion to St. Michael the Archangel and Our Lady, Mediatrix of All Graces, through our consecration to her. (Please see Appendix J, *How to Practice the Devotion*, on pg. 298.)

4. Do good and avoid evil—the basis of the moral law. Behave as Jesus asked in the Beatitudes and with a be-attitude: be poor in spirit, be meek, be for righteousness, be merciful, be clean of heart, be peacemakers, and be accepting of persecution for the sake of righteousness.

5. Practice Christian charity. Love one another. Help one another. Sacrifice yourselves.

6. Never fear or despair, because they destroy hope which is needed as the darkness and chastisements continue. Have faith and trust the promises of protection of Jesus King of All Nations.

7. Consecrate yourself to the Immaculate Heart of Mary and wear the Brown Scapular as a sign of your consecration.

8. Sacrifice through fasting on bread and water on Wednesdays and Fridays, if you are able, or make other acts of self-denial, such as renouncing addictive behavior, not watching television, or using computers, smartphones, smoking, drinking, etc.

9. Practice the First Friday Devotion of attending Mass and receiving Communion on nine consecutive First Fridays of the month in reparation for the offenses against the Sacred Heart of Jesus.

10. Practice the First Saturday Devotion of praying the Rosary, meditating for 15 minutes on the mysteries, attending Mass, and receiving Holy Communion in reparation for the offenses against the Immaculate Heart of Mary on five consecutive First Saturdays of the month with confession within eight days of each First Saturday.

11. Practice the First Wednesday Devotion in honor of St. Joseph by attending Mass and receiving Communion in the same way that he received the child Jesus in his home in Nazareth and by praying the Joyful Mysteries of the Rosary in honor of his protection of the Holy Family.

12. Learn the Catholic Church's teachings on faith and morals by reading the *Catechism of the Catholic Church* and the Scriptures.

13. Practice personal purity in our minds, our hearts, and our bodies, especially sexual purity.

14. Avoid persons, places, and things that are near occasions of sin.

For Our Home We Should,

1. Have our home blessed by a priest.

2. Enthrone the Image of Jesus King of All Nations for His promised protection of our homes.

3. Install and venerate the Image of Our Lady of America as her promised safeguard for our homes.

4. Pray the family Rosary and pray together every day as a family before meals. Use Holy Water to bless ourselves, our children, and our spouse.

5. Wear the Medal of Jesus King of All Nations for His promised protection from chastisements and the Medal of Our Lady of America for her promised protection from evil spirits.

6. Refrain from opening ourselves to demonic influences by viewing pornography, violence, and horror; by listening to demonic music; or by engaging in occult practices, such as horoscopes, fortune-telling, and demonic games, or violent video games.

We Should Practice Apostolic Action Such As,

1. Practice personal holiness, St. John Paul II's *Plan for the Third Millennium*. In *Novo Millennio Ineunte (At the Beginning of the New Millennium)*, he wrote,

   > We are certainly not seduced by the naive expectation that, faced with the great challenges of our time, we shall find some magic formula. No, we shall not be saved by a formula but by a person [Jesus Christ], and the assurance which He gives us: I am with you! This program for all times is our program for the third millennium. First of all, I have no hesitation in saying that all pastoral initiatives must be set in relation to holiness....Holiness remains more than ever an urgent pastoral task.

2. Be missionaries to the culture by speaking and writing seeds of truth in our own environment of family, neighbors, friends, and co-workers. You may be the only Gospel that someone ever sees or hears!

3. Communicate with your political representatives in favor of good laws and in protest against bad ones.

4. Communicate with the media or sponsors in protest against any immoral entertainment.

5. Serve in your parishes on the parish council, or as lector, usher, sacristan, singer, teacher of CCD, youth, or OCIA (formerly RCIA), in a prayer group or Scripture study group, or help with maintenance and repairs.

6. Serve in your communities by works of mercy of visiting the sick, the poor, and the prisoners, feeding the hungry, comforting the sorrowful, and instructing the ignorant.

7. Host a Visitation of the Missionary Image of Our Lady of Guadalupe to your parish or home.

8. Host a Visitation of an Image of Jesus King of All Nations to your parish or home.

9. Host a Visitation of an Image of Our Lady of America to your home.

10. Be a volunteer promoter of devotion to Our Lady of Guadalupe.

11. Be a volunteer promoter of the Jesus King of All Nations Devotion.

12. Be a volunteer promoter of devotion to Our Lady of America.

13. Use whatever talents that God has given you to bring His Good News to our Culture of Death in the New Evangelization!

14. Stand up for Christ the King, like the Cristeros!

In the 1920s, Mexican President Plutarco Calles began a violent Secularist persecution against the Catholic Church. It was inspired by the French Revolution and followed its methods of killing Catholic priests and the faithful and destroying their churches, as in the genocide against Catholics in the Vendée region of France.

In defense of their lives and their faith, many Catholics known as Cristeros arose and resisted the persecution. They were known as Cristeros because of their rallying cry, *"Viva Cristo Rey!"* (*"Long Live Christ the King!"* in Spanish).

Pope Pius XI condemned the "cruel persecution" and "great evils" of the Mexican government in his 1926 Encyclical, *Iniquis Afflictisque (On the Persecution of the Church in Mexico)*. He wrote, "We can scarcely keep back our tears, some of these young men and boys have gladly met death, the Rosary in their hands and the name of Christ the King on their lips." He also said, "The blood of martyrs has always been the seed of blessings from heaven."

When some of the Cristeros were captured, the Commandant asked them for whom they had taken up arms to create such disorder. They replied that it was not to create disorder that they had taken up arms, but to defend Christ the King, who was no longer on the altars. They were immediately shot and killed.

By 1930, over 200,000 people had been killed in the persecution, which ended with a treaty that the Vatican mandated the Cristeros sign or be excommunicated. The treaty simply and unjustly provided for an immediate cease-fire and the reopening of Catholic Churches, but left in effect the anti-Catholic laws.

On May 21, 2000, St. John Paul II canonized 25 of the Cristeros as martyrs. Thirteen more martyrs were beatified on the Solemnity of Christ the King, on November 20, 2005.

If the Secularists come for us, like the Mexican government came for Blessed Fr. Miguel Pro, a priest dressed as a layman, on November 22, 1927, let us stand up for Christ the King as he and the Cristeros did — with fortitude. As Fr. Pro, with no prior charges, trial, or judicial judgment, faced a firing squad, he forgave his enemies, stood in a crucified posture against a log wall (see the photo on the next page) and, as they aimed their guns at him, shouted out, *"Viva Cristo Rey!"* and died a martyr's death.

Martyr priest Fr. Miguel Pro shouting before his execution,
"Viva Christo Rey!" (*"Long Live Christ the King!"*)

18. The End

We now come to the end of this book and look forward to our end in this world while in the Kingdom of God on earth, as we persevere toward the Kingdom of God in heaven through love of God, neighbors, and enemies and through obedience and faith with prayer, fasting, almsgiving, and works of mercy to our destiny of eternal life and rest with Jesus King of All Nations. Let us be mindful of St. Augustine's fourth century description of this rest, as he described it in his spiritual autobiography, *Confessions*,

> You have made us for yourself, and our hearts are restless until they rest in you....

> O Lord God, grant your peace unto us, for you have supplied us with all things — the peace of rest, the peace of the Sabbath, which has no evening...in unbroken rest you made them that the voice of your Book may speak beforehand unto us, that we also after our works (therefore very good, because you have given them unto us) may repose in you also in the Sabbath of eternal life....

> But you, being the Good, needing no good, art ever at rest, because you yourself art your rest...Let it be asked of you, sought in you, knocked for at you; so, even so shall it be received, so shall it be found, so shall it be opened.

This "rest" and the following words of the author of the Letter to the Hebrews can be applied to the Sabbath of eternal rest in heaven for those who believe, but, for those who do not believe and who were disobedient, they shall not enter into that rest.

> And to him whom did he "swear that they should not enter into His rest," if not to those who were disobedient? And we see that they could not enter for lack of faith. Therefore, let us be on our guard while the promise of entering into His rest remains, that none of you seem to have failed. For in fact, we have received the good news just as they did. But the word that they heard did not profit

them, for they were not united in faith with those who listened. For we who believed enter into [that] rest, just as He has said, "As I swore in my wrath, 'they shall not enter into my rest.'" (Hebrews 3:18–19; 4:1–3; Psalms 95:11).

So, by our obedience, faith, and good works may we all enter into that eternal rest that Jesus King of All Nations has promised to us.

The *Catholic Catechism,* quoting the Third Council of Lyon in 1274, calmly teaches, "The most Holy Roman Church believes and confesses firmly that on the day of judgment all men will appear together with their own bodies before the judgment seat of Christ to render an account of their works." With the result that "...the Kingdom of God will arrive in all its fullness. Then the just will reign with Christ forever, glorified in body and soul, and the material universe itself will be transformed. Then God will be 'all in all' (1 Corinthians 15:28), in eternal life." (CCC 1059–1060).

Pope Benedict XVI wrote in his *Spiritual Testament,* dated August 29, 2006, opened after his death on December 31, 2022,

"Stand firm in the faith! Do not let yourselves be confused!...

"Jesus Christ is truly the way, the truth and the life – and the Church, with all its insufficiencies, is truly His body."

Appendices

A. Bishops' Support

Bishop Enrique Hernández Rivera, D. D., former Bishop of Caguas, Puerto Rico, wrote, "I recognize the need to foster more devotion to Our Lord and Savior, Jesus the Christ, True King of All Nations. I wish the promoters of the Jesus King of All Nations Devotion all the best in your efforts of spreading the message of Christ to all who invoke Him by this title."

Bishop Rivera granted the original revelations of the Devotion the *Nihil Obstat*, on August 15, 1993. The *Nihil Obstat* is an official declaration that a book (The *Journal*) is free of doctrinal or moral error.

Bishop Roman Danylak, now deceased, was the spiritual advisor of the Jesus King of All Nations Devotion apostolate. He presided over a consecration to Jesus King of All Nations and the crowning of His Visitation Image at a Mass celebrated at the Basilica Shrine of Our Lady of Guadalupe in Mexico City.

He wrote in his letter (on the next page,) "I encourage you to promote and help to spread the Devotion so that the Reign of Jesus King of All Nations will be recognized on earth."

Jesus King of All Nations

September 9, 1998

To Whom It May Concern:

Praised be Jesus and Mary!

I am the spiritual advisor to the apostolate of the Jesus King of All Nations. This devotion promotes the recognition as Jesus King of Our Hearts. It is found in scripture, and founded in the teaching of the Church.

The Director of the apostolate is Daniel J. Lynch. Mr. Lynch is a Catholic in good standing with the Church, father of nine children, a Judge of the State of Vermont and a lawyer who gave up his law practice to serve as the Director of the apostolate. Mr. Lynch is also the author of several books, a producer of videos and audios, and a public speaker and evangelist who has spread this mission throughout the world. Please help him to spread this mission.

The apostolate sponsors Visitations of a large Traveling Image of Jesus King of All Nations. I presided over a consecration to Jesus and the crowning of this Image at a Mass celebrated at the Basilica Shrine of Our Lady of Guadalupe in Mexico City.

These Visitations have resulted in many conversions, healings and testimonies of divine protection. The fruits of this devotion are good. I encourage you to promote and help to spread this devotion so that the reign of Jesus King of All Nations will be recognized on earth.

Sincerely in Christ

+ Roman Danylak, bishop

+ Roman Danylak, bishop

244

B. The Prayers and Promises of the Devotion

The Morning Offering to Jesus King of All Nations

This prayer is a good way to start your day! Jesus revealed it, but it was not recorded in the Journal.

Lord Jesus, my adorable King, I offer to you, through Mary, the Mediatrix of All Graces, my day, my every moment, my very self with all of my faculties.

May your most holy and sovereign Will be done in me today, that you may be glorified in me and that your Reign be extended in the hearts of all mankind.

I adore you Lord Jesus, really and truly present in every consecrated Host throughout the entire world. Shine forth from this your throne on earth into my heart and the hearts of all people.

Saint Michael bring your spear. Protect the advancement of the Lord's Devotion of Jesus King of All Nations; the Devotion of Justice which is the compliment to His Mercy and Love.

O Jesus, our King of All Nations, may your Reign be recognized on earth! Amen.

The Novena in Honor of Jesus as True King

This Novena consists of praying once a day, over a period of nine days, a set of one Our Father, one Hail Mary and one Glory Be, along with the following Novena Prayer,

O Lord our God, you alone are the most holy King and ruler of all nations. We pray to you, Lord, in the great expectation of receiving from you, O Divine King, mercy, peace, justice, and all good things.

Protect, O Lord our King, our families and the land of our birth. Guard us, we pray, most faithful one! Protect us from our enemies and from your just judgment.

Forgive us, O Sovereign King, our sins against you. Jesus, you are a King of mercy. We have deserved your just judgment. Have mercy on us, Lord, and forgive us. We trust in your great mercy.

O most awe-inspiring King, we bow before you and pray; may your Reign, your Kingdom, be recognized on earth! Amen. (*Journal* 29).

The Novena in Honor of Jesus as True King Promises

Jesus told His Secretary to write His words. "*...all these words that are written*" (Jeremiah 51:60). "I thank you...my little one, for your efforts for my Image which must be done! "*...what thy hand and thy counsel decreed to be done.*" (Acts 4:28). My child, do you remember my saying that I would tell you something of great importance? "Yes, my Lord." My little one, every time you say the prayers I taught you in connection with my Image as Jesus King of All Nations, I promise that I will convert ten sinners, bring ten souls into the one true faith, release ten souls from purgatory, and be less severe in my judgment of your nation, the United States of America. "*Thou hast obtained mercy.*" (Hosea 2:1). My little one, this not only applies to your nation, but also all other nations. "*...all the countries...*" (Ezekiel 36:24). My child, each time you say these prayers, "*my house is a house of prayer...*" (Luke 19:46) I will mitigate the severity of the chastisements upon your country." "*I am the Lord that exercises mercy, and judgment, and justice in the earth: for these things please me, saith the Lord.*" (Jeremiah 9:24). (*Journal* 41).

"Whenever there is the threat of severe weather, recite these prayers along with the prayers I will later teach you, and no harm will come to you or to those you pray for. "*...as the Lord thy God promised...*" (Deuteronomy 10:9). This, my little one, applies not only to weather, but all forms of my justice. "*Put us not to confusion, but deal with us according to thy meekness, and according to the multitude of thy mercies. And* *deliver us according to thy wonderful works, and give glory to thy name, O Lord…"* (Daniel 3:42–43). This is why these prayers, along with my Image as Jesus King of All Nations, must become known. *"…make Him known."* (Mark 3:12). Those trusting souls who pray this Devotion, *"a most sweet odor to the Lord…"* (Numbers 28:24) especially efficacious when prayed before my Image, will also be granted these promises of mine." *"For the Lord fulfills His Word…"* (Romans 9:28). (*Journal* 42).

The Chaplet of Unity

The Chaplet of Unity is a series of prayers. Jesus said, "I promise to give this *Chaplet of Unity* great power over my wounded Sacred Heart when prayed with faith and confidence to heal the brokenness of my people's lives caused by so much sin, selfishness, error, division, and disunity." *"For the end of these things is death."* (Romans 6:21). (*Journal* 47).

The Chaplet is recited on ordinary Rosary beads. Groups may divide the recitation between Leader (**L**) and Responders (**R**). If you are alone, recite both parts.

Recite on the large bead before each of five decades,

L: God our Heavenly Father, through Your Son Jesus, our Victim-High Priest, True Prophet, and Sovereign King,

R: Pour forth the power of Your Holy Spirit upon us and open our hearts. In Your Great Mercy, through the Motherly Mediation of the Blessed Virgin Mary, our Queen, forgive our sinfulness, heal our brokenness, and renew our hearts in the faith, and peace, and love, and joy of Your Kingdom, that we may be one in You.

Recite on the ten small beads of each of the five decades,

L: In Your Great Mercy,

R: Forgive our sinfulness, heal our brokenness, and renew our hearts that we may be one in You.

Conclude in unison,

Hear, O Israel! The Lord Our God is One God!

O Jesus, King of All Nations, may Your Reign be recognized on earth!

Mary, Our Mother and Mediatrix of All Graces, pray and intercede for us your children!

St. Michael, great prince and guardian of your people, come with the holy angels and saints and protect us!

The Chaplet of Unity Promises

Jesus said, "Yes, in this Devotion to me as Jesus King of All Nations, entreat my kingly Heart with the prayer of this *Chaplet of Unity* that I myself, your Sovereign Lord Jesus Christ, have given you! Pray and ask for the spiritual wholeness and the healing of your own souls, for the union of your own will with God's Will, for the healing of your families, friends, enemies, relationships, religious orders, communities, countries, nations, the world, and unity within my Church under the Holy Father! I shall grant many spiritual, physical, emotional, and psychological healings for those who pray this prayer if it is beneficial to their salvation according to my most Holy Will! Unity and oneness in spirit was my own prayer for all mankind and my Church as my own last testament before I gave my life as Savior of all mankind! As I am one with my Father and the Holy Spirit, my Will is that all mankind be one in me, so that one faith, one fold, and one shepherd will be gathered together under my sovereign Kingship as Lord." (*Journal* 50–52).

"I promise to give this *Chaplet of Unity* great power over my wounded Sacred Heart '...*his Heart...*' (Zechariah 7:10) when prayed with faith and confidence to heal the brokenness of my people's lives '*I heal them...*' (John 12:40) caused by so much sin, selfishness, error, division, and disunity." "*For the end of these things is death.*" (Romans 6:21). (*Journal* 47).

"Confession, Confession, Confession, my children! Confess your sins to me through my priests that I may cover you with my mercy. '*When He had said this, He breathed upon them and He said to them, "Receive the Holy Spirit; whose sins you shall forgive, they are forgiven them; and whose sins you shall retain, they are retained".*' (John 20:22-23). Pray this Chaplet that a renewal of your hearts and minds by the Holy Spirit will lead to a daily conversion in faith, peace, love, and joy within your souls. '...*being sanctified by the Holy Spirit.*'

248

(Romans 15:16). I promise you 'my peace, my divine presence within your souls', which the worldly-minded cannot and does not understand! *'To you it is given to know the mysteries of the Kingdom of Heaven, but to them it is not given.'* (Matthew 13:11). My peace knows no bounds or limits! By imploring me in this manner, you will turn away from sin and its destructive effects, *'...you will be free indeed.'* (John 8:36) and toward a continual greater and greater abundance of graces from me in my mercy." *"Let us therefore draw near with confidence to the throne of grace, that we may obtain mercy and find grace to help in time of need."* (Hebrews 4:16). (*Journal* 49).

"I shall grant many spiritual, physical, emotional, and psychological healings for those who pray this prayer if it is beneficial to their salvation according to my most Holy Will!" *"...great crowds gathered together to hear Him and to be cured of their sicknesses."* (Luke 5:15). (*Journal* 51).

"Those special souls *'the great and the small, standing before the throne...'* (Revelation 20:12) who honor me in this Devotion will do the same, and to them I promise to grant my kingly blessings! *'...that I may enrich them that love me, and may fill their treasures.'* (Proverbs 8:21). I, Jesus, *'...the Lord Jesus Christ...'* (Philippians 2:11) Son of the Most High God, *'...the Son of God.'* (John 5:28) who AM Sovereign Lord, *'...Lord and Savior.'* (2 Peter 3:2) promise to hold out to the souls who pray my *Chaplet of Unity* the scepter of my Kingship *"...thou dost stretch forth thy hand..."* (Psalms 137:7) and grant them mercy, pardon, and protection in times of severe weather and plagues." *"...and I will have mercy..."* (Hosea 3:23). (*Journal* 54).

"I extend this promise not only for yourselves, but also for individuals for whom you pray. *'...His brethren...'* (Mark 3:31). No, my beloved, sin and the evils committed by mankind are too great, no longer will I spare my judgment to correct the conscience of mankind as a whole, *'And a throne shall be prepared in mercy, and one shall sit upon it in truth in the tabernacle of David, judging and seeking judgment and quickly rendering that which is just.'* (Isaiah 16:5) but this Devotion and Chaplet prayed with repentance, confidence, and love, will heal, save, and unite souls to my mercy who otherwise would be lost." *"...for thy mercy came and healed them."* (Wisdom 16:10). (*Journal* 55).

"Any harm or danger, spiritual or physical, whether it be to soul, mind, or body, will I protect these souls against, *'The Lord watches over thee, the Lord is thy protection at thy right hand.'* (Psalms 120:5) and clothe them over with my own Mantle of Kingly Mercy. *'...as waters covering the sea.'* (Habakkuk 2:14). To this I add the promise of the assistance of my most holy Mother's mediation on their behalf. *'...her children.'* (Matthew 11:19). Even if you die, you shall not be lost, for you shall know salvation and union with me in the Kingdom of my Father where we reign with the Holy Spirit, eternally the Divine Trinity, One God." *"We then who have believed shall enter into his rest."* (Hebrews 4:3). *(Journal* 56).

"My child, little one of my most Sacred Heart, I come to you tonight to entrust to you a beautiful promise that I will grant in my great mercy, *'according to the multitude of thy tender mercies.'* (Nehemiah 13:22) to those souls who will recite my Chaplet. I promise my most powerful protection to those souls who, in time of danger, whether it be to mind, body, or soul, shall recite my Chaplet with confidence, *'with confidence'* (Hebrews 4:16) thus imploring my great mercy through my most holy Mother. *'His Mother'* (John 2:5). I also promise to those souls who shall recite my Chaplet, my peace, which knows no bounds. *'Peace I leave with you, my peace I give to you...'* (John 14:27). My little one, so many hearts in this world are without peace. They must come to me, their true peace, if they would have peace!!!" *"He who has ears to hear, let him hear."* (Luke 14:35). *(Journal* 211).

Jesus said, "My child, by praying the Chaplet I have taught you, you will replace my great sorrow with infinite joy, *'with joy'* (Luke 8:13) and obtain the extension of my Reign in the hearts of men. *'...of all nations and tribes and peoples and tongues...'* (Revelation 7:9). Yes, my child, this also is my promise to all who will recite this Chaplet with love, faith, and confidence. My child, I will grant my kingly blessing to all who will pray this Chaplet of mine." *"I will surely bless thee..."* (Hebrews 6:14). *(Journal* 235).

The Chaplet of Unity Daily Intentions

Jesus taught His Secretary His daily intentions for us to offer His *Chaplet of Unity.* He said, "My daughter, as my most holy Church enters the month dedicated to Mary, my holy Mother, I come again to teach you seven intentions, one for each day of the week, for which I ask you to offer my *Chaplet of Unity*. After making the general intention I have already taught you, you are to add the particular intention I am about to give you." (*Journal* 329).

The numbers below refer to the paragraph numbers in the Journal.

330. We begin, my little one, with <u>Sunday</u>. On this day dedicated to the Lord, your God, I ask that you pray for my holy Church upon earth, the Church Militant, and, in particular, for my Vicar, the Pope, all cardinals, bishops, and priests that, together with the faithful, they may be one in me as I AM one with the Father and the Holy Spirit. *"I am in my Father and you are in me and I in you."* (John 14:20). My Spouse, the Church, is wounded by the many sins of disunity arising from pride, selfish desires, and a great lack of charity. The enemy seeks anew to destroy my spotless bride. He shall not prevail! Pray fervently my Chaplet for this intention on Sundays. Every chaplet you offer me on this day is to be for this intention. *"He taught me, and said to me: "Let your heart hold fast my words:"* (Proverbs 4:4).

331. On <u>Mondays</u>, my little one, I desire that you pray my *Chaplet of Unity* for the Poor Souls in Purgatory, the Church Suffering. Pray for their relief and deliverance, that they may soon come into my Kingdom and reign with me eternally. *"Let us enter into His dwelling, let us worship at His footstool."* (Psalms 132:7). Show them great charity as they depend upon your prayers.

332. On <u>Tuesdays</u>, my child, you are to offer my *Chaplet of Unity* for those who promote my Devotion of Jesus King of All Nations. These souls are most special in my sight and to them I will give to know the secrets of my love in a particular way in heaven. They will share intimately in the glory of my Kingship. Joy shall be theirs as they witness the subjection of all my enemies. They shall reign with me, their King and Lord, forever. *"Rise up in splendor! Your light has come, the glory of the Lord shines upon you."* (Isaiah 60:1). I will return. My blessing to you and to those you love.

334. On <u>Wednesdays,</u> my child, form the intention of pleading for my kingly mercy for all those afflicted in these latter days with hopelessness. These souls are overcome in

mind, body, and soul by the darkness that presently envelops the world. The darkness of sin engulfs the nations. Materialism and self-seeking deafen souls to my voice and blind their eyes from seeing the light of truth. I AM Truth! I AM the Light! I AM the Way for all souls, all nations to follow. Pray that this great number of souls may not yield to the temptation to despair.

335. On _Thursdays_, my little one, offer my _Chaplet of Unity_ for greater devotion to me, the King of All Nations, in the Holy Eucharist. The light which enlightens the world of souls, which enlightens the nations, streams forth from the Holy Eucharist. I AM among you! It is I! Come to me. This is the day upon which I instituted the Sacrament of the Holy Eucharist. Pray that souls will worship me in this most excellent Sacrament! Where there is adoration of my Real Presence, graces abound! _"For thus says the Lord to me: I will quietly look on from where I dwell, like the glowing heat of sunshine, like a cloud of dew at harvest time."_ (Isaiah 18:4). Love me in my Sacrament of Love!

336. On _Fridays_, my child, offer my _Chaplet of Unity_ for true repentance of sin in all souls. Let souls seek and obtain my great mercy through the forgiveness of their sins in the holy Sacrament of Confession. _"Those who are well do not need a physician, but the sick do. I did not come to call the righteous but sinners."_ (Mark 2:17). This is the day on which I gave my life for the salvation of all. May my Passion and death be no more in vain for a number of souls. Behold! The King of Glory hanging upon a cross! All of His divine beauty is marred, hidden. All for love of you, my children.

337. Finally, little one, offer my _Chaplet of Unity_ on _Saturdays_ for the proclamation of the dogma of Mary, Mediatrix of All Graces and Co-Redemptrix. My holy Mother will receive this honor from my Church. It is my Will. So it shall be. _"these things are recorded in the chronicle of his pontificate,"_ (1 Maccabees 16:24). This dogma is to be a great light for the nations and usher in the Era of Peace. The enemy is furious at the prospect of this dogma and is ferociously fighting to prevent it. Legions of demons have been assigned the task of destroying this work, so much do

they fear Mary, the Woman of Revelation. The gates of hell shall not prevail against my Holy Will. Amen, amen, so I say, so it shall be. For I AM the Eternal One, the Only One, the Lord of all. *"They will fight with the Lamb, but the Lamb will conquer them, for He is Lord of lords and king of kings, and those with Him are called, chosen, and faithful."* (Revelation 17:14). My blessing to you.

[Author's note: These are general intentions and do not replace the individual's personal intentions held within their heart for which they would offer the Chaplet. Our Lord pours out tremendous graces in the power of His Holy Spirit through this *Chaplet of Unity.*]

The Novena of Holy Communions

This Novena consists of offering nine consecutive Holy Communions in honor of Jesus King of All Nations. Jesus said, "I desire that the faithful souls who embrace this devotion to me...make a *Novena of Holy Communions*. They, therefore, shall offer nine (9) consecutive Holy Communions in honor of me as Jesus King of All Nations." (*Journal* 220). "Consecutive" means nine Communions, uninterrupted, one after another, that the souls would receive. They need not be on nine calendar days in a row, just each Communion received, one after the other.

Jesus King of All Nations did not reveal how we should honor Him during the *Novena of Holy Communions* in honor of Him. I [the Author] suggest that, before you receive Holy Communion, you pray an Our Father, a Hail Mary, and a Glory Be. I also suggest that after Holy Communion, you pray the *Novena Prayer in Honor of Jesus as True King* and that you name the intention of your Holy Communion and the name of the person to whom you wish the angel to be sent.

The Novena of Holy Communions Promises

Jesus showed His Secretary the powerful effects of this Novena in a vision. She saw Jesus gazing up to heaven. Nine times, He gave a command and an angel came to earth. Jesus explained, "My daughter, for those souls who will offer me [this] Devotion, I will bid an angel of each of the Nine Choirs, one with each Holy Communion, to guard the soul for the rest of its life on this earth." (*Journal* 223).

Jesus revealed the following additional promises for the practice of the *Novena of Holy Communions,*

> I extend a most beautiful promise to the souls who shall offer me this Devotion [of practicing the *Novena of Holy Communions*]. I promise, my child, to grant these souls a particular power over my kingly Heart. *"He that maketh the earth by His power, that prepareth the world by His wisdom, and stretcheth out like the heavens by His knowledge."* (Jeremiah 10:12). What they ask for in this *Novena of Holy Communions,* if it be according to my most Holy Will, I will surely grant it. *"...yet not what I will, but what thou willest."* (Mark 14:36). Let these souls ask from me without reservation. I am waiting to shower untold blessings upon souls who receive me with love in Holy Communion. *"Lord, do not trouble thyself, for I am not worthy that thou shouldst come under my roof; this is why I did not think myself worthy to come to thee. But say the word, and my servant will be healed."* (Luke 7:6–7). Yes, my child, let them receive me with love and humility. Then will my blessings of healing for their minds, bodies, and souls come upon them. *"...and I heal them."* (John 12:40). Let them offer me within their very souls, *"The Son of Man must be lifted up..."* (John 12:34) through my Immaculate Mother, to my Heavenly Father, who will then smile down upon them benevolently and who will grant these souls His Fatherly Blessing. *"...because of the loving-kindness of our God..."* (Luke 1:78). (*Journal* 221).

> Novenas of additional Holy Communions, repeated by that soul, will increase the ardor of that soul to love me, their God, through these angelic servants of mine. This Novena may be prayed with its promises for another soul and that soul will also receive additional angelic protection. The praying of this Novena for communities, nations, and the world will also call down my angelic protection upon them. Because of the many evils in these end-times, it is my desire that you pray to me to send my angelic hosts to guide, guard, and protect you. *"The Lord watches over thee, the Lord*

is thy protection at thy right hand." (Psalms 120:5). This then is my solemn promise. *"I will give you the holy and sure promises..."* (Acts 13:34). *(Journal* 224).

I urge my faithful ones to make this Novena a constant prayer. I will grant them the additional angels to guard them individually, as I have promised, *"Christ is faithful"* (Hebrews 3:6) but I ask that they not be satisfied with this, but that they continue to offer me this Novena again and again, (even after they have completed the first nine Holy Communions,) so that I may continue to send down my holy angels for the protection and assistance of other souls who cannot do this for themselves for one reason or another. *"...be assiduous in prayer, being wakeful therein with thanksgiving. At the same time pray for us also..."* (Colossians 4:2, 3). This would be a great charity on their part *"But above all these things have charity, which is the bond of perfection."* (Colossians 3:14) and would truly be a reflection of their God, *"according to the image of his Creator."* (Colossians 3:10) who is Divine Charity. *"For our God is a consuming fire."* (Hebrews 12:29). *(Journal* 228).

The Consecration to Mary, Mediatrix of All Graces

Jesus asks those who embrace this Devotion to consecrate themselves to His Mother under her title as "Mary, Mediatrix of All Graces." He said,

> My beloved little daughter, your Lord and God comes to you to give you a message of great importance. I desire that the souls who embrace my devotion to "Jesus King of All Nations" make a special consecration to my most holy Mother under her title of "Mary, Mediatrix of All Graces," which it has pleased me in my great love for her to give her. People must acknowledge her indispensable role as the Mediatrix, the Channel, of all of my grace to mankind. Only when this dogma is officially proclaimed by my Church will I truly establish my Reign on earth. *(Journal* 239–240).

Then the Blessed Virgin Mary appeared to the Secretary and said, "Daughter, know that I have obtained this prayer for my children from the Heart of my Divine Son." "...*the works of my hands*..." (Judith 13:7). Then Jesus revealed to [her] the following prayer of consecration to be prayed by those who embrace His Devotion of Jesus King of All Nations.

O Mary, Most Holy and Immaculate Mother of God, of Jesus, our Victim-High Priest, True Prophet, and Sovereign King, I come to you as the Mediatrix of All Graces, for that is truly what you are. O Fountain of All Graces! O Fairest of Roses! Most Pure Spring! Unsullied Channel of all of God's grace! Receive me, most holy Mother! Present me and my every need to the most Holy Trinity! That having been made pure and holy in His sight through your hands, they may return to me, through you, as graces and blessing. I give and consecrate myself to you, Mary, Mediatrix of All Graces, that Jesus, our one true Mediator, who is the King of All Nations, may reign in every heart. Amen. (*Journal* 244).

The Litany in Honor of Jesus King of All Nations

Jesus told His Secretary, "*I promise...that whosoever shall recite this Litany of mine shall die in my arms with my smile upon them. I myself will appear to these souls as 'King of All Nations' before their death.*" (*Journal* 283).

The Litany invocations are prayed by the individual praying or by a Leader, if any. The Litany responses are indicated by the letter "**R**" and are made after <u>each</u> invocation by all who are praying, except the Leader, if any.

<u>The individual or leader begins:</u>

Lord, have mercy on us.

Christ, have mercy on us.

Lord, have mercy on us.

<u>R – *Have mercy on us.*</u>

God, our Heavenly Father, who has made firm for all ages your Son's throne,

God, the Son, Jesus, our Victim-High Priest, True Prophet, and Sovereign King,

God, the Holy Spirit, poured out upon us with abundant newness,

Holy Trinity, Three Persons, yet One God, in the Beauty of your Eternal Unity.

R—Reign in our Hearts.

O Jesus, our Eternal King,

O Jesus, most Merciful King,

O Jesus, extending to us the Golden Scepter of your mercy,

O Jesus, in whose great mercy we have been given the Sacrament of Confession,

O Jesus, Loving King who offers us your healing grace,

O Jesus, our Eucharistic King,

O Jesus, the King foretold by the prophets,

O Jesus, King of Heaven and Earth,

O Jesus, King and Ruler of All Nations,

O Jesus, Delight of the Heavenly Court,

O Jesus, King Most Compassionate toward your subjects,

O Jesus, King from whom proceeds all authority,

O Jesus, in whom, with the Father and the Holy Spirit, we are one,

O Jesus, King whose Kingdom is not of this world,

O Jesus, King whose Sacred Heart burns with love for all of mankind,

O Jesus, King who is the Beginning and the End, the Alpha and the Omega,

O Jesus, King who has given us Mary, the Queen, to be our dear Mother,

O Jesus, King who will come upon the clouds of heaven with power and great glory,

O Jesus, King whose throne we are to approach with confidence,

O Jesus, King truly present in the most Blessed Sacrament,

O Jesus, King who made Mary the Mediatrix of All Graces,

O Jesus, King who made Mary Co-Redemptrix, your partner in the Plan of Salvation,

O Jesus, King who desires to heal us of all division and disunity,

O Jesus, King wounded by mankind's indifference,

O Jesus, King who gives us the balm of your love with which to console your Wounded Heart,

O Jesus, King who is the Great I AM within us, our Wellspring of Pure Delight,

R – May we serve you.

Jesus King of All Nations, True Sovereign of all earthly powers,

Jesus King of All Nations, subjecting under your feet forever the powers of hell,

Jesus King of All Nations, the light beyond all light, enlightening us in the darkness that surrounds us,

Jesus King of All Nations, whose mercy is so great as to mitigate the punishments our sins deserve,

Jesus King of All Nations, recognized by the Magi as the True King,

Jesus King of All Nations, the Only Remedy for a world so ill,

Jesus King of All Nations, who blesses with peace those souls and nations that acknowledge you as True King,

Jesus King of All Nations, who mercifully sends us your holy angels to protect us,

Jesus King of All Nations, whose Chief Prince is St. Michael the Archangel,

Jesus King of All Nations, who teaches us that to reign is to serve,

Jesus King of All Nations, Just Judge who will separate the wicked from the good,

Jesus King of All Nations, before whom every knee shall bend,

Jesus King of All Nations, whose dominion is an everlasting dominion,

Jesus King of All Nations, Lamb who will shepherd us,

Jesus King of All Nations, who, after having destroyed every sovereignty, authority, and power, will hand over the Kingdom to your God and Father,

Jesus King of All Nations, whose Reign is without end,

Jesus King of All Nations, whose kindness toward us is steadfast, and whose fidelity endures forever,

R – We praise and thank you.

Eternal Father, who has given us your Only Begotten Son, to be our Redeemer, One True Mediator, and Sovereign King,

Loving Jesus, Sovereign King, who humbled yourself for love of us and took the form of a servant,

Holy Spirit, Third Person of the Trinity, Love of the Father and the Son, who sanctifies us and gives us life,

Mary, our Queen and Mother, who mediates to Jesus on our behalf,

R – Pray for us.

Mary, our Queen and Mother, through whom all Graces come to us,

R – Pray for us.

Mary, our Queen and Mother, Singular Jewel of the Holy Trinity,

R – We love you.

Holy angels and saints of our Divine King,

R – Pray for us and protect us. Amen.

The Litany Promises

Jesus attached a beautiful promise to the faithful recitation of this Litany. "I promise my child, that whosoever shall recite this Litany of mine shall die in my arms with my smile upon them. *'I heard a voice from heaven say, "Write this: Blessed are the dead who die in the Lord from now on." "Yes", said the Spirit, "Let them find rest from their labors, for their works accompany them."'* (Revelation 14:13). I myself will appear to these souls as 'King of All Nations' before their death. *'...unfailing, you stood by them in every time and circumstance.'* (Wisdom 19:22). Graciously, and with great tenderness, I will extend to them the golden scepter, the symbol of my mercy. I promise them a peaceful death. My child, I ask that souls recite my Litany with love and fervor. Let them pray it not only for themselves but for all souls. *'Whoever has two cloaks should share with the person who has none.'* (Luke 3:11). Children, I need your help to save the greater number!" *"I wish that where I am they also may be with me..."* (John 17:24). *(Journal* 283).

The Special Blessing

The *Special Blessing* of Jesus King of All Nations was revealed by Our Lady when she appeared to His Secretary's Spiritual Mother holding the Child Jesus in her arms. The Child was plucking roses one by one from His Sacred Heart, kissing them, and holding them to His Mother's lips. Our Lady kissed each rose, took it from Jesus' hands, touched it to her Heart, then gave it to the "Spiritual Mother" who placed each rose within Our Lady's Immaculate Heart. From there the roses were distributed to peoples of all nations for all time — billions upon billions of roses. The roses are the graces of the *Special Blessing,* and the passing of the graces from Jesus to Mary to her children illustrates Our Lady's role as Mediatrix of All Graces.

To Give the Special Blessing

The *Special Blessing* may be passed on by anyone to others in person or at a distance in prayer. If in person, place your hands on the person's head with your right thumb on his/her forehead. If at a distance, hold your hands over, or in the direction of, the person or group and pray:

May the Reign of Jesus King of All Nations be recognized in your heart;

May the Reign of Jesus King of All Nations be lived in your heart;

May the Reign of Jesus King of All Nations be given through your heart to other hearts;

So that the Reign of Jesus King of All Nations may be lived in every heart all over the world.

I ask this *Special Blessing* through Our Lady, Mediatrix of All Graces, who, as Queen and Mother of All Nations, has obtained it for you as a tremendous grace from the Sacred Heart of her Divine Son, in the name of the Father and of the Son and of the Holy Spirit. Amen.

Make the sign of the cross on the person's forehead with your thumb, or make the sign of the cross with your hand in his/her direction.

The gifts of the *Special Blessing* are the gift of receiving, understanding, and living Jesus' Word in Scripture; the gifts of intimacy with Jesus, Mary, and souls as partners in the Body of Christ; and the gift of knowing the secrets of God's love. The *Special Blessing* also grants healing and brings unity to the Body of Christ.

Jesus wants everyone to receive the graces of this kingly *Special Blessing*. Pray it for your family, your friends, your priests, the lost, the sick, the dying—everyone who is in need of God's mercy.

The Enthronement of His Image

Jesus told His Secretary, "Enthrone this my Image everywhere for I shall be powerfully present there and the power of my sovereign Kingship shall surely shield you from my just judgment. Be strong and do not lose hope. I AM with you to save you." (*Journal* 418–419).

"Let my holy Image be enthroned everywhere! Within shrines, churches, homes, religious communities, hospitals, offices, and, indeed, within the very heart of man! This Image represents the totality of my divine offices—Victim-High Priest, True Prophet, and Sovereign King—and, as such, calls down the blessing of my Almighty Father." (*Journal* 561). "When one venerates this Image, my Sacred Heart and my Divine Mercy are also venerated." (*Journal* 554).

Enthronement of the Image of Jesus King of All Nations is a solemn act by which the participants (family, office, parish, etc.) enthrone, display, honor, and venerate His Image. They give formal recognition of the Kingship of Christ over their lives, families, home, offices, parishes, etc. The Enthronement Ceremony is the official, ceremonial beginning of their commitment to live out the effects of their recognition of Christ's Kingship.

Jesus King of All Nations told His Secretary, "My daughter, great are the graces which will be granted through the proper veneration of this Image of mine." (*Journal* 6–7). "This Image is to be a sign that I rule heaven and earth, and my Kingdom, my Reign, is near at hand....I give this Image to mankind as a source of graces and of peace." (*Journal* 7, 14). "This Image, my child, must become known. My daughter, those souls who venerate this Image of mine will be blessed with my peace." (*Journal* 14–15).

Jesus invited us to pray before His Image, "My children, come before my Image of Jesus King of All Nations and pray for your countries. Pray for your people. Pray for your families. Pray for my mercy which I will graciously grant to those peoples and nations that acknowledge me as True King! I AM your sure refuge in these most evil and truly dangerous times." (*Journal* 24).

The enthronement and veneration of His Image will help to realize Jesus' requests. We can make reparation for the enemies of Jesus who mockingly adored Him in His Passion. We can recognize Him as our True King in this ceremony.

In the Rite of Solemn Enthronement, we pray,

> Almighty and everlasting God, who approves the painting of images of Jesus so that as often as we gaze upon them we are reminded to honor Him as our True King, grant, we implore you, to bless and sanctify this Image made in honor and in memory of Jesus King of All Nations, your Only Begotten Son; and grant that whosoever, in its presence, will venerate and worship Him may obtain, through His merits and intercession, graces and peace in this life and everlasting glory in the world to come. Through Christ Our Lord. Amen.

Then the leader sprinkles the Image with holy water and enthrones (displays) the Image in the place of honor prepared for it. This is the symbolic *Act of Enthronement*. Then the people pray the following prayer,

> Jesus, you told us in a parable that the people said, "We will not have this man to reign over us." (Luke 19:14). In your Passion, the soldiers stripped you and clothed you in a scarlet robe, thrust a reed into your right hand, and crowned you with a crown of thorns. They knelt in front of you and mocked you saying, "Hail, King of the Jews!" (Matthew 27: 28–29).

> Pontius Pilate said to the crowd, "Behold your King!" (John 19:14). But the people who clamored for your crucifixion yelled, "We have no king but Caesar!" (John 19:15). Your executioners pierced your hands and feet with nails. The Roman soldier thrust his spear and pierced your Heart from which flowed blood and water. (John 19:34).

> Jesus, unlike these people and those like them, we wish to make reparation for them. We want to have you to reign over us and we recognize no King but you! We recognize you as our True King. We see you in this Image of Jesus King of All Nations in your glorified body from which flow graces of love and mercy from your pierced hands and Sacred Heart from which flows blood and water. You are clothed in true royal splendor of scarlet, holding the scepter of your mercy out to us from your right hand and crowned with the golden crown of your authority.

> We stand before you, adore and honor you, and hail you as the True King of All Nations. We recognize your Reign in our hearts and on earth. We recognize your sovereign rights over all humanity and all nations. May we honor you as much in this Devotion as you were dishonored, despised, humiliated, and outraged in your Passion.

> O Jesus, King of All Nations, you said, "My children, come before my Image of Jesus King of All Nations and pray for your countries. Pray for your people. Pray for your families. Pray for my mercy which I will graciously grant to those peoples and nations that acknowledge me as True King!" (*Journal* 24).

So, we have come before your Image for that purpose and we acknowledge you as True King. We recognize your Reign on earth. We recognize your Mother as Mary, Mediatrix of All Graces. We recognize St. Michael the Archangel as the Protector of your Church, your Kingdom on earth. We ask them to intercede with us for your reign in all hearts and for the recognition of your Reign on earth.

Jesus King of All Nations, you told us, "Great are the graces which will be granted through the proper veneration of this Image of mine....I give this Image to mankind as a source of graces and of peace....The Image of myself as Jesus King of All Nations is a gift of love from my Heart to my children, intended to put before their minds the remembrance of me and therefore help them to hold me close in their hearts as my most holy Mother did so perfectly when she was on earth." (*Journal* 6, 14, Preface).

We accept the gift of your Image and hold you close in our hearts as we implore you for these promised graces through our proper veneration of your Image by our solemn enthronement of it. We acknowledge and proclaim you as King of our hearts, our families, our parishes, our dioceses, our country, and all nations.

As you requested, we have enthroned your Image here, relying on your promise to us, "For I shall be powerfully present there and the power of my sovereign Kingship shall surely shield you from my just judgment. Be strong and do not lose hope. I AM with you to save you." (*Journal* 418–419).

The Enthronement Ceremony concludes with the following pledge,

Jesus King of All Nations, I come before your Image to acknowledge you as True King and to pray for your mercy for myself, my family, my parish, my diocese, my country, and all nations.

I pledge to you that I will recognize your Reign on earth. I will love, honor, and obey you and your Church, your Kingdom on earth. I will recognize your Mother as Mary, Mediatrix of All Graces. I will recognize St. Michael the

Archangel as the protector of your Church, your Kingdom on earth. I will ask them to intercede with us for your reign in all hearts and for the recognition of your Kingdom on earth. I will properly adore, love, thank, praise, and worship you in the Holy Eucharist, your most glorious Blessed Sacrament.

I accept the gift of your Image and pledge to hold you close in my heart as your most holy Mother did so perfectly when she was on earth.

As a constant reminder of this pledge, I will try to wear or carry your Medal in reverence, relying on your promises of protection and final perseverance if I do so. I implore you for your promised graces and peace through my proper veneration of your Image. I acknowledge and proclaim you as King of myself, my family, my parish, my diocese, my country, and all nations. Amen.

Please see Appendix J, *How to Practice the Devotion*, on page 298 to obtain the Enthronement Booklet.

C. The Medal and Promises

"My daughter, it is my most Holy Will and desire that there be a Medal struck according to the likeness you have seen. I promise to offer the precious grace of final perseverance to every soul who will faithfully embrace this Devotion. '...*unto the praise of the glory of His grace...*' (Ephesians 1:6). My daughter, I am very anxious to have this done." "...*we will do the things which you have spoken.*" (Judith 7:25). (*Journal* 75).

"Jesus returned [to His Secretary] and gave what would be the beginning of additional promises to the faithful wearing of the Medal. *'All these things Jesus spoke...'* (Matthew 13:34). 'My little one, I, your Jesus, come to you tonight to extend an additional promise to the faithful wearing of the Medal honoring me as Jesus King of All Nations. My daughter, Secretary of my merciful love, "...*the Lord is gracious and merciful*" (Psalms 144:8) I solemnly promise to those souls who faithfully wear this Medal, and thus honor me as True King, the tremendous grace of my peace in their hearts and their homes. *"These things I have spoken to you that in me you may have peace."* (John 16:33). I will pour my grace into them, making their soul to blossom as a precious flower in my sight.'" *"Israel shall blossom and bud..."* (Isaiah 27:6). (*Journal* 158).

"I add, my child, yet another promise to the faithful wearing of this Medal. I promise, to every soul who faithfully wears this Medal, the tremendous grace of total forgiveness of all their sins, both mortal and venial. This is not to, in any way, replace the frequent reception of the Sacrament of Confession!!! I urge souls to receive this Sacrament of my great mercy often. There will they be healed." "...*and He cured them there.*" (Matthew 19:2). (*Journal* 164).

"A couple of days later, Our Lord was to clarify this last promise. Jesus continued, 'This Devotion to me as Jesus King of All Nations is to be a companion devotion to that of my mercy as given to my beloved daughter, [St.] Faustina, and to that of my Sacred Heart as given to my beloved daughter, [St.] Margaret Mary.'" *"the saints"* (2 Corinthians 9:12). (*Journal* 165).

"On the Feast of St. Margaret Mary Alacoque, Our Lord came and clarified for me [the Secretary] the last promise. 'My daughter, I have come to clarify the last promise that I gave you concerning the wearing of the Medal in honor of me as Jesus King of All Nations. My child, the grace that I will grant to those souls who faithfully wear this Medal is the grace of daily repentance, which, if they are faithful to, will lead, (in the way of salvation,) to the forgiveness by me of all their sins.' '...*in whom we have our redemption, the remission of our sins.*' (Colossians 1:14). Jesus was to explain this promise even further." (*Journal* 167).

"For the sake of continuity, I [His Secretary] will record here what Our Lord spoke concerning this.... 'I promise the graces of daily repentance, unto conversion, unto salvation, into eternal life to the soul who will faithfully wear this Medal.'" "*For the sorrow that is according to God produces repentance that surely tends to salvation...*" (2 Corinthians 7:10). (*Journal* 168).

"Our Lord...has extended His mercy to us by no longer requiring that the Medal be worn. Obviously, this is the preference, since He first requested its wearing. But He loves us so much, and understands our weaknesses, that He has 'bent over backwards' to accommodate us in His great mercy. He now extends these promises to those who 'embrace' this Devotion, and keep His Medal 'in reverence'. Praised be Jesus in His love and mercy!" "*And you yourselves are witnesses of these things.*" (Luke 24:48). (*Journal* 169).

"Our Savior, in His great mercy and love, continued to extend wonderful promises to those who would faithfully wear His Medal. ...Jesus gave the following promises. 'My child, I come to you this day to add another promise to the faithful wearing of this Medal. I promise the souls who thus wear this Medal a special power over my Sacred Heart. "*...by reason of His very great love wherewith He has loved us...*" (Ephesians 2:4). I will readily hear their petitions and prayers "*We will hear thee...*" (Acts 17:32) and pour out upon them my grace, according to my most Holy Will.'" "*...in accord with all the Will of God.*" (Colossians 4:12). (*Journal* 170).

"Our Lord continued to give promises. 'My daughter, yet another promise do I attach to the faithful wearing of my Medal. I extend, little one, to the soul who faithfully wears my Medal, the grace to understand the efficacy of praying to me as King. "*...this is the gift of God.*" (Ecclesiastes 3:13). I also promise, to the soul who faithfully wears this Medal, the grace to trust in my mercy. "*I will trust in*

Him." (Hebrews 2:13). The more the soul trusts in my power and mercy, the greater will I reward their confidence.'" *"Therefore, I say to you, all things whatever you ask for in prayer, believe that you shall receive, and they shall come to you."* (Mark 11:24). *(Journal* 173).

Medal Promises of St. Michael

"St. Michael came and gave further promises of his own for the wearing of the Medal. 'My dear friend, I come to you this night to deliver the promise I spoke of the other night. I, the Archangel Michael, *"Michael, one of the chief princes..."* (Daniel 10:13) promise to obtain for those faithful Catholic souls who faithfully wear this Medal honoring the Most High God as Jesus King of All Nations, the reverse of which bears my image, the beautiful grace of an angelic escort to the table of the Lord Jesus Christ.'" *"...for they are the ministers of God, serving unto this very end."* (Romans 13:6). *(Journal* 174).

"I myself will accompany these souls who approach Our Lord in Holy Communion, with reverence, faith and love. *'...in holiness and honor...'* (Thessalonians 4:4). I will bear these souls upon my hands. *'For the hand of the Lord was with him.'* (Luke 1:66). I will watch over them with a most special vigilance. I will be their special protector in their journey toward eternity. Let the faithful approach Our Lord in the most Blessed Sacrament with love, devotion, and reverence. *'...with thanksgiving.'* (Colossians 4:2). Let them at least desire these things." *(Journal* 175).

"To those ministers of His who do reverence Christ, the God-Man King, in the Blessed Sacrament, as He should be, I give my most loving thanks and promise to them my special presence and protection. He must be loved, adored, reverenced, and worshiped properly in this, the most Excellent Sacrament. *'Thanks be to God for His unspeakable gift!'* (2 Corinthians 9:15). Let those sacred places where they worship our Sacramental Lord and King call upon me for the continuation and spread of this Devotion most pleasing to Almighty God! I am the guardian of the most Blessed Sacrament." *"Blessed is he who watches..."* (Revelation 16:15). *(Journal* 177).

"My friend, one of the most beautiful graces Almighty God shall grant, through the faithful wearing of this Medal, is that I myself will obtain these souls the grace of coming to the belief of the divine truth of the Real Presence of Jesus Christ, the God-Man, in the most Blessed Sacrament. *'And He said to them, "But who do you say that I am?" Simon Peter answered and said, "The Christ of God."'* (Luke 9:20). This grace not only applies to those souls within the bosom of Holy Mother, the Catholic Church, *'the Church of God, which He has purchased with His own blood.'* (Acts 20:28) but also to those faithful souls who love Christ and are presently affiliated with another church or belief. *'...thy brethren are standing outside, wishing to see thee.'* (Luke 8:20). Hence, this grace I am speaking of is that of daily conversion for those already in the Church, *'Now you are the body of Christ, member for member.'* (1 Corinthians 12:27) and also that of conversion to the One True Faith of those souls, whom Christ loves dearly, who are presently estranged from Holy Mother Catholic Church. *'I will heal their breaches, I will love them freely, for my wrath is turned away from them. I will be as the dew, Israel shall spring as the lily, and his root shall shoot forth as that of Libanus. His branches shall spread, and his glory shall be as the olive tree, and his smell as that of Libanus. They shall be converted that sit under his shadow; they shall live upon wheat; and shall blossom as a vine; his memorial shall be as the wine of Libanus.'* (Hosea 14:5–8). When St. Michael was explaining this latter part, with folded hands, he gazed up to heaven with a tremendous look of gratitude and thanksgiving." *"...rendering thanks abundantly."* (Colossians 2:7). *(Journal* 178).

St. Michael the Archangel said, "I promise to those souls who give glory and honor to God in this Devotion, and invoke me under this title [Protector of the Church on Earth], protection from the enemy during life and especially at the hour of their death when the assaults of the enemy are most violent." *"...my eye has seen my enemies confounded."* (Psalms 53:9). *(Journal* 80).

"Let souls turn to me for renewed devotion to Our Lord in the Blessed Sacrament! He must be properly adored, loved, thanked, praised, and worshiped in this the most glorious Sacrament. *'This is the Holy of Holies.'* (Ezekiel 41:4). Let souls call upon me whenever sacrileges and abominations are being committed against the Most High God in this Sacrament of His love. *'...and He Himself will crush our enemies.'* (Psalms 59:14). I promise to put to flight His every enemy. *'...and He chased from her the evil spirit.'* (Tobit 12:3) Great is my zeal for the glory of God!" *"...before whose face I stand..."* (1 Kings 18:15). *(Journal* 86).

D. More Promises to Those Who Embrace the Devotion

Promises to Priests

"My child, beloved one of my most Sacred Heart, I extend yet another promise to the devotional wearing of my Medal. I promise to my ministers, my priests, the grace of greater devotion in ministering the Sacraments. '...*thou wilt be a good minister of Christ Jesus,*' (1 Timothy 4:6). I also promise to those priests who will promote devotion to me as Jesus King of All Nations, the grace of converting souls in great numbers. '*And the multitude of men and women who believed in the Lord increased still more...*' (Acts 5:14). Let them preach to their flocks that I AM King over all! '*Thou art of great authority indeed, and governest well the Kingdom of Israel.*' (1 Kings 21:7). Nonetheless, I AM a merciful King!!!" "*Power belongs to God, and to thee, O Lord, mercy...*" (Psalms 61:12, 13). (*Journal* 181).

"My child, with this I voice another promise to the faithful wearing of my Medal. I will grant to those priests of mine, who desire it, the grace to come to the understanding of holy obedience '...*for the Lord will give thee understanding...*' (2 Timothy 2:7) and how this virtue is not only pleasing to me, but absolutely necessary for these brothers of mine to live in peace and unity." "*Let everyone be subject to the higher authorities, for there exists no authority except from God, and those who exist have been appointed by God. Therefore, he who resists the authority resists the ordinance of God; and they that resist bring on themselves condemnation.*" (Romans 13:1–2). (*Journal* 186).

Reaffirmation of Promise of Protection and Completion of Promises

"A day or so later, Jesus answered a question that had been going through my [the Secretary's] mind. '*And it came to pass, while they were wondering...*' (Luke 24:4). My child, you have been wondering whether or not the promise I once made to you for the praying of the prayers to me as Jesus King of All Nations, (that of my protection from severe storms and all forms of my justice,) '*Watch, then, praying at all times, that you may be accounted worthy to escape all these things that are to be…'* (Luke 21:36) is also to be granted to those who faithfully wear my Medal. My child, I tell you, that I do extend this promise of mine to the devotional wearing of my Medal." *"And thou hast dealt with us, O Lord our God, according to all thy goodness, and according to all that great mercy of thine…"* (Baruch 2:27). (*Journal* 188).

"Here I repeat and clarify the promise. *'And I testify again…'* (Galatians 5:3). I promise to the souls who will faithfully wear my Medal, the grace of protection from harm from all forms of my justice. *'How great is the mercy of the Lord, and His forgiveness to them that turn to Him!'* (Ecclesiastes 17:28). This will especially be true of danger coming from natural disasters." *"…and all things that have been written by the prophets concerning the Son of Man will be accomplished."* (Luke 18:31). (*Journal* 189).

"During the several days that followed, Our Lord revealed yet more promises to the wearing of the Medal and restated others. 'My little one, I come to you again *"I have many things to speak…"* (John 8:26) to add another promise to the faithful wearing of my Medal. I promise, my child, to these souls, the grace of receiving in abundance the gifts of the Holy Spirit.'" *"…spiritual gifts,…abundantly…"* (1 Corinthians 14:12). (*Journal* 190).

"My child, all who faithfully wear my Medal will receive a special degree of glory in heaven. *'A high and glorious throne…'* (Jeremiah 17:12). These souls shall be crowned by me and shall reign with me, their Eternal King. *'And the king turned his face, and blessed all the assembly of Israel…'* (1 Kings 8:14). Also, I promise that these souls will be granted a special power over my Sacred Heart and the Immaculate Heart of my Mother. (These souls will be most special in my sight.) *'…found favor in His sight.'* (Esther 2:9). I promise to the souls who shall faithfully wear my Medal, the desire to please me in all things and thus come to perfection." *"…because I do always the things that are pleasing to Him."* (John 8:29). (*Journal* 191).

"Jesus gave the final promise. *'I will give you the holy and sure promises…'* (Acts 13:34). 'My child, I come to you to give you the last of my promises that I will grant to those souls who faithfully wear my Medal. My daughter, I solemnly promise to the soul who faithfully wears my Medal, the grace to come to know the secrets of my love. *"…the secrets of His Heart are made manifest…"* (1 Corinthians 14:25). With this, my child, my promises to those who faithfully wear my Medal are complete.'" *"Heaven and earth will pass away, but my words will not pass away."* (Mark 13:31). *(Journal 193).*

"Our Lord returned to extend a promise in connection with praying the Chaplet. 'My child, little one of my most Sacred Heart, I come to you tonight to entrust to you a beautiful promise that I will grant in my great mercy *"according to the multitude of thy tender mercies."* (Nehemiah 13:22) to those souls who will recite my Chaplet. I promise my most powerful protection to those souls who, in time of danger, whether it be to mind, body, or soul, shall recite my Chaplet with confidence, *"with confidence"* (Hebrews 4:16) thus imploring my great mercy through my most holy Mother. *"His Mother"* (John 2:5). I also promise to those souls who shall recite my Chaplet, my peace, which knows no bounds. *"Peace I leave with you, my peace I give to you…"* (John 14:27). My little one, so many hearts in this world are without peace. They must come to me, their true peace, if they would have peace!!!'" *"He who has ears to hear, let him hear."* (Luke 14:35). *(Journal 211).*

Promises for Venerators of the Visitation Image

"(As Jesus stood before me [the Secretary] in a vision, He spoke.) 'My daughter, littlest of my little ones, your Jesus desires to show you in a vision some of the miracles He will grant to those souls who come before His Image in the painting of Jesus King of All Nations' (Our Lord is here specifically speaking of the Visitation Image of Himself as King of All Nations. It has traveled around the world already. Our Lord has had this particular Image of Himself exude a beautiful fragrance from His Heart and the wounds in the wrists and feet. Many have witnessed this, including priests. I was blessed to have experienced it twice in the presence of the Image.)" *(Journal 289).*

"At this point in the vision, I saw miracles of conversion represented by a soul kneeling before the Image and crying with face in hands. I saw miracles of physical healing represented by Our Lord stretching forth His hand from the Image and healing the somehow diseased face of a young woman. As He did so, He said gently, 'Be healed, my daughter, be healed.' Her face then turned a smooth white." *(Journal 290).*

"Our Lord gave me this powerful conviction, that no soul who enters the presence of this Image of Jesus King of All Nations will leave without having been touched in their heart. '...*He placed His hands on them...*' (Matthew 19:15). Although I feel Our Lord is speaking in a particular way about the Visitation Image, I also believe that this vision represents the miracles that will be given in the overall Devotion." "*...you have answered well.*" (Luke 20:39). (*Journal* 291).

"Jesus also spoke the following about His priests. 'My priests, who come before this particular Image of mine, will receive from my sovereign Kingship a singular grace.'" "*...for building you up, beloved.*" (2 Corinthians 12:19). (*Journal* 292).

Promises of the Third Millennium

"Come and receive the merciful balm of my love so that you may be healed of your spiritual ills, your mental ills, and your physical ills. Oh, my children, I love you!!!" "*You are my people.*" (Isaiah 51:16). (*Journal* 309).

"Child, I have given a great remedy in my Devotion of Jesus King of All Nations. I ask my children to embrace this Devotion; to pray this Devotion; and to invoke me as Jesus King of All Nations. My mercy and protection will cover those souls, families, and nations that invoke me thus. I will stretch forth to them my scepter of mercy that they may take firm hold and not let go of my Divine Will and law. I will cover them with my kingly mantle that my perfect justice may not reach them as it will reach those who have abandoned my law." "*Indeed the Lord will be there with us, majestic; yes, the Lord our judge, the Lord our lawgiver, the Lord our King, He it is who will save us.*" (Isaiah 33:22). (*Journal* 318).

"Let souls embrace my Devotion of Jesus King of All Nations, and thereby obtain for themselves all of my great promises contained therein. No, my people, I have not forgotten you, for I love you with an everlasting love." "*I have loved you says the Lord; but you say, 'How have you loved us?'*" (Malachi 1:2). (*Journal* 362).

"These particular graces are powerfully offered to you in my Devotion of Jesus King of All Nations. Seize this opportunity given by heaven and embrace my Devotion that you may receive my great promises and find forgiveness, peace, and renewal of your minds, hearts, and souls." *"I will fulfill the promise I made."* (Jeremiah 33:14). (*Journal* 364).

"The promised graces and mercy stand at the ready, waiting to be poured out upon my Church, individual souls, religious communities, all nations, and, indeed, truly upon the entirety of creation and yet are being withheld due to the absence of recognition and approval by my holy Church." (*Journal* 381).

"Pray and trust in me, my faithful ones. I will not abandon you in the dark and cloudy day which rapidly approaches. Stay close to my Immaculate Mother; cling to her holy Rosary, invoke her Immaculate Heart." (*Journal* 416).

"Take up my Devotion of Jesus King of All Nations for in its practice you shall find for yourselves a haven of grace, mercy, and protection. Enthrone this my Image everywhere for I shall be powerfully present there and the power of my sovereign Kingship shall surely shield you from my just judgment. (*Journal* 418).

"Be strong and do not lose hope. I am with you to save you." (*Journal* 419).

E. Jesus King of All Nations' Prophecies of Chastisements

Jesus King of All Nations revealed many prophecies of chastisements to His Secretary, the mystic of the Devotion, including the ones below.

The numbers refer to the paragraph numbers in the Journal.

23. My children, your God appeals to you. *"I have not come to call the just, but sinners, to repentance."* (Luke 5:32). Now is the time of great mercy. *"I will show mercies to you..."* (Jeremiah 42:12). Take heed and benefit from it. *"...let him who reads understand..."* (Mark 13:14). If you do not, a most grievous chastisement will suddenly fall upon you. *"...for in one hour has thy judgment come!"* (Revelation 18:10).

317. Will they hear? Will they wake from their sleep in sin? *"For as it was in the day of Noah, so it will be at the coming of the Son of Man. In those days before the Flood, they were eating and drinking, marrying and giving in marriage, up to the day that Noah entered the ark. They did not know until the Flood came and carried them all away. So will it be also at the coming of the Son of Man....Therefore, stay awake! For you do not know on which day your Lord will come."* (Matthew 24:37–39, 42). If they do not, a yet more terrible catastrophe will befall mankind. Pray! Sacrifice! Invoke my most Sacred, Eucharistic, and kingly Heart through my most holy Mother! *"The Mother of my Lord."* (Luke 1:43).

319. My children, dear children, do not despair. There is always hope. *"Take courage, it is I, do not be afraid! He got into the boat with them and the wind died down."* (Mark 6:50–51). My holy and dear Mother has instructed you many times in many places how to bring down my mercy upon the world. This Woman of Hope still pleads for you all, her children. *"Blessed are you, daughter, by the Most High God, above all the women on earth; and blessed be the Lord God, the creator of heaven and earth who guided your blow at the head of the chief of our enemies. Your deed of hope will never be forgotten by those who tell of the might of God. May God make this redound to your everlasting honor, rewarding you with blessings,...you averted our disaster, walking uprightly before our God."* (Judith 13:18–20). Souls underestimate the power of Mary's prayers. One glance from my dear Mother is

enough to disarm my perfect justice. She is the channel of my mercy. Through her flows my life to mankind. Trust your Mother. Honor your Mother. Beseech your Mother to pray for the world. She gathers your prayers and sacrifices and presents them to me perfumed with the fragrant incense of her love.

320. Children, my children, do not despair. *"Rejoice in hope, endure in affliction, persevere in prayer."* (Romans 12:12). Come to my throne of mercy, confident that I will hear you. I reign in the most Blessed Sacrament. Adore me there. Receive me with hearts full of love and submission to my Holy Will. I need you my faithful ones. Help me to save souls. *"These alone are my co-workers for the Kingdom of God, and they have been a comfort to me."* (1 Thessalonians 4:11). Many are perishing due to obstinate hearts. They must desire salvation; I will not force it upon them for I will not take away their free will. However, my grace and mercy can melt even the most obstinate heart, but you must pray for these graces. *"Just as you once disobeyed God but have now received mercy because of their disobedience, so they have now disobeyed in order that, by virtue of the mercy shown to you, they too may now receive mercy. For God delivered all to disobedience, that He might have mercy upon all."* (Romans 11:30–32).

326. Remain faithful. Anchor yourselves to me by means of the holy Sacraments, my holy Mother's Rosary, and my *Chaplet of Unity*. This Chaplet is a great and powerful prayer given to my children in my mercy. I say again: I have given it great power over my Sacred Heart.

339. My child, I call you powerfully to once more take up the work of writing my Words for my dear, erring children! *"Say to daughter Zion, 'Behold, your King comes to you,'"* (Matthew 21:5). The world is in great danger, great peril due to the weight of its sins! My children! Open your hearts and minds to the influence of my grace! Children of men, you are blinded by sin! You are blinded by pride! Never in the history of the world has mankind been so laden down with sin. Noise is everywhere. Confusion abounds. The idolatry of modern technology is a tool of the enemy with which he withdraws hearts and minds from hearing the gentle, loving voice of God. *"For those times will have tribulations such as has not been since the beginning of God's Creation until now, nor ever will be."* (Mark 13:19).

341. A great catastrophe is about to descend on the world. *"Fire, sent from on high"* (Baruch 6:63). *"the time of trial that is going to come to the whole world to test the inhabitants of the earth."* (Revelation 3:10). Lessen this punishment with the spiritual weapons of frequent reception of the holy Sacraments; loving, reverent attendance at the holy Sacrifice of the Mass; and constant praying of the holy Rosary. When my Mother came to Fatima, she requested the praying of the Rosary daily. I now say constant! Let this prayer encompass your very hearts, minds, and souls, offering it to me through my dear Mother for the salvation of souls.

348. My child, take this message of mine quickly to your director. *"God has told me to hasten."* (2 Chronicles 35:21). I call upon all the faithful and in particular my consecrated ones to offer prayers and sacrifices to lessen a great chastisement that is about to fall upon mankind. Many souls will be unprepared and they need desperately the charity of others. *"Jerusalem is mindful of the days of her wretched homelessness, when her people fell into enemy hands, and she had no one to help her; when her foes gloated over her, laughed at her ruin."* (Lamentations 1:7). I have been patient for so long, listening to the pleading of my holy Mother for her erring children. The cup is overflowing. My justice must be poured out. Yet my mercy is ever present even when my justice is revealed. *"Turn to me and be safe, all you ends of the earth, for I am God; there is no other! By myself I swear, uttering my just decree and my unalterable Word:"* (Isaiah 45:22-23). Pray, pray, pray. *Novum!* (Latin for "in a new way") Extend your prayers yet further. Help me to save your brothers and sisters who are in danger of being eternally lost. *"For the Son of Man has come to seek and to save what was lost."* (Luke 19:10).

366. Urgency! Urgency my people! *"Thus says the Lord God: See, I will lift up my hand to the nations, and raise my signal to the peoples;"* (Isaiah 49:22). Great is the chastisement that is ready to descend upon this sinful world to correct the consciences of individuals and the conscience of mankind as a whole! My Sacred, kingly, and Eucharistic Heart which burns as a conflagration of Divine Love for mankind urges me on to mercy, yet the weightiness of mankind's sins compels my perfect justice to be poured out. *"Because you are haughty of heart, and say, 'A god am I! I occupy a godly throne in the heart of the sea!' And yet you are a man, and not a god, however you may think yourself like a god."* (Ezekiel 28:2).

370. I correct my children out of love for them. *"Those whom I love, I reprove and chastise. Be earnest, therefore, and repent."* (Revelation 3:19). I delight not in the suffering of my children. I desire to awaken their darkened consciences that they may recognize their sinfulness and be converted [so] that there may be a renewal of hearts and minds thereby causing the world itself to be renewed. *"The one who sat on the throne said, 'Behold, I make all things new.' Then He said, 'Write these words down, for they are trustworthy and true.'"* (Revelation 21:5).

372. Until the heart of man changes, the world will not and cannot change. Greater and greater will be the catastrophes in nature which itself rebels against the sinfulness of the children of men. The earth itself writhes in horror at the weight of corruption and uncleanness it supports. It cries out for justice against its inhabitants.

381. The promised graces and mercy stand at the ready, waiting to be poured out upon my Church, individual souls, religious communities, all nations, and, indeed, truly upon the entirety of creation and yet are being withheld due to the absence of recognition and approval by my holy Church.

414. Therefore, let it also be known that a Great Renewal of my Holy Church, of Mankind, and, indeed, of All Creation will follow the cleansing action of my justice. How greatly I love my people! It is for your good, O mankind, that I allow my justice to be poured out in order to awaken your conscience and correct your sinful behavior. Yet you see how dearly I love you in that I continually warn you and even seek to comfort you in the pain of the cleansing which is almost upon you.

418. Take up my Devotion of Jesus King of All Nations for in its practice you shall find for yourselves a haven of grace, mercy, and protection. Enthrone this my Image everywhere for I shall be powerfully present there and the power of my sovereign Kingship shall surely shield you from my just judgment.

453. I promised by holy covenant never to flood the earth in totality again; no, this time my all-holy justice shall come through fire.

496. My Spirit shall once more descend in a new Pentecost; a new Pentecost replete with the cleansing fire of His love. A fire ablaze with the love and justice of God.

664. Awake! Lift up your heads, my people! Do you not see the signs all around you?! A great catastrophe is about to befall you!

826. Seek my great mercy while there is yet time. Terror will fall upon this world while consciences sleep. Pray that the greater number shall be saved.

827. *"The Lord does not delay His promise, as some regard 'delay,' but He is patient with you, not wishing that any should perish but that all should come to repentance. But the day of the Lord will come like a thief, and then the heavens will pass away with a mighty roar and the elements will be dissolved by fire, and the earth and everything done on it will be found out."* (2 Peter 3:9–10).

F. The Spiritual Mother's Message of Aversion of a Prophesied Seaquake Chastisement in Puerto Rico

On May 22, 1992, in answer to the prayers of His Devotion, Jesus King of All Nations averted a seaquake chastisement in Puerto Rico that He had prophesied. Below is the message that He revealed to the "Spiritual Mother" regarding this. The Spiritual Mother was a spiritual advisor of the Secretary.

She said,

I am, at Our Lord's request, *"And you, O child, shall be called prophet of the Most High; For you shall go before the Lord to prepare straight paths for Him, giving His people a knowledge of salvation in freedom from their sins, All this is the work of the kindness of our God; He, the Dayspring, shall visit us in His mercy to shine on those who sit in darkness and in the shadow of death, to guide our feet into the way of peace."* (Luke 1:76–79) typing this message that He, as my sovereign Eucharistic King, dictated to me as I was before Him in the Blessed Sacrament at St. Michael's Church *"from the house of God"* (Daniel 5:3) between the afternoon hours of twelve and one o'clock today. I have read this message to Fr. José on the telephone and he can bear witness of what I have spoken that Our Lord said to me today and what my Jesus also said to me last night, May 21, 1992. *"She reported what He had said to her."* (John 20:18).

Our Lord said,

Daughter of my Father *"your Father"* (Mark 11:26), my beloved, my spouse *"He who is of God hears the words of God"* (John 8:47), tell my beloved priest sons, tell my beloved bishop *"Now it was...Joanna...*[Author's note: the Spiritual Mother's first name was Johanna.]*who was telling these things to the apostles."* (Luke 24:10) that in my great mercy I, yes, it is I myself *"and He interpreted to them the things...referring to Himself."* (Luke 24:27), your sovereign Lord and God, who has mitigated this chastisement *"But you, our God are good and true, slow to anger, and governing all with mercy."*

(Wisdom 15:1) to my people in the islands, my people of Puerto Rico! *"that it might be an evident and manifest sign of the help of God."* (2 Maccabees 15:35). "Why?", I will tell them, for you already know the reason my beloved. *"for we cannot but speak of what we have seen and heard."* (Acts 4:20). Because in this place, some have already received me as their Lord and King *"For even as Jonah was a sign to the Ninevites, so will also the Son of Man be to this generation for they repented at the preaching of Jonah, and behold, a greater than Jonah is here."* (Luke 11:30, 32) in the Devotion that I have given you and [my Secretary] *"His servants"* (Luke 19:13) to give to the world, that of Jesus King of All Nations." *"It is what I desired"* (2 Maccabees 15:39).

My beloved priest sons, José and Jaime, along with my daughters, my spouses in the Order of the Virgin of the Aurora, received my message with living hearts open to my Words, open to my love, and brought my message to my beloved Bishop Enrique *"here we are, at your service"* (Job 38:35) who received you with an open heart, with an open soul, with open physical manifestations of charity toward you! *"The favors of the Lord I will recall, the glorious deeds of the Lord, because of all He has done for us; for He is good to the house of Israel, He has favored us according to His mercy and great kindness. He said: 'They are indeed my people, children who are not disloyal;' So He became their Savior in their every affliction."* (Isaiah 63:7–9).

This most beloved Bishop, Prince of my Church, and priest son of mine *"A wise magistrate lends stability to his people, and the government of a prudent man is well ordered. As the people's judge, so are his ministers; as the head of a city, its inhabitants. A wanton king destroys his people, but a city grows through the wisdom of its princes. Sovereignty over the earth is in the hand of God, who raises up on it the man of the hour; sovereignty over every man is in the hand of God, who imparts His majesty to the ruler."* (Sirach 10:1–5) did not receive you with scorn, indifference, mock the messages that I have sent, or refuse to listen!!! *"He will not speak on his own, but will speak only what he hears, and will announce to you the things to come. In doing this, he will give glory to me, because he will* have received from me what he will announce to you." (John 16:13-14).

As I told you last night [May 21, 1992], *"what have I been telling you"* (John 8:26) speaking about my people in Puerto Rico, "I will have mercy on whom I will have mercy!!" I have heard the prayers of my people in repentance, and my most holy Mother has interceded on their behalf, for these children recognize and honor my Mother! I have stopped the seaquake at this time, for it would have devastated the lands and the peoples *"Mighty are you, O Lord, and your faithfulness surrounds you. You rule over the surging of the sea; you still the swelling of its waves...yours are the heavens and the earth; the world and its fullness you have founded;....Yours is a mighty arm; strong is your hand, exalted your right hand."* (Psalms 89:9-10, 12, 14); with the merciful scepter of my Kingship I have done this! Yes, indeed! My messengers were correct that I sent to tell my people of the devastation of the chastisement that was to occur today, the 22nd of May! In my justice, their horrible sins have justly deserved much more than this! *"Your hands are full of blood! Wash yourselves clean! Put away your misdeeds from before my eyes; cease doing evil; learn to do good. Make justice your aim: redress the wronged, hear the orphan's plea, defend the widow. Come now, let us set things right says the Lord: though your sins be like scarlet, they may become white as snow; Though they be crimson red, they may become white as wool. If you are willing, and obey, you shall eat the good things of the land; But if you refuse and resist, the sword shall consume you: for the mouth of the Lord has spoken!"* (Isaiah 1:15-20). But my faithful souls have prayed to me and recognized me as King of All Nations, and have spread my glory in this recognition! *"Rise, O God; judge the earth, for yours are all the nations."* (Psalms 82:8).

No, not all are praying, but enough have prayed to mitigate, as you know so well my beloved, that it is my promise to those who honor me, and have embraced me in my Devotion as King of All Nations! *"and instruction is to be sought from His mouth"* (Malachi 2:7). Yes, chastisements will come..., but let them see, let them experience, let them bear witness to the mercy that I have given them that they were not harmed! *"it shall not hurt them."* (Mark 16:18). I did not allow you to tell them ahead of time, for it is their faith and trust in me that I wish to receive! Through their prayers of imploring my merciful graces upon them through my Mother, they have prayed with a sincere heart! *"no dishonesty was found upon his lips."* (Malachi 2:6). For there are those who would not have prayed with a sincere heart to me, or not have prayed at all, both are the same to me....I do not hear this lip service! *"He has sent empty away."* (Luke 1:53). I have shown them what my kingly mercy does! I have shown them what prayers with sincere hearts can do! *"And in His name will the Gentiles hope."* (Matthew 12:21). I have shown them that if they turn to me, their Merciful King who desires to reign in their hearts, that I am a King of Mercy, a Father of Mercy, a Lord of Love who does not want their unnecessary deaths and condemnation of their souls because of their sins and stubbornness and pride! *"So be on watch. Pray constantly for the strength to escape whatever is in prospect, and to stand secure before the Son of Man."* (Luke 21:36).

Have no doubt—the thunder of my justice was going to be heard!!! As thunder comes before the rain...so the thunder of my just judgment upon them was going to be heard first! Will my children *wake up* and see the lightning first? The Lightning of the Merciful Rays of my mercy that I wish to strike their hearts with!!! Will they notice me who AM? *"named Jesus"* (Matthew 1:25). Will my people finally see with the light of my grace so that I can reign in their hearts?! Yes, I wish to be the light that comes before the Reign! The Reign of my Merciful Kingship! *"'Yes, when you seek me with all of your heart, you will find me with you,' says the Lord, 'and I will change your lot;'"* (Jeremiah 29:13-14). Choose my people; choose how you wish to serve me! *"And I saw that wisdom has the advantage over folly as much as light has the advantage over darkness."* (Ecclesiastes 2:13). I who AM Jesus, your True High-Priest Victim, Prophet who cries out to you now, and Sovereign King who invites you to reign with me in mercy and love and unity, who wishes to acknowledge those who have prayed for all of my people, for they are most dear to my kingly Heart! *"That whole night they called upon the God of Israel for help."* (Judith 6:21). It is you, my special little ones, who have found the fulfillment of my promises not only for yourselves, but for your whole nation! *"My people is Israel, who cried to God and was saved. The Lord saved your people and delivered us from all these evils. God worked signs and great wonders, such as have not occurred among the nation. For this purpose, He arranged two lots: one for the people of God, the second for all the other nations...God remembered His people and rendered justice to His inheritance."* (Esther 10:6–9).

Remember what I have done for you, my people, of how I have spared you this time! *"Gathering together with joy and happiness before God, they shall celebrate"* (Esther 10:10). Honor my Mother, who has stood by the foot of your cross, like she stood at the foot of mine, and prayed and interceded and mediated to me for your sakes! She is the Mediatrix of All of my Graces! She is my Co-Redemptrix! *"You are the glory of Jerusalem, the surpassing joy of Israel; you are the splendid boast of our people. With your own hands you have done this; you have done good to Israel, and God is pleased with what you have wrought. May you be blessed by the Lord Almighty forever and ever! And all the people answered, 'Amen!'"* (Judith 15:9–10). I bless you all my children. Remember the things that I have said to you! *"The child learns to reject the bad and choose the good."* (Isaiah 7:16).

The Spiritual Mother concluded her Message, "I pray with all of you with Our Blessed Mother a song of praise to Jesus Our King for how He has been merciful to us! *'Judith led all Israel in this song of Thanksgiving, and the people swelled this hymn of praise:'* (Judith 15:14). I sing with all of you Our Lord's Word in Judith 16:1–17."

Judith said,

Begin a song to my God with tambourines,
    sing to my Lord with cymbals.
Raise to Him a new psalm;
    exalt Him, and call upon His name.
For the Lord is a God who crushes wars;
    He sets up His camp among His people;
    He delivered me from the hands of my pursuers.
The Assyrian came down from the mountains of the north;
    he came with myriads of his warriors;

their numbers blocked up the wadis,
   and their cavalry covered the hills. He boasted that he
      would burn up my territory,
   and kill my young men with the sword,
and dash my infants to the ground,
   and seize my children as booty,
   and take my virgins as spoil.

But the Lord Almighty has foiled them
   by the hand of a woman.
For their mighty one did not fall by the hands of the young
     men,
   nor did the sons of the Titans strike him down,
   nor did tall giants set upon him;
but Judith, daughter of Merari,
   with the beauty of her countenance undid him.

For she put away her widow's clothing
   to exalt the oppressed in Israel.
She anointed her face with perfume;
   she fastened her hair with a tiara
   and put on a linen gown to beguile him.
Her sandal ravished his eyes,
   her beauty captivated his mind,
   and the sword severed his neck!
The Persians trembled at her boldness,
   the Medes were daunted at her daring.

Then my oppressed people shouted;
   my weak people cried out, and the enemy trembled;
   they lifted up their voices, and the enemy were turned back.
Sons of slave girls pierced them through
   and wounded them like the children of fugitives;
   they perished before the army of my Lord.

I will sing to my God a new song:
O Lord, you are great and glorious,
   wonderful in strength, invincible.
Let all your creatures serve you,
   for you spoke, and they were made.

You sent forth your spirit, and it formed them;
  there is none that can resist your voice.
For the mountains shall be shaken to their foundations with
    the waters;
  before your glance the rocks shall melt like wax.
But to those who fear you,
  you show mercy.
For every sacrifice as a fragrant offering is a small thing,
  and the fat of all whole burnt offerings to you is a very little
    thing;
but whoever fears the Lord is great forever.

Woe to the nations that rise up against my people!
The Lord Almighty will take vengeance on them in the day of
  judgment;
He will send fire and worms into their flesh;
  they shall weep in pain forever.

G. The Spiritual Mother's Message of the Aversion and Mitigation of Nuclear War

On May 11 and 13, 1998, India conducted a total of five underground nuclear tests, breaking a 24-year self-imposed moratorium on nuclear testing. Pakistan followed, claiming five tests on May 28, 1998 and an additional test on May 30, for a total of six, to get one up on India. The Indian tests, which completely surprised the U.S. intelligence and policy community, set off a world-wide storm of criticism. Many analysts judged that, by conducting nuclear tests, the Indian government hoped to consolidate its power by rallying strong national, pro-nuclear sentiment.

On May 29, 1998, the Spiritual Mother of the Jesus King of All Nations Devotion phoned me and told me that she and others had been praying for peace between India and Pakistan. She said that Jesus King of All Nations gave her a message concerning their nuclear confrontation and the threat of nuclear war.

Jesus King of All Nations averted a nuclear chastisement and mitigated it to a lesser chastisement of conventional warfare because of the prayers of the people.

Our Lord: Beloved, thank you and those whom you asked to pray, and did so, over the situation of India's and Pakistan's nuclear testing. *"He told them, 'To you the mystery of the Reign of God has been confided.'"* (Mark 4:11). Although they persisted, the prayers were used to mitigate the *"wicked design"* (Mark 7:21) of these pride-filled and arrogant nations.

Sacrificial prayer to and with me, your merciful God, *"Jesus was at prayer"* (Luke 3:21) does change situations and hearts for the better! I, your Jesus, your merciful, Sovereign King of all the nations and peoples of this world *"God declared"* (Acts 13:34) tell you this plainly! *"Do not my words promise good to him who walks uprightly?"* (Micah 2:7). Nuclear arms that mankind makes only hold death and destruction for men, women, children, animals, plants, and the planet earth itself that I have created. *"For from Him and through Him and for Him are all things. To Him be glory forever. Amen."* (Romans 11:36).

Nuclear explosions also do harm to the earth on which you live, to its core, and to its very course. Here the Lord showed me a vision of an orange with a bomb exploding inside that tore at the very flesh of the orange. *"appeared to me"* (Genesis 48:3). He was trying to make a point that these explosions do harm the very skin of the planet and its inside of dirt and rocks and waters and on the outside its position in space. *"For suddenly arises the destruction they send and the ruin from either one, who can measure?"* (Proverbs 24:22).

Then Our Lord said,

No, mankind cannot even begin to measure the evil and destructive forces of nuclear armaments. It is arms of love that you need, mankind. When little children came to me, I held them in my arms and I touched them lovingly and blessed them. *"They even brought babies to be touched by Him."* (Luke 18:15). My arms of love bring true peace and love of the Holy Spirit. *"And my spirit continues in your midst; do not fear."* (Haggai 2:5).

Beloved, even in your own country today, teachers in school systems and others cannot put their arms of comfort around hurting children for fear of false civil lawsuits of abuse filed by greedy parents. This is upside down! This is not the example of goodness I gave you; it is the way of the evil one. *"Who diverted you from the path of truth? Such enticements do not come from Him who called you."* (Galatians 5:7–8).

I tell you, unless you change the attitude of your hearts, put aside bitterness and rivalry, and your personal and generational traditions of hate and anger toward one another, you, mankind, will make the entire earth become a potter's field. Yes, I said it is you, mankind, who will make it a potter's field, a field of blood. *"Those who inhabit a land overshadowed by death."* (Matthew 4:16). Judas sold me out for 30 pieces of silver. *"Yes, that was the sum."* (Acts 5:8). Humanity is selling out parents, brothers, sisters, children, unborn babies, neighbors, and nations in greed to gain power, wealth, and freedom from God-given responsibilities. *"He who seeks only himself brings himself to ruin, whereas he who brings himself to naught for me discovers who he is."* (Matthew 10:39). It is time and past time to reconcile with your wife, reconcile with your husband, and *"heed carefully what you hear."* (Matthew 11:13) reconcile with your children, reconcile with your neighbors, reconcile peoples and nations with one another. *"If you bring your gift to the altar and there recall that your brother has anything against you, leave your gift at the altar, go first and be reconciled with your brother and then come and offer your gift. Lose no time, settle with your opponent."* (Matthew 5:23–25).

Pray for those my people, pray for those who will not be reconciled, pray for those who are your enemies and I, your merciful King of All Nations and peoples, will heal them. I will forgive their sinfulness, heal their brokenness, and renew their hearts [Author's note: As we petition Him to do in the *Chaplet of Unity*] in the power of the Holy Spirit that there may be unity and love amongst all peoples and nations, neighbors, and families for my sake, for I AM God. AM I speaking plainly enough my people? I AM.

My love for you is infinitely merciful, for I love you more than you can ever possibly know love.

H. The Act of Entrustment of the United States of America to Jesus King of All Nations

On November 21, 2021, on the Solemnity of Jesus Christ, King of the Universe, in his Cathedral of St. Francis Xavier, Bishop David Ricken of the Diocese of Green Bay, Wisconsin, entrusted the United States of America to Jesus King of All Nations. His priests and pastoral leaders joined Bishop Ricken in reciting a Special Litany for Christ to reign.

O Immortal King of Ages, Lord Jesus Christ, our God and Savior! We kneel before you to acknowledge your Reign, to submit ourselves to your law, to entrust and consecrate to you our Diocese and all of our people.

We confess before heaven and earth that we need your rule. We acknowledge that you alone have a holy and perennial law for us. Therefore, humbly bowing our heads before you, the King of the Universe, we recognize your sovereignty over this Diocese and all who live within it. We recognize that you are the Sovereign King, the King of All Nations, the King of this Nation, the United States of America. Desirous to worship the majesty of your power and glory, with great faith and love, we cry out to you: **Christ, reign over us!** (All bold lettering is by Bishop Ricken.)

Bishop/Pastor	Everyone
In our hearts	**Christ, reign over us!**
In our families	**Christ, reign over us!**
In our parishes	**Christ, reign over us!**
In our schools and universities	**Christ, reign over us!**
In the means of social communication	**Christ, reign over us!**
In our offices, places of work, service, and rest	**Christ, reign over us!**
In our cities and villages	**Christ, reign over us!**
On our farms and in the countryside	**Christ, reign over us!**
Throughout this Nation of the United States of America and the State of Wisconsin	**Christ, reign over us!**

We bless you and give you thanks, Lord Jesus Christ:

Bishop/Pastor	Everyone
For the unfathomable love of your Sacred Heart	**Christ, reign over us!**
For the grace of baptism and the covenant of all sacramental grace	**Christ, reign over us!**
For the maternal and royal presence of Mary in our history	**Christ, reign over us!**
For the great Divine Mercy that you constantly extend to us	**Christ, reign over us!**
For the love pouring out of your Sacred Heart	**Christ, reign over us!**
For your faithfulness despite our betrayals and weaknesses	**Christ, reign over us!**

Aware of our faults and abuse inflicted on your Sacred Heart, we ask forgiveness for all our sins, and, in particular, for turning away from the holy faith, for our lack of love for you and our neighbor. We ask you to forgive the social sins of our nation, all its defects, addictions, and enslavement. We renounce the Devil and all his works.

We humbly submit ourselves to your Lordship and your law. We commit ourselves to ordering our entire personal, family, parish, diocesan, and national life according to your law:

Bishop/Pastor	Everyone
We pledge to defend your holy worship and to preach your royal glory	**Christ our King, we beseech you, hear us!**
We pledge to do your Will and to protect the integrity of our consciences	**Christ our King, we beseech you, hear us!**
We pledge to care for the sanctity of our families and the Christian education of our children	**Christ our King, we beseech you, hear us!**
We pledge to build your Kingdom and to defend it in our nation	**Christ our King, we beseech you, hear us!**

Bishop/Pastor	Everyone

We pledge to engage actively in the life of the Church and to protect her rights. **Christ our King, we beseech you, hear us!**

You, the only Ruler of states, nations, and of all creation, the King of kings and the Lord of lords! We entrust to you the Diocese of Green Bay and all church and civil leaders. Make all those who exercise power do so with justice and govern rightly in accordance with your laws.

Christ our King, we confidently entrust to your mercy all people of this land, the United States of America, and especially those of the people who do not follow your ways. Give them your grace, enlighten them through the power of the Holy Spirit, and lead us all to the eternal communion with the Father.

In the name of brotherly love, we entrust to you all the world's nations. Make them recognize you as their rightful Lord and King and use this time given to them by the Father to submit voluntarily to your Lordship.

Lord Jesus Christ, King of our hearts, make our hearts like your Sacred Heart. Let your Holy Spirit descend and renew the face of the earth. May your Holy Spirit support us as we accomplish the obligations that are the consequences of this Diocesan act, protect us from evil, and bring about our sanctification.

In the Immaculate Conception, we place our decisions and commitments. We all entrust to the maternal care of the Queen of Heaven, Our Lady of Good Help, and to the intercession of our patron saint, St. Francis Xavier.

Everyone:

Christ, reign over us! Reign over our country, and reign in every nation—for the greater glory of the most Holy Trinity and the salvation of humanity. Make our homeland and the entire world into your Kingdom: a Kingdom of truth and life, a Kingdom of holiness and grace, a Kingdom of justice, love, and peace. Amen.

I. Books by Dan Lynch

The Coming Great Chastisement and The Great Renewal

www.JKMI.com

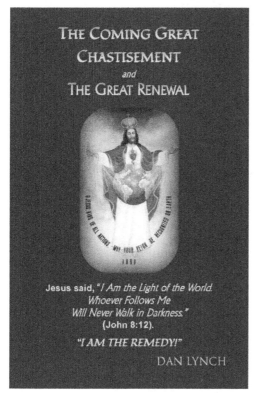

"I have had the privilege of studying the Jesus King of All Nations revelations with great care. This study has left me no doubts, not even minor, concerning the authenticity of these revelations as revelations directly dictated by Jesus to His Secretary and the truth of their content as a remedy for the imminent chastisement under way."

Fr. Peter Damian Fehlner, OFM Conv., S.T.D.

"I believe that Dan Lynch has done us a great service in linking historical facts and prophetic revelations over the past two centuries with the teachings of the Holy Scriptures and of the Roman Pontiffs about what is being manifested in our own era. He illustrates very well that the teaching of Pius XI in *Quas Primas (On the Feast of Christ the King)* on the Kingship of Christ, is more highly relevant than ever and that it accords remarkably with the (private) revelations on Jesus King of All Nations.

"It seems impossible to me to escape the conclusion that we are at a very crucial stage in the Church and in the United States and in the world. The Devotion to Jesus King of All Nations certainly seems to be a divinely-ordained remedy for our present chaotic situation."

Monsignor Arthur Calkins, Mariologist and named Chaplain of His Holiness and Prelate of Honor of His Holiness

"Dan Lynch has done a masterful job to summarize not only the critical times we are living, but the even more critical *response* needed. One way or another, the world *will* acknowledge that Jesus is Lord."

Mark Mallett, Evangelist and Author,
The Final Confrontation

"What Dan presents to us is not the *Eschatology of Despair* promoted today by a few, but rather he prophetically proclaims the same thing Pope Pius XI did almost 100 years ago in *Quas Primas (On the Feast of Christ the King)*: Our Lord Jesus Christ is the King of All Nations, and we must acknowledge Him as such so as to hasten His Reign on earth."

Daniel O'Connor, Professor of Philosophy and Author, *The Crown of History* and *The Crown of Sanctity*

Medjugorje's Ten Secrets — How to Prepare

- The Most Comprehensive Book in the World about Medjugorje's Ten Secrets.

- Explains How to Prepare for the Secrets and Chastisements That Will Soon Come to the World.

- Jesus King of All Nations said, "What You See Happening Around You [The COVID–19 Pandemic] is the Beginning of the Chastisements Foretold by Me to Correct the Conscience of Mankind."

Fr. Petar, designated recipient of Mirjana's First Secret, said, "Everything is closer and closer. Never in the whole world has the situation been so sad and so bad....Never in history have there been so many sinners and unbelievers. We are feeling that something has to happen very quickly. It cannot continue like this much longer. God has to do something very quickly!"

Catherine Grinn, a Catholic School Principal, said, "This book is an amazing tool to evangelize our younger generation!

"It pulls you in and you want to keep reading it as you are taught how to equip yourself to help bring the Triumph of the Immaculate Heart of Mary.

"Most importantly, it answers so many questions that people now have. Dan has connected us to the apparitions, messages, and secrets of Medjugorje and shows us that they are about us, and for us, and for this time.

"My 19-year-old daughter picked up the book and read it. She said, 'This book is very inspirational! Why don't the Catholic schools or the priests teach us these things?'"

Our Lady of America, Our Hope for the States

- The only canonically approved private devotion of Our Lady from the United States.
- Approved messages and requests for Purity and Peace and the promise of Protection.
- The Divine Indwelling of the Most Holy Trinity.

Our Lady of Guadalupe, Hope for the World

"This book will instruct, encourage, and inspire a wide variety of people in the Church and outside the Church. You may be a priest seeking new ways to call your people to a deeper faith.

"Whoever you are, give this book some of your time, and it will repay you abundantly."

Fr. Frank Pavone, National Director, *Priests for Life*

I Will Sing of Mercy: The Journal of the Secretary of the Jesus King of All Nations Devotion

Known as the *Journal*, it contains all of the visions, revelations, and messages of Jesus in the Jesus King of All Nations Devotion.

"One must read the full account of the *Journal* to have a comprehensive view and insight concerning the rich spiritual treasures of the Devotion, and the vital apostolate outlined there for our times, NOW TIMES! And get the Medal!" Rev. Albert J. Hebert

Saints of the States

"This book is a wonderful contribution to appreciate the rich spiritual heritage we possess in the lives of so many heroic men and women of America. Dan Lynch traces the historical development, both secular and religious, through the centuries.

"Dan Lynch has produced a very enjoyable, enriching, and inspiring book. It challenges us to do in our times what these holy men and women did in their own."

Fr. Andrew Apostoli, CFR

The Gospel of Love

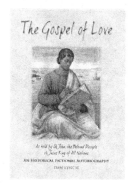

"*The Gospel of Love* is unlike any other book about St. John the Evangelist. It's an accurate, historical, fictional autobiography written from John's own point of view. While reading your way through it, you will feel like you are right there with John in 1st-century Israel and Ephesus.

"This is a fabulous book! I really hope that it inspires many people who will share it with their friends and relatives.

"When I read my Foreword aloud to my 91-year-old mother, she said, 'I want to read that book just from listening to what you said about it.' Bravo Dan!"

—From the Foreword by Erin von Uffel, DM
(Dame in the Order of Malta)
Vice Postulator of the cause for the canonization of
Sr. Marie de Mandat-Grancey

"You will experience John's life as if you were with him nearly 2000 years ago. You will experience John's innermost thoughts and doubts as he struggles to accept Jesus Christ as the Messiah, the Son of Man, and the Son of God, and His teachings that constitute the Gospel of Love. You will see John's transformation from tempestuousness to tranquility as he gradually comes to know and believe in the love that God has for all of us.

"More importantly, you will come away with a deeper understanding of how the Gospel of Love taught by Jesus affected John's character and growth in sanctity and how its reading can do the same for you.

"Nothing is so important in life as to grow in holiness by fulfilling the first and second laws of the Gospel: love of God who is love itself and love of neighbor as oneself made in the image and likeness of God. Nothing in life is so sad as not to have become a saint by loving God and neighbor as Jesus does.

"Our thanks to Dan Lynch for this inspiring work!"

—Fr. Peter M. Damian Fehlner, OFM Conv., Author and Theologian

J. How to Practice the Devotion Through Its Images, Prayers, Medal, Promises, and Graces

www.JKMI.com

READ The Booklet!

THE REMEDY for our times! Newly revised. Read about the origin of the Devotion, the Kingship of Jesus, how *we* can recognize Jesus as King of All Nations, and the promises and prayers of the Devotion. Read about signs, wonders, healings, and conversions!

HEAR
The Story and
PRAY
The Prayers

READ The *Journal*

The *Journal* contains all of the visions, revelations, and messages of Jesus in this Devotion.

"One must read the full account of the Journal *to have a comprehensive view and insight concerning the rich spiritual treasures of the Devotion, and the vital apostolate outlined there for our times, NOW TIMES! And get the Medal!"* Rev. Albert J. Hebert

Granted the *Nihil Obstat,* which declares that The *Journal* contains nothing contrary to faith and morals.

CARRY
The Package

Jesus said,
"Enthrone this my Image everywhere for I shall be powerfully present there..."

WEAR The Medal

SPREAD the Introductory Pamphlet to others.

Display and Venerate
The Image

Jesus said,
"This Image, my child, must become known. Tremendous will be the miracles of grace that I will work through this Image and Devotion of mine."

K. Help the Reign of Jesus King of All Nations to be Recognized on Earth by Enthroning His Image!

www.JKMI.com

"Take up my Devotion of Jesus King of All Nations for in its practice you shall find for yourselves a haven of grace, mercy, and protection. **Enthrone this my Image everywhere** *for I shall be powerfully present there and the power of my sovereign Kingship shall surely shield you from my just judgment." (Journal* 418).

Honor Jesus by enthroning His Image in your home, parish, or school! Dan Lynch shares with you the *Jesus King of All Nations Devotion* and then guides you step-by-step through the process of enthroning and consecrating your home, parish, or school to Jesus King of All Nations. We have everything you will need to make your enthronement. Pass this tradition to the next generation to ensure continued devotion to and trust in Jesus, well into the future.

| Beautiful Color Images of Jesus King of All Nations on canvas | 8 x 13 Unframed Jesus King of All Nations Image | Framed Jesus King of All Nations Image | The ONLY Medal revealed by Jesus for protection! This unique Medal is manufactured exclusively for us. |

L. Perhaps Jesus King of All Nations is Calling _You_ to Host a Visitation of His Image.

Visitations of the Image of Jesus King of All Nations are for the mission of bringing the recognition of His Reign on earth. Our apostolate coordinates Visitations of the Image to parishes and homes. We train local Guardian Teams for Parish Visitations. These Teams prepare for the Visitations in cooperation with the local pastors.

The Visitations consist of Holy Hours of Prayer for Life, Peace, and Protection from a booklet with the recitation of the prayers of the Jesus King of All Nations Devotion and veneration of the Image. There is a talk explaining the Image and the messages of Jesus. Religious goods are available for sale to promote the Devotion.

The Image is surrounded by signs, wonders, healings, and conversions.

For more information, sign up on our website at www.JKMI.com.

M. Perhaps Our Lady of Guadalupe is Calling _You_ to Host a Visitation of her Missionary Image.

St. John Paul II said, "May Our Lady of Guadalupe cross this continent bringing it life, sweetness, and hope!"

He also prophesied, "Through Our Lady of Guadalupe's powerful intercession, the Gospel will penetrate the hearts of the men and women of America and permeate their cultures, transforming them from within."

You may help fulfill St. John Paul II's prophecy by hosting Visitations of the Missionary Image of Our Lady of Guadalupe and celebrating with Masses, holy hours, processions, and merciful visits to parishes, schools, abortion centers, prisons, convents, hospitals, and nursing homes.

The Image is surrounded by signs, wonders, healings, and conversions.

Commissioned, blessed, and certified by the Basilica Shrine of Our Lady of Guadalupe in Mexico City, it has been traveling the world since 1991.

For more information, sign up on our website at www.JKMI.com.

N. About the Author

Dan Lynch is a former judge who is the founder of Dan Lynch Apostolates, which promotes devotion to Our Lady of Guadalupe, Jesus King of All Nations, Our Lady of America, and St. John Paul II. He coordinates journeys of Missionary Images for veneration and Holy Hours of Prayer for Life, Peace, and Protection. He is an author and a public speaker on radio and television and at conferences, missions, and retreats. He is pictured here with the Visitation Image of Jesus King of All Nations.

He produced the video, *Our Lady of Guadalupe, Mother of Hope*, and is also the author of,

The Coming Great Chastisement and the Great Renewal, the only book that summarizes the evils of the Culture of Death and provides the remedy to conquer them.

Medjugorje's Ten Secrets—How To Prepare, the most comprehensive book in the world about Medjugorje's Ten Secrets and how to prepare for them, based upon interviews of Medjugorje visionary Mirjana Soldo by the author and others.

Our Lady of Guadalupe, Hope for the World, which explains the history of Our Lady of Guadalupe and her modern mission to end abortion and bring a Culture of Life through conversions in the New Evangelization.

Our Lady of America, Our Hope for the States, which explains the only canonically approved private devotion from the United States and contains prayers and requests.

Saints of the States, which tells the story of the development of Catholicism in the United States through biographies of its saints and blesseds.

I Will Sing of Mercy: The Journal of the Secretary of the Jesus King of All Nations Devotion (editor), that contains all of the visions, revelations, and messages of Jesus King of All Nations.

The Gospel of Love, an historical, fictional autobiography of St. John, the Beloved Disciple of Jesus King of All Nations.

Dan enjoys hiking, biking, kayaking, boating, and fishing. He and his wife, Sue, live in Vermont. They are the parents of nine children, the grandparents of twenty-five, and the great-grandparents of two.